# ■ *Best Little Stories From World War II*

### By C. Brian Kelly

**BEST LITTLE STORIES FROM WORLD WAR II**, a journalistic history of World War II in the form of 101 vignettes reflecting the humor and the pathos, the triumph and the tragedy of the war as it affected soldier and civilian, leader and "common man," world-wide. True stories derived from a variety of sources and written as short narratives by C. Brian Kelly, former editor of *World War II* and *Military History* magazines.

Published by Montpelier Publishing,
P.O. Box 3384, University Station,
Charlottesville, Va. 22903-0384

First Printing   November 1989
Second Printing   October 1990
Third Printing   May 1992
Fourth Printing   February 1993
Fifth Printing   May 1994
Sixth Printing   February 1995
Seventh Printing   March 1996

Cover design by Stephen S. Vann

Cover photo
The USS *Bunker Hill* moments after she was hit by a pair
of Japanese kamikaze suicide planes off *Okinawa,*
May 11, 1945.

*U.S. Navy Photo*

Papercraft Printing & Design Company, Inc.
Charlottesville, Virginia, USA

*To the children—yours, mine, everybody's,
with the hope that they'll never have
to experience such a war.
But let us revere those who,
for the right reasons, did.*

# ■ *Acknowledgements:*

How could this book have been written without the support, encouragement, logistical aid and/or moral buttressing of Ingrid Smyer, co-publisher at Montpelier; Ruth Estep and Joi Estep at the University of Virginia; Lani Boaz and John Conover at Papercraft Printing & Design Company, and—at the magazine-publishing emporium that I serve—Carl Gnam, Gregg Oehler, Stephen S. Vann, Jon Guttman, Ralph U. Scherer and wife Janet, Kenneth and Roberta Phillips, Sandy Cochran, Marge Fowler, Jennifer Keen, Patricia Allen, Tamara Seneff, Cynthia Cooper, Phyllis Hutchison, and so many others, all at Empire Press, Leesburg, Virginia, plus, by definition more first than last, my mother, Claire Burke?

# ■ Author's Note

As any reader knows, there are a million and one "best" stories from an event so epic as World War II, an upheaval affecting so many millions around the world. To the extent that these 101 vignettes make *some* point or tell *some* thing that is worthwhile, they strike me as among the best . . . while yet recognizing there are so many more.

Nor does "best" mean to say the war, any war, was good. These are not all happy, light-hearted stories. They are meant, on the contrary, to show war in its many, so very countless piecemeal parts, all the bad and the occasional good. Thus, I have picked small situations that struck me for their poignancy, their inspiration, their humor and, of course, their unhappy but meaningful tragedy.

They come from a variety of sources in terms of the facts or direct quotes cited herein, but all were written by yours truly as short narratives in search of that small point . . . or sometimes simply for the *storytelling* in it. Many of the original sources are obscure and beyond the average reader's reach, but many books, journals or other publications cited here as fact-sources are attainable—even if only slightly stirred, the reader is urged to seek them out, by all means!

Meanwhile, with many thanks to the historians who toiled among the primary sources or did the interviews long before me, allow me to offer this one collection of historical vignettes written and gathered under one roof for the first time. Please do enjoy.

C. Brian Kelly
Charlottesville, Virginia
September 1990

# ■ Contents

# ■ *Ambassador's Briefcase Purloined*

Once upon a time, in a slow and seemingly peaceful era for America, a coastal steamer regularly plied the docile waters between Washington, D.C., and Norfolk, Virginia. Oldtimers still say the overnight voyage was a delight. For young U.S. Navy Ensign John D. Bulkeley, though, it would be the beginning of his own personal war with Japan. Neither the Japanese—nor even the U.S. Navy, it seems—ever quite knew what hit them.

Assigned to the cruiser *Indianapolis*, the 24-year-old Bulkeley was aboard the Wilson Lines steamer in July 1936. His ship was tied up at the huge U.S. Navy base in Norfolk, and he was looking forward to an off-duty weekend in Washington and Baltimore.

Entering the dining salon that evening in his white dress uniform, Bulkeley was struck by the sight of four Japanese, all well dressed, sitting at one of the tables. A steward told the curious young officer that one of them was the Japanese ambassador to the United States. To Bulkeley, the other three looked very much like military officers in mufti.

The steward also told Bulkeley the foursome often made the same round trip—Washington to Norfolk and back.

The young American's suspicions were aroused. Why would an ambassador spend so much time travelling to Norfolk? Didn't he have enough to occupy him in the diplomatic world of Washington? And why those three men of obvious military bearing as his frequent companions?

To Bulkeley, the answer seemed obvious enough. The naval base at Norfolk! They must be spying on the base and all the American warships that docked there. In fact, the briefcase so carefully kept by the ambassador's feet, even during dinner, must contain the most recent fruit of their labors.

Never one to waffle in the toils of indecision, Bulkeley made up his mind on the spot. He must get his hands on that briefcase!

1

He formed his plan as he watched the foursome through dinner, which for the Japanese meant the consumption, the copious consumption, of tea. Enough, Bulkeley said later, "to float a battleship."

Surely they would have to awaken during the night and use the common head—there were no such facilities in the steamer's small, individual cabins.

No one in official Washington was aware of the high drama that unfolded later that night as the young ensign from the *Indianapolis* posted himself at a vantage point on the deck near the ambassador's cabin and waited in the darkness.

For four or five hours, nothing happened. The coastal steamer by now had entered the Potomac River, her passengers peacefully bedded down—except for the waiting Bulkeley. Finally, about 4 a.m., the ambassador emerged from his cabin. Exactly as anticipated, he "walked down the deck toward the sandbox to heed the call of nature."

Exactly as planned also, Ensign Bulkeley swung into action. "Moments later, I scrambled through the hatch of the Jap's cabin, grabbed his briefcase, and barreled back through the hatch."

Bulkeley slipped out of sight, toward the stern of the small ship. What next? Would the ambassador return, sleepily crawl back into bed without noticing the briefcase was gone? Or—? Unfortunately for Bulkeley, it was *or*. He did notice the theft. "He began screaming and hollering and raising holy hell. Then the other Japs joined in the screaming. The racket was so loud, they no doubt heard it in Tokyo."

Bulkeley again wasted no time. With the river shoreline dimly in sight on either side, and he still in his dress whites, he went over the rail and into the water. Sidestroking and holding the briefcase above the water, he plugged for the Maryland shore while the Wilson "liner" pulled steadily away, in the direction of Washington.

Minutes later, soaked shoes squishy from their bath, Annapolis grad Bulkeley was trudging along a dirt road with his precious cargo, the Japanese briefcase. Reaching a larger road, he managed to hitch a ride into the Federal City, which in those pre-war days was well shut down for the weekend.

Bulkeley hid himself in a seedy hotel until Monday morning, the briefcase still his constant companion. And on Monday morning, he took a taxi to the U.S. Navy headquarters on Constitution Avenue. Safe inside, he found his way to an unmarked door that was Navy Intelligence. He knocked.

"Some old gent—he must have been 106 years old and going down for the third time—cautiously opened the door. He was stone-faced, and wearing civilian clothes. I found out later that he was a captain in Naval intelligence. He never invited me inside. Merely said, 'Yes?' and stood there while I told him of events on the Norfolk-Washington steamer. Then I proudly held up the Jap ambassador's briefcase. The old bastard turned ashen—I thought he was going to faint. Finally, he asked my name, rank and duty station, then slammed the door shut in my face."

Bulkeley was stunned. Before he could react, however, the door suddenly re-opened, "and the same gent snatched the briefcase out of my hand, told me to report back to the *Indianapolis* immediately and again slammed the door."

Back in Norfolk, Bulkeley discovered that word of his adventure had travelled ahead of him. Boarding his ship, he was hailed before its skipper. The skipper said he didn't want to know any details and informed Bulkeley he was being transferred, right then, to the transport *Chaumont*. In 24 hours, the *Chaumont* cast loose its lines at Norfolk and sailed for Shanghai, China. Bulkeley was gone from sight of official Washington and the outraged Japanese.

The Japanese, though, would feel his sting again. Regaining a naval state of grace in Shanghai, he conducted intelligence against them there. Then, with war openly underway after Pearl Harbor, he commanded the tiny PT-boat "fleet" that harassed the invading Japanese in the Philippines—that also carried Douglas MacArthur to safety in his dramatic escape from embattled Corregidor.

He earned the Medal of Honor for his unrelenting gallantry and leadership in those waters; he continued his wartime commands in the landings in the Tobriand Islands of the Pacific (1943); at Normandy and on the French Riviera (June and August 1944). In all, the future admiral finished the war as one of the U.S. Navy's most highly decorated combat commanders.

But he never did find out what was in the Japanese ambassador's purloined briefcase.

From *Sea Wolf: A Biography of John D. Bulkeley, USN*
by William B. Breuer (Presidio Press, Novato,
Calif., 1989)

# ■ *Underground War*

"Anyone who still works against Germany today is shoveling his own grave." The speaker, behind a cluttered desk at the Gestapo headquarters in Hamburg, was Inspector Paul Kraus. As a petty tyrant in the Gestapo's Foreign Division, he ran a "world-wide network of agents and man-hunters." He held life-and-death power over thousands who fell into Gestapo hands during the mid- to late 1930s.

As Jan Valtin sat before him, routine calls would interrupt. Business calls . . . *Gestapo business*. A female aide, Hertha Jens, would take the calls and tell him.

Someone from a distant prison or bureaucratic cranny. Convict Meier has finished serving his sentence. What to do with him now?

Kraus would think and mumble aloud. Meier . . . Meier? What had been his alleged crime against the state? Oh, yes. That. How did he behave in prison? He "behaved" fine, it seems. "All right, let him go, he seems to have become sensible."

But not a man named Schultz. "Schultz? . . . He was a stubborn customer. We'll send him to Sachsenhausen. Put him on ice for another year or so." And so, "an anti-Nazi's fate was decided."

The fact was that Valtin, himself, had been a prisoner for four years, since 1933. He, himself, was both an anti-Nazi and a victim of the Gestapo; he was, in fact, an agent of the Communist Comintern headquartered in Moscow, and his apparent defection to the Gestapo in 1937 was only a ruse ordered by his Comintern superiors through a world-wide network of their own that reached even into the Gestapo's most tightly secured prisons.

Valtin, Kraus, the woman Jens and thousands more, both inside and outside Nazi Germany . . . all, the cruel, the cynical and the still idealistic, were warriors in an underground, little-known war that raged between the rival Comintern and Gestapo for years before the outbreak of World War II.

For his own lifelong commitment to the apparently glowing panacea of exported communism, Valtin had been tortured, imprisoned, vilified, cut off from his family, threatened with death countless times and forced to witness unspeakable brutality and the deaths of many others.

The cynicism and brutality, he was coming to realize by 1937, were on both sides in this unrelenting war. But Valtin kept such

4

thoughts to himself even as he was released by the Gestapo and allowed to rejoin his *comrades* in Denmark, ostensibly as an agent for the Nazis but in reality still working for the Comintern and "feeding" the Gestapo harmless bits of information.

Valtin's disillusionment was still burrowing into his soul, undermining years of resolve, when, by chance, a key Comintern agent was captured in Germany by the Gestapo, a genuine Russian named Popoff. It was only a matter of time before he would give in to torture and talk. Valtin's Communist colleagues laid plans to kidnap a key Gestapo agent and later propose a swap of the respective prisoners.

Valtin's role could endanger his wife, still in Germany and under surveillance as a guarantee of his loyalty to the Gestapo. When Valtin mentioned this, one of the *comrades* said: "The Party comes first. We must rescue Popoff before he goes to the dogs."

*The Party comes first!* wrote Valtin later. *Mountains of wrecked lives are buried beneath that epitaph!*

The plan went forward. With Valtin's help, a Gestapo man called "Oskar" was lured to Copenhagen for a meeting. He was attacked in a side street, knocked unconscious and carried off in a taxi driven by a Party member. A few days later, again knocked unconscious, he was carried aboard a Soviet steamer in Copenhagen harbor, the *Kama*. He was still aboard when it set sail the next morning for Archangel, final fate unknown.

Soon, Valtin broke with his comrades, was himself taken prisoner and held in a cottage outside of Copenhagen, his own final fate precarious in the extreme. ("I knew too much and had to be destroyed.")

After three weeks under guard in the seaside cottage, and about to be placed aboard another USSR-bound ship, he escaped one morning by setting the small house on fire and mingling with the crowd of onlookers who gathered outside. He hitched a ride to Copenhagen, where he dropped out of sight—a fugitive from both the Gestapo and the world-wide agents of Moscow.

In Germany, his hostage wife was thrown into prison, where she died. "Did she, herself, put an end to her life? Was she murdered in cold blood? 'The Gestapo never jokes!' Neither does it give explanations. Our son, Jan, became a ward of the Third Reich. I have not heard of him again."

From *Out of the Night* by Jan Valtin (Alliance Book Corporation, New York, 1941)

# ■ *Movie Show In Shanghai*

August 21, 1937, would be American sailor Freddie John Falgout's 21st birthday. Stationed aboard the cruiser *Augusta*, flagship of the U.S. Asiatic Fleet, he would be spending that special day far from his hometown of Raceland on the Louisiana Bayou.

He and his ship were at exotic Shanghai, on Central China's Whangpoo River . . . but in the midst of fierce battle. Shanghai's celebrated Bund commercial center by the docks, its strip of prestige shops along Nanking Road and its other allurements were not merely exotic, they were dangerous. Although the international sectors of the teeming Chinese city, sixth largest in the world, supposedly were exempt from the struggle between attacking Japanese forces and Chinese defenders, the frequent stray round did take its toll.

A stray Japanese shell killed 300 civilians on Nanking Road shortly after the fighting began August 13, and another 500 died in the Great World Amusement Palace when it was struck by an errant Chinese bomb.

The *Augusta* had arrived August 14, "Bloody Saturday," at Shanghai, as part of a flotilla dispatched to protect Americans and others in the city's international settlements. With Japanese warships deployed nearby on the Whangpoo, the *Augusta* and her men more or less saw the shells of the opposing sides whistle by, but with no harm done, for several days.

On the evening of August 20, the off-duty men of the American cruiser gathered on the well deck, protected by smokestacks and seaplane catapults, for the showing of a movie. Freddie John Falgout, on mess duty that day, was among the men who carried benches topside from the galley. The movie-showing was routine, a morale-boosting measure ordered by the skipper, Captain Harold V. McKittrick.

Freddie Falgout, however, had brought along a book to read until darkness fell in earnest and the movie began to roll. "Not far away, a Japanese gun crew fired 36-millimeter 'pom-pom' shells at low-flying Chinese planes."

One of the shells, its trajectory spent without a target found, fell at 6:38 p.m. among the American sailors, almost at Freddie Falgout's feet. The flying shrapnel struck 19 men in all, but only one was killed—Freddie Falgout. And he only by a fragment the size of a dime, except that he was so close, and it struck him in the heart.

His widowed father heard about it in Louisiana the next day, from a neighbor who had heard on the radio about the American sailor killed in Shanghai. An official telegram then confirmed the news.

After Freddie Falgout's body came home six weeks later, more than 10,000 persons attended his smalltown funeral on the Bayou—full military honors. How could they know? Later, another 300,000 American service personnel would die in World War II, but Freddie . . . Freddie Falgout, on the eve of his 21st birthday, apparently was the first American casualty of the entire war.

From Douglas and Jan Baldwin in *Military: The Press of Freedom*, Vol. IV, No. 7, December 1987

# ■ *A Monster Is Created*

The onetime corporal who commanded the generals of Germany during World War II, who very nearly "owned" them, body and soul, was in an odd and ironic way a creature of the military establishment's own making. As is well-known, the Austrian-born Hitler served the German army in World War I as a lowly corporal. Living in Munich at the outbreak of war, he was allowed to join the 16th Bavarian *Landwehr* (Infantry) Regiment after petitioning the King of Bavaria for permission to enlist.

He was decorated for bravery in combat, earning nearly every available medal up to and including the Iron Cross First Class. He was wounded and, in October of 1918, was blinded by gas. At war's end, still assigned to his regiment, he found Bavaria in political upheaval, as was all of defeated Germany. In Bavaria's case, a socialist regime had taken over the provincial government, and Hitler's regimental barracks had fallen under the sway of a revolutionary soldiers' council.

Hitler himself wore the red markings of the revolutionaries.

Still a soldier, he voluntarily took on duties as a guard at a prisoner-of-war camp, but the POWs soon were gone, sent home. He stayed on in his barracks as Bavaria went from a socialist regime to a communist one, as a "soviet republic." Such a state of affairs was intolerable to both the shrunken, post-war German

Army and to closely allied private armies that had sprung up all over the politically unstable country. Often composed of embittered war veterans, mixed with street toughs, these Free Corps (*Freikorps*) tended to be right-wing in their ideology and of like mind with the tightly restricted military establishment. Awaiting them in Munich, entirely unknown, was their man of destiny.

At the moment, though, he was still a mere corporal and housed in a barracks controlled by members of a so-called Red Army. In May 1919, a combined *Reichwehr* (German Army) and *Freikorps* force stormed Munich—and Hitler's own regimental barracks. Hitler was among those marched off as prisoners. He then turned informer, and on his word ten men were executed for their left-wing activities.

Still housed in the regimental barracks, Hitler now became a confidential agent for the *Reichwehr's* Munich Command, Political Department. His job was to monitor and infiltrate radical political groups. The assignment one night (September 12, 1919) was to listen in on a public meeting of a little-known, rightist group, the German Workers' Party (DAP).

The meeting in a beer hall only attracted about 40 persons and Hitler, unimpressed so far, was about to leave quietly when another onlooker rose to propose that Bavaria realign itself with Austria as part of a Catholic union. That stopped Hitler, a rabid pan-Germanist, in his tracks.

The impromptu rejoinder that he then heatedly delivered was a fateful one—the DAP fell all over itself in its haste to enlist Hitler as a member, while his *Reichwehr* superiors also hastened to insert "their" man in a potentially supportive right-wing workers' group. Even the WWI luminary General Erich Ludendorff was involved in the plans for the undistinguished corporal. He, the same man responsible for "inserting" the exiled Lenin into Czarist Russia, proposed not only that Hitler should join the DAP, but also that he should strive to strengthen it.

Hitler, of course, carried out both "assignments" remarkably well. He gained control of the small DAP, which in time became the much more potent National Socialist German Workers' Party (NSDAP) and vaulted him to command of Nazi Germany, with the generals then at the feet of their onetime corporal and political informer.

From David T. Zabecki, *World War II* Magazine, July 1987

# ■ Street Fights And Bombs

Born in the German Palatinate on the west side of the Rhine, Gertrud Breier was about 10 years old when she saw the first visible sign of the evils soon to visit her homeland. Her family and their close friends, the von Bassmanns, had walked to a fair in Ludwigshafen-Rhine, a pleasant two-hour trek from their own town of Frankenthal.

In their verdant province of vegetable fields and vineyards, such walks—or long strolls in the forest—were a common family activity. This one, in the early 1930s, would always stand out in Gertrud's memory.

"On the way home, on the outskirts of the city, some motorcycles appeared suddenly out of nowhere. The men asked everyone to step back . . . .The men were in uniforms and their arm bands each had a swastika. I had never seen that symbol before, and I didn't know what it meant."

Moments later, a Mercedes convertible appeared, "and a lot of people on the street started to exclaim 'Heil! Heil! Heil!' "

Dark-haired and dressed in a brown uniform, a man in the car "raised his hand to salute and the people cheered."

Gertrud's father turned to von Bassmann: "That is Adolf Hitler, the leader of the new National Socialist Party. What is he doing on the left [west] side of the Rhine River?" Von Bassmann, a Jew, said that was a bad sign, and the two men fell to whispering with one another.

At home that night, Gertrud's mother told her to forget the incident and described Hitler as a mixed-up man and troublemaker who had been in jail and liked to show off. At school the next day, Gertrud's teacher said not to talk about such a person, who belonged on the other side of the Rhine anyway. (By terms of the Versailles Treaty, the French had occupied the Palatinate after World War I; in the early 1930s, the French troops had left.)

Life in the Palatinate remained fairly tranquil for another two years or so, but momentous events were brewing. Gertrud's "politician" father was an advisor to German Chancellor Heinrich Bruening, and in 1932 Bruening was forced out of office, due in large part to pressures from the politically powerful National Socialists. Thereafter, Gertrud's father was a restless, "deeply worried" man.

Then, in January 1933, Hitler was named Chancellor. The effects even in tiny Frankenthal of the Palatinate were immediate.

"Street fights between members of different parties and violence in some of the factories disturbed our once quiet and peaceful old town."

With Gertrud's father now in hiding, Nazi thugs descended on the family home at bedtime, January 31. They ransacked the place, yelled at Gertrud's mother, shoved her around and even kicked her. In February, the family was forced to move to a smaller house in Ludwigshafen, where Gertrud's father found a court job as an executor of wills. At her new school, Gertrud had a member of the Nazi women's league for a teacher. "She divided the class into two groups. One group she favored: the children of her fellow Nazi party members. The other group was very small: children like me from the *good* and silent anti-Nazi families. We were about eight girls; we sat at the right front side of the classroom. Since there were two Jews among us, we called ourselves the 'chosen elite.' "

Life in the Palatinate no longer was so tranquil: the von Bassmanns, being Jewish, emigrated to America. Most of the school children joined the Hitler Youth (but not Gertrud and her friends). Books were burned. Children had to attend Saturday classes on "nationalism." Parents became afraid of their own children as potential informers. "More and more people disappeared—presumably arrested just for being 'politically unreliable,' without any concrete proof."

Austria was annexed. Next door to Gertrud's family home, Jewish neighbors had their house burned and they themselves were taken away in a green police wagon (to be cremated at Dachau).

With the invasion of Poland on September 1, 1939, came, finally, The War. Soon after: "One small French aircraft dropped a few bombs on Frankenthal, my hometown and birthplace. The house that belonged to my mother's family for 300 years was destroyed."

With the war, came a vigorous—and expensive—black market for food and other necessities. And, as time passed, more and more air raids. Finding shelter was a major concern—school children went to bed at night dressed and with a few key belongings beside them. "When the first alarm sounded, we would jump out of bed, run out of the house, and get to the shelter as fast as we could. Many a night's sleep was interrupted."

One time, Gertrud, a teen-aged girl by now, was caught in the country by an air raid. "I couldn't get to a shelter. I just didn't know where to run. It was during the day and I found a hole—

maybe it was an empty water hole or a hole left by an uprooted tree. I threw myself in that hole as the earth shook and bombs fell and exploded all around me. People were screaming. When it was all over, there were wounded and dead people all around me—a horrible sight. I asked myself, 'Is that the promise the Third Reich made—the great victory?' "

Another time, Gertrud and her father were in a bomb shelter shaken as never before with explosion after explosion close by. It seemed endless, and near them in the shelter was a young woman with a newborn baby in her arms. She screamed hysterically. "The bombs kept exploding, and the mother squeezed her baby so hard that it died in her arms."

From The Governess by Gertrud Breier (Vantage Press,<br>
New York, 1988)

# ■ War Of Nerves

Early one afternoon in 1936, Werner von Blomberg, a tall, broad man in his early 50s, obviously was consumed with nervous tension as he walked his two dogs in Berlin's Tiergarten. An American correspondent who came across the German War Minister noticed that Blomberg's face was white, "his cheeks twitching."

The same correspondent had seen Blomberg just a few hours earlier on March 7, 1936—at an historic meeting of the German Reichstag in the city's Kroll Opera House. Blomberg had been one of the men on the stage, and he had been nervous then, too, his fingers drumming in silent agitation.

Seated on the stage with War Minister Blomberg had been the rest of Adolf Hitler's Cabinet; ranged in rows before them had been the 600 deputies of the Reichstag, or national legislature.

Addressing them all was Hitler himself. At times speaking in low, hoarse voice, and at others rising to shrill, hysterical scream, Hitler announced the German occupation of the demilitarized Rhineland—his first military adventure as head of the new Nazi state.

It wasn't much of an adventure—only three German battalions

actually crossed the Rhine in violation of the Versailles Treaty of 1919. But it was enough, quite possibly, to provoke a strong French reaction; enough, by Hitler's own confession later, to provoke the most nerve-wracking 48 hours of his life.

The *Führer* had no need to worry about the reaction of his rubber-stamp parliamentary body, for at the news of German troops on the march, the deputies sprang to their feet with wild cries of delight. "Their hands are raised in slavish salute," wrote William L. Shirer in his *Berlin Diary*, "their faces now contorted with hysteria, their mouths wide open, shouting, shouting, their eyes burning with fanaticism, glued on the new God, the Messiah."

Overnight, France did *not* mobilize in response. The crisis appeared safely passed—Hitler's first external coup. And at the State Opera on March 8, as the "New Germany's" leadership gathered anew for Heroes Memorial Day, a braver-looking General Blomberg delivered the main address in honor of the country's dead from World War I, 20 years earlier.

"We do not want an offensive war," he told his audience (and the world), "but we do not fear a defensive war." He dismissed "whispers" of the German Army's poor rapport with Hitler's Nazi Party. "We in the army are National Socialists," Blomberg proclaimed. "The party and the army are now closer together."

According to the politically naive war minister, the Nazi revolution in Germany differed from history's earlier revolutions by "recreating" the army, rather than destroying it. More than that, "The National Socialist state places at our disposal its entire economic strength, its people, its entire male youth."

In all, quite a responsibility had been placed on the army's shoulders. And the burden was likely to grow heavier, "because we may be placed before new tasks."

The last, as onetime Corporal Adolf Hitler led his nation and his generals into war with nations on either side of Germany, was certainly true, but Blomberg would not be on hand to take part. He had dragged his feet over the proposed Rhineland adventure. As it unfolded, he visibly blinked in fear. By chance, he recently had married a typist from his office. At first, Hitler had welcomed such a "democratic" romance. After the Rhineland affair, by odd coincidence, reports suddenly circulated that she had a past as a prostitute. Blomberg, for whatever reason, then became the first of many professional officers serving Hitler to be forced out of his entourage.

From *Berlin Diary* by William L. Shirer
(Alfred A. Knopf, New York, 1941)

# ■ 'Inspection' Interrupted

Offered a three-month contract to "inspect" China's fledgling air force in the spring of 1937, aviator Claire Chennault accepted retirement for deafness from a United States Army that was, itself, deaf to his theories of air combat. He was a longtime advocate of coordinated fighter tactics, but winners for the moment were the believers in the "invincible bomber."

Japan already was nibbling at China following the outright occupation of Manchuria in late 1931 and establishment of the puppet Manchuko regime in early 1932.

Retired Major Chennault boldly sailed into Kobe, Japan, aboard the *President Garfield*. He was greeted at dockside by fellow American and former flying colleague Billy MacDonald, who had arrived in China the year before as a volunteer instructor for the Chinese Air Force flying school at Hangchow.

"How is it an instructor in the Chinese Air Force can move about freely in Japan?" asked Chennault.

MacDonald had an obviously rehearsed answer—ready not so much for Chennault, but for the Japanese. "You're mistaken, Major. I'm an assistant manager of a troupe of acrobats. See, it says so right here in my passport!"

It seems that "assistant manager" MacDonald had left the "troupe" in Osaka and gone ahead to meet Chennault. "For the next few days you and I are going to be 'tourists'—like the Japanese tourists that wander around the U.S. Ever noticed them?"

Chennault nodded. Since he already expected real war between China and Japan, and then the same between the United States and Japan, he of course had noticed the Japanese "tourists" MacDonald referred to. "Especially around harbors and airfields," he now rejoined.

"We'll return the compliment."

And they did. For the next few days they traveled about Japan in a rented car, visiting construction sites, industrial centers, shipping facilities and anything else that could be a potential bombing target. More than simply visiting, they also shot reels of photographs with cameras hidden under their coats.

If they were noticed officially, no one stopped them.

Four years later, with full-scale war raging, Claire Chennault found his own photos and notes on potential Japanese targets more informative and useful than like material supplied by the U.S. War Department.

His inspection trip in China shortly afterwards revealed a woefully inadequate and unprepared air arm, but Chennault was unable to finish his three-month tour. He was at the Italian Flying School (for the Chinese) at Loyang in July when the Japanese used an incident near the Marco Polo Bridge outside of Peking as their reason for open assault upon China—with no declaration of war.

From Loyang, Chennault immediately dispatched a telegram to China's Generalissimo Chiang Kai-shek offering his services in any capacity the Chinese might like.

In two days, Chiang wired back: "Your voluntary offer of services gratefully accepted. Proceed to Nanchang. Direct final combat trainer fighter groups there."

Chennault, for a time placed in charge of the Chinese Air Force, was thrilled at the opportunity to test his theories of air warfare in actual combat. More important, though: "I was convinced that the Sino-Japanese War would be a prelude to a great Pacific war involving the United States. I felt that the more I could learn about the Japanese and the more damage I could inflict in the early stages of the conflict, the better I would be able to serve my country eventually."

> From *Chennault and the Flying Tigers* by Anna Chennault
> (Paul S. Eriksson, Inc., New York, 1963)

# ■ *Diplomacy Under Physical Duress*

Emil Hacha, 66 and suffering from a heart condition, was not exactly a prisoner undergoing relentless interrogation, but he might as well have been.

He was, instead, the head of one state conferring with the head of a neighboring state—a conference in the wee hours of the morning that was more like a Gestapo interrogation.

In November 1938, as Chief Justice of Czechoslovakia's Supreme Court, he led a relatively quiet life outside the turbulent mainstream of pre-war European politics. His safe isolation ended when his country's National Assembly named him to replace Eduard Benes as president.

That change, brought about by Benes' post-Munich resignation, meant that the failing Hacha would be the man to stand up to Hitler on behalf of a nation.

He was not up to it, but it could be said that he tried. With German troops massing along the borders of Bohemia in early March 1939, he sought an audience with Hitler and was indeed "invited" to Berlin. He and his Foreign Minister, Frantisek Chvalkovsky, arrived in the evening of March 14 and were received with military honors.

The visitors then were summoned before Hitler at the unusual hour of 1:15 a.m., March 15. In the *Führer's* study at the newly built Chancellery, the two Czechs next were subjected to one of the most extraordinary browbeatings in the history of diplomacy.

Hitler; his own Foreign Minister, Joachim von Ribbentrop; Herman Goering and General Wilhelm Keitel all were present for the merciless hounding, which went on for the next three hours. The two Czechs were told that their country was to be "introduced" into Nazi Germany's Third Reich, and they must sign documents of surrender or see Prague pulverized by bombing at daybreak . . . just hours off.

Hacha pleaded with Hitler that his people "have a right to live a national life." But Hitler and his henchmen were not to be appeased. In and out of the room at different times, Hitler himself warned them that for every Czech battalion attempting to stem an invasion, there would be a German division ready to overcome it.

By one informed account, the Germans pressed their two visitors brutally. "They literally hounded Dr. Hacha and Mr. Chvalkovsky round the table on which the documents were lying, thrusting them continually before them, pushing pens into their hands, incessantly repeating that if they continued in their refusal half of Prague would be in ruins from bombing within two hours."

The pressure, obviously, was unbearable. Hacha, resisting for hours, passed out—fainted. Revived by Hitler's personal physician, Dr. Theodore Morell, the Czech leader fainted a second time a few minutes later. Morell stabbed again with a reviving injection of some kind.

In the meantime, a Hitler-dictated document had been hurriedly translated into Czech. At 4 a.m, Hacha finally signed, agreeing, for the sake of "calm, order and peace in Central Europe," to place his country "under the protection of the German Reich."

Hitler was exultant at his first "conquest" of a non-German country (he already had taken over Austria and the Sudentenland).

15

Rushing into his nearby office, he exclaimed to the secretaries present: "Children! This is the greatest day of my life! I shall go down in history as the greatest German."

That evening, as his forces occupied Czechoslovakia, Hitler publicly announced: "Czechoslovakia has ceased to exist!"

Hacha, for his part, returned home as State President of the Reich Protectorate of Bohemia and Moravia, a puppet's role he would hold until his country was overrun by the Red Army at war's end. He was in a Prague prison when he died on June 27, 1945, his country soon to become a "protectorate" again, this time under Soviet dictate.

From various sources

# ■ *War's First Battle*

The war in Europe began with the German invasion of Poland on September 1, 1939. True? Not entirely. The first "battle" of World War II was fought—in Poland, to be sure—six days earlier. Moreover, the ultimate commander of the German combat team that fought the little-known battle of Mosty in Polish Silesia on August 26, 1939, was a displaced admiral of the German Navy, one Wilhelm Franz Canaris.

As any history buff knows, Canaris was chief of Nazi Germany's *Abwehr*, or military secret service. With the attack on Poland originally scheduled for 4:15 a.m., August 26, a Saturday, the Admiral's *Abwehr* was supposed to send 16 *Kampfgruppen* (combat teams) into Poland 12 hours ahead of the German armies for a series of raids on Polish communication and transportation facilities, such as telephone lines or bridges. In other cases, the special K-teams were to seize and hold certain facilities intact for their own *Wehrmacht's* use.

Late on August 25, the teams were assembled and ready at their jump-off points—Canaris and his staff had done their homework and followed their orders explicitly. But late on the 25th, an agitated aide from the Chief of Staff's office called to report that Hitler had postponed the invasion because of political developments. "You must do everything humanly possible to halt your combat teams," said the aide.

Fifteen of the K-teams were halted in time, but one, headed by Lieutenant Albrecht Herzner, already, irrevocably, was on its way. Herzner, striking out from a German base at Zilina in Slovakia, had been ordered to seize the railroad station at Mosty and secure the Jablunkov Pass in the Beskids. The rail line here ran from Slovakia, past Mosty and on deeper into Polish Silesia. Following his original orders, Herzner positioned his team and gave the signal to attack. Opening fire at 1 a.m. on August 26, his K-group overwhelmed the Poles guarding Mosty, capturing the rail station and securing the pass as planned. The Germans then settled down to await the arrival of an entire invading division.

When no division appeared after a time, the young German commander approached the Polish colonel he and the K-team had taken prisoner. What's going on, Herzner asked, weren't the two countries at war? "I told you they aren't," the Polish officer replied. He suggested that Herzner call his home base on the telephone in the stationhouse and find out the facts. Herzner did—and was told to return to Zilina immediately. The war had not started after all.

It was a ludicrous situation, but no joke. In the war that did start six days later, Herzner was among the millions of casualties. So was Poland, which collapsed in just 27 days of assault by the new German *Blitzkrieg*.

From *The Game of the Foxes* by Ladislas Farago
(David McKay Company, Inc., New York, 1971)

# ■ *An Eagle's Brief Flight*

Like five orphans, the submarines *Vulture*, *Wild Cat*, *Lynx*, *Wolf* and *Eagle* had been cast into a hostile world, entirely on their own, with nowhere to go—not even home.

For them, home was Poland, and under the crushing weight of the German *Blitzkrieg*, Poland was sinking from sight. All five boats of the Polish Navy had been able to escape their base at Gdynia in the Gulf of Gdansk after it was struck by German divebombers at the onset of Hitler's Poland campaign (September 1, 1939).

While Poland's land forces reeled before the German steam-roller, the five submarines then roamed the nearby sectors of the Baltic Sea to do what they could in defense of their homeland even if confined to their own watery environment.

Since the Germans sent few ships eastward into the Baltic, the Polish underwater flotilla found little action in its guard duty—specifically in Puck's Bay, which controlled the sea approach to Gdansk. The real action was provided by the wide-ranging *Luftwaffe*, whose deadly aircraft had to be avoided at all costs.

In only a few days, the home waters were swept clear of Polish surface ships, and on September 12 Gdynia itself was abandoned. "Only the five submarines remained to continue the war at sea."

For the orphaned submarines, however, *continuing the war* meant merely surviving, and one by one they each were confronted by a final moment of truth. For the *Sep (Vulture)*, it came on September 15. Badly damaged by *Luftwaffe* bombing, *Sep* had only one choice. She must turn for Stockholm in neutral Sweden and accept internment for the duration of the war.

Likewise, a bomb-damaged *Rys (Lynx)* limped into Swedish waters on September 17 for safe haven and internment. *Zbik (Wild Cat)* managed to stay on the loose until September 25, but by then she, too, was forced to give up the fight as, at home, Warsaw was about to surrender.

That left just two of the orphans roaming the seas, both unaccounted for and neither aware of the other's whereabouts or activities. *Wilk (Wolf)*, in fact, had set out for England in hopes of joining up with the Free Polish Navy there. Thus, *Orzel (Eagle)* would be the last of the five still in home waters.

Like her sisters of the sea, *Orzel* had left her berth at Gdynia in the first hours of the war. On station in Puck's Bay, she had found no targets, but she managed to elude the roaming *Luftwaffe* for days. She spent part of the time laying mines and once barely avoided a German trap signalled by false calls for help from another "submarine."

She then cruised the Baltic beyond Puck's Bay until all communication with Gdynia ceased as of September 12. From then on, *Orzel* would be on her own.

Double disaster struck the same day. Her hydraulic system collapsed, and so did her skipper, a Commander Kloczkowski. As the boat's executive officer, Lieut. Cmdr. Jan Grudzinski, took over the helm, the *Orzel* headed for Tallinn in ostensibly neutral Estonia, both to make repairs and to place Kloczkowski in a hospital for treatment of his serious illness. Under prevailing international law, the Poles expected they would be allowed a belligerent ship's right to remain in port 24 hours, make their repairs, and sail again.

At first, their Estonian hosts appeared to agree. The skipper was hospitalized and repairs to the hydraulic system were completed in just a few hours. Refueled and her stores replenished, *Orzel* was ready to depart long before the 24 hours expired.

But now the Estonians said she must wait for six hours after a German freighter cleared the harbor waters. After long—and it seemed deliberate—delay, the freighter finally turned her back to Tallinn and headed to sea. In theory, *Orzel* could follow in just six hours.

But no, the Estonians now said, a new accord binding upon the three Baltic states required disarmament and internment of any belligerent's warship appearing in their waters. (Estonia, Latvia and Lithuania, it should be recalled, were tiny countries pressed on one side by Nazi Germany and on the other by the Soviet behemoth; in the end, they were occupied by the Soviets, next by the Germans, then "liberated" again by the Soviets.)

The latest edict was enforced by armed guards placed on board the Polish *Orzel*. The Estonians removed new Captain Grudzinski's charts, navigational instruments and vital components of the boat's deck guns. Next, her torpedoes would be removed, but that couldn't be done until the following day.

The Poles made use of the respite to plan their own next move—more exactly, to plot an escape. They were heartened the next morning by a message written on the back of a visiting card from the capital city's British naval attaché. "Good luck and God Bless you," it said.

As dockyard workers struggled at removing the boat's 20 torpedoes, the *Orzel*'s Polish crew was busy, too. One crewman apparently fishing from a dingy in the harbor waters was instead plotting an escape channel to the boat's rear. Another, unobserved, sabotaged the hawsers holding the sub in place—a strong pull would snap the last uncut strands.

The boat's radio was dismantled before watching Estonians, but a contrived short circuit and small electrical fire persuaded them it must be reassembled in order to trace the short circuit. Grudzinski himself, meanwhile, sabotaged the torpedo hoist after 14 of the deadly "fish" had been lifted out of his boat, leaving six. He blamed the Estonian workers, whose foreman then agreed to call off the job for the day—a Sunday—and return the next morning to remove the final six fish.

By such ruses, the friendly and cooperative Poles made their preparations for the coming night. By then, the Estonians were so lulled that they left only two armed guards on board the submarine.

They were easily disarmed, with no harm to either one, and after a crewman cut the dockyard's main electricity cable with an axe, the boat simply backed away from her berth in the suddenly prevailing darkness. Under quiet electrical power, she scraped over a mudbank for one tense moment before she could turn, bow on, for the open sea.

As her diesels then roared to life, the harbor guns responded loudly, but *Orzel* cleared a gauntlet of shells, machine-gun and rifle fire until reaching deep water and plunging into a dive that put her beyond reach.

The orphan still remained in an entirely hostile environment, however, and she was bereft of charts, navigational equipment and usable deck guns.

She sailed first for the Swedish coast, where she dropped off her two Estonian prisoners in a collapsible rubber boat. She then headed back to sea—and a war patrol.

The officers, in the meantime, got together and drew up a set of homemade charts based upon each man's best memory. The salvaged radio told the crew of Warsaw's surrender and their country's sad fate.

Soon, the *Orzel* had spent 16 days patrolling the Baltic without encountering a single enemy target (she still had her six unsullied torpedoes aboard). And now a BBC broadcast informed the crew of sister-boat *Wilk*'s successful flight to England. Why shouldn't *Orzel* attempt the same, despite her navigational shortcomings and short supply of remaining fuel?

The proposal meant traversing heavily patrolled waters, threading a navigational needle between Sweden and Danish territory to escape the Baltic, then crossing the danger-filled North Sea to enter English waters—it would not be easy even in a fully equipped submarine.

Nonetheless, by mid-October, the *Orzel* ran that gauntlet safely, too. Her skipper Grudzinski was awarded Poland's highest military decoration, the *Virtuti Militari*, for his remarkable feat in guiding her to safety—and to renewed chance to fight the common German enemy.

*Orzel* had her opportunity to fight, as part of the Royal Navy's

2nd Submarine Flotilla, when Germany launched her lightning invasion of Norway the following April. On station off the Norwegian coast the morning of April 8, *Orzel* launched her torpedoes against a German troop transport and thus became the first Allied sub to sink an enemy ship taking part in the invasion of Norway.

That campaign lasted until well after Nazi Germany's next move, the invasion of France and the Low Countries on May 10. The Norwegian campaign was marked by various naval engagements and significant ship losses on both sides. One, her exact fate never known, was the *Orzel*. Long overdue, reported the Polish Admiralty-in-exile on June 11, the orphaned *Orzel* and all her crew were "presumed lost." The *Eagle*, after brief flight, was gone.

From *Submarine Warriors* by Edwyn Gray
(Presidio Press, Novato, Calif., 1988)

# ■ *Revolting Visit To Poland*

With the smoke of Warsaw barely clearing, a German colonel leading a tour of stunned foreign correspondents explained such total, unprecedented military success could be attributed not only to "our irresistible arms" but also "to our superior intelligence service."

Here was a public plaudit for Admiral Wilhelm Canaris, whose *Abwehr* indeed had done its homework well and contributed materially to the outcome in Poland.

Canaris, a mysterious and enigmatic figure whose true loyalties are hotly debated by historians even today, was in fact typical of the schizophrenic impulses that marked so many of Hitler's commanders.

At 9:15 the morning of the Poland invasion, Canaris, obviously excited, even elated, called his staff officers into a Berlin auditorium for a briefing in which he fervently told them, "I demand unquestioning and unconditionally positive loyalty to the *Führer*." He ended with the familiar refrain, "Heil Hitler."

Minutes afterward, on his way back to his office, he was told that Britain had ordered total mobilization. "My God," said Canaris. "If England comes into this, it will be the end of our poor Germany."

Ten days later, touring the field of battle in Poland, Canaris found himself questioning his own demands for loyalty to Hitler. In the field, his men reported massacres of Poles by the SS and the Gestapo. Canaris was shown a directive from SS Chief Heinrich Himmler calling for the systematic extermination of Polish civilians, especially the aristocracy and the Roman Catholic clergy. The same directive cited an order from Hitler himself as its authority. Canaris couldn't believe it.

He hurried to Chief of Staff Wilhelm Keitel's office in Hitler's personal train, parked at Ilnau, to "report" his information about "these unheard-of atrocities." But Keitel, who obviously knew all about them, was unreceptive. "If I were you, Herr Canaris," said the Hitler lackey, "I would not get mixed up in this business. This 'thing' has been decided upon by the *Führer* himself."

Keitel went on to explain that since the *Wehrmacht* had no stomach for "this 'thing'," Hitler had ordered the SS and the Gestapo to handle it. "As a matter of fact, every military command in Poland will from now on have a civilian chief besides its military head, the former to be in charge of the 'racial extermination' program."

Stunned, Canaris was about to protest when Hitler himself entered the railroad car. Here was the intelligence chief's chance to take his complaint to the very top—but, as Keitel put his finger to his lips to signal silence, Canaris' nerve failed him. Numb, he replied to Hitler's questions about French intentions to the west without really thinking. When he returned to Berlin four days later, Canaris was physically sick.

From *The Game of the Foxes* by Ladislas Farago
(David McKay Company, Inc., New York, 1971)

# ■ *The Incredible, Ubiquitous Samaritan*

The last thing on William M. Miller's mind the night of February 21, 1940, was the stalled Phony War in Europe. "I had just purchased my first car, a Lincoln Zephyr V 12," recalls the Pennsylvania native.

On the way home from an evening in the state capital of Harrisburg, the exuberant young American decided to see how fast his new car would go. Three feet of snow covered the ground, but during the day the roads had been clear. He forgot that melting snow would have seeped onto the roadways and frozen into sheets of ice by the 2 a.m. hour.

"The last time I looked down at the speedometer, I was going 110." The predictable happened.

"I slowed down for a curve, and my brakes locked because I was on a sheet of ice and had no control of the car. I hit a concrete culvert head-on and flew through the windshield as if I had been shot out of a cannon. I eventually sold the car for $85 junk value with a 24-inch circular hole in the windshield."

In a coma for four days, Miller later learned that a passing stranger, Warren Felty, had found him lodged in a snowbank, unconscious. Accompanied by a friend, Felty hurriedly placed Miller in their car and rushed him to a Harrisburg hospital.

But that's not the end of the story.

Five years later, the war in Europe now very much on captured B-17 pilot Miller's mind, he was one of the half-starved Allied POWs forced to undertake a "death march" of 75 miles to Spremberg, Germany, to avoid liberation by the advancing Red Army. This time (January 1945), two feet of snow covered the ground; the temperatures were "zero or below," and the "worst blizzard in that part of Germany in 80 years" struck at the shuffling column.

"Prisoners were falling to the ground, unable to continue. Our German guards were older men and just could not keep up. I actually saw American officers carrying the German guards' rifles, as well as supporting them along the line of march."

By the second day, conditions only worsened. "It seemed as if we had been on the road for a week. Everyone seemed to be in a daze. Friends whom you had made in camp didn't recognize you and wouldn't even talk to you. It was every man for himself, and later our senior officers admitted they had lost all control over the situation. At this point, no one could help anyone. You were on your own."

With a promised stopping point five miles ahead, Miller was on his very last legs. "I had discarded everything that I was carrying except a small amount of food. I just could not go any farther. I couldn't put one foot in front of the other. My hands and feet were numb."

Predictably, the exhausted Miller collapsed—into a snow-bank. "I had fallen behind my camp unit, and the last thing I remembered was the sight of all the prisoners passing by and none stopping to help. Either I passed out or went off to sleep, both certain death in the snow."

But no, Bill Miller was to escape certain death a second time. Call it a miracle. "Someone was kicking and shaking me and pulling me to my feet. Incredible as it may be, it was Warren Felty of Middletown, Pennsylvania, the same person who had saved my life five years and 4,000 miles away, under just about identical circumstances."

How could it be? Well, as a B-17 pilot with the 94th U.S. Bomb Group at Bury St. Edmonds, England, Miller had been shot down October 20, 1943, while flying his first mission over Germany. Captured after bailing out of his stricken plane, he spent the rest of the war at Stalag Luft III at Sagan, Germany, the same POW camp that produced the "Great Escape."

Felty, in the meantime, also had become a B-17 pilot—with the 96th Bomb Group in England—and he also had been shot down and taken prisoner. Both men were held at Stalag Luft III, but in different compounds. Only on the death march to Spremberg had they been reunited.

Felty, of course, helped Miller finish the second day's journey to the stopping place five miles ahead. While there were many more difficult moments before the POWs were liberated at the end of April, the stop enabled Miller to regain his strength for the rest of the ordeal—to survive.

After the war, he accidentally ran into Felty once more—back home in Pennsylvania. On the verge of losing a job for lack of a local distributor for his company's products, Miller was having breakfast in a roadside restaurant at Harrisburg and wondering what to do about his job situation. Outside, a passing motorist who had never before been to the restaurant decided to stop and go in.

It was Felty, and in just two hours he had made arrangements with his own company to be the distributor that Miller needed. Miller's job had been salvaged.

"He was just driving by and something compelled him to stop."

From *World War II* Magazine, May 1988

# ■ *Jockeying For Position*

Erwin Rommel was furious. Only three days since German forces invaded Poland, Hitler, arriving aboard his special train, was visiting the front. He wanted a tour of the battlefields, so he, his staff and various official escorts, Rommel included, packed into seven heavy-duty Mercedes automobiles (equipped with not four, but six wheels).

The small motorcade was led into the danger zones by two armored scout cars. Following close behind was a huge column of 70 additional vehicles carrying the *Führer*'s entourage of Nazi Party hacks and governmental "dignitaries," all anxious to have lead positions. At stopping points, they rushed from their cars for photographs at Hitler's side if at all possible, then ran pell mell back to their autos for the next lap in the journey to Fourth Army headquarters—and further jockeying for position in the convoy.

Since the rough and primitive back roads of Poland were not built for such traffic, clouds of dust roiled up in protest.

Rommel was Hitler's Headquarters Commandant at the time, and when Martin Bormann complained about the unruly motorcade activities, Rommel shot back: "I'm not a kindergarten teacher. You sort them out if you want!"

That was on September 4, 1939, three days after the war's start, but by September 20, the same sort of fawning behavior was still going on. By then, Hitler had moved from his train to the Casino Hotel in Zoppot.

Watching in considerable astonishment was the German general Walter Warlimont, a visitor to the Hitler headquarters. As he looked on one morning, 20 to 30 cars were assembled "two abreast" in the hotel driveway for a trip to a battle area north of Gdingen. "It was the job of General Rommel, the Headquarters Commandant, to get this cortege moving, with Hitler at its head."

When Warlimont asked Rommel why two abreast, "Rommel replied that, after many unhappy experiences, he had laid on this 'order of march' because it offered the best hope of satisfying the precedence and protocol requirements of the large number of nonmilitary visitors who had meanwhile flowed into the headquarters."

Thus, with cars two abreast, six or eight exalted personages could travel "level with each other and at the same distance from Hitler, and for them that was more important than anything."

But Rommel's best-laid plans went awry that very day. "The cortege went down a narrow track where the two-abreast formation was no longer possible and the majority of the cars were held up at a barrier while Hitler and the leaders drove on."

Even though word was passed among those left behind that the tour had been interrupted for a quick Hitlerian visit to a field hospital, Bormann, for one, was again outraged. "Nevertheless, although they were almost on the battlefield, Martin Bormann, the Head of the Party Chancellery, made a fearful scene and cursed General Rommel in outrageous language because of the supposed slight inflicted on him."

Once again, the future "Desert Fox" was fuming. But he had to hold his tongue. "There was nothing Rommel could do in answer to such insolence. When I straightaway gave vent to my indignation . . . Rommel merely asked me to tell Schumndt, the senior military aide, equally forcibly what I thought about it."

From *Inside Hitler's Headquarters, 1939-45* by Walter Warlimont (Weiden Feld and Nicolson, London, 1964) and *Hitler's War* by David Irving (Hodder and Stoughton, London, 1977)

# ■ Hitler 'Accepts' The Credit

The man who came to dinner one night was General Erich von Manstein, Prussian to the core and easily one of the most brilliant military strategists Hitler had fallen heir to as the master of Nazi Germany. The dinner host was Hitler himself.

It was February of 1940, and after many delays, the plan for the invasion of France was still on, exact date uncertain. Despite its premature disclosure to the Allies as a result of an errant plane's crash in Belgium January 10, the plan still was an imitation of Germany's World War I Schlieffen strategy of looping into northern France by way of neutral Belgium.

Von Manstein, however, carried with him the seeds of another plan, *Sichelschnitt*, or "cut of the sickle." For months now, von Manstein had been pushing his alternative scheme to plunge into the eastern rib cage of France by way of the Ardennes, while feinting in the direction of Belgium.

The blade thus plunging into France from unexpected quarter would be German armor.

It so happened that few in Nazi Germany's military hierarchy, Hitler included, were all that happy with their variation of the old Schlieffen plan, especially after it was revealed by the plane crash. Still, it was THE plan, and for months now von Manstein's efforts to sell the High Command on *his* scheme had been thwarted. No less than seven Manstein memos sent up the chain of command had been pigeon-holed.

There the matter might have ended, there the Nazi conquest of France *might* have been averted, and there World War II might have fallen into the same sort of frozen stalemate that characterized the Western Front of World War I. Might have . . . except that Hitler got wind of the Manstein scheme, had him for dinner one night, then took the General into the study to hear the details.

The apparent fallacy of Manstein's vision was the rough, heavily forested terrain of the Ardennes. How could German tanks operate on its few roads leading into French territory?

In November, however, Manstein already had posed that question to the key man in development of Germany's panzer forces, General Heinz Guderian. "Manstein asked me if tank movements would be possible through the Ardennes in the direction of Sedan," Guderian recalled after the war. "He explained his plan of breaking through the extension of the Maginot Line near Sedan, in order to avoid the old-fashioned Schlieffen plan, familiar to the enemy and likely to be expected once more. I knew the terrain from World War I, and, after studying the map, confirmed his view."

So, in effect, did Hitler following the dinner *tête-à-tête*. By February 24, 1940, the plan for subduing France had been changed—the strategy would be von Manstein's own *Sichelschnitt*. As history since has recorded, it was indeed the plunge of the dagger that brought France to her knees.

Hitler was so pleased that he gladly took full credit for himself. As for von Manstein's contribution, Hitler disdainfully explained: "Among all the generals I talked to about the new plan in the West, Manstein was the only one who understood me."

From various sources

# ■ Bold Gamble Supported?

The action in early April of 1940 was in Norway and Denmark, along with their adjacent waters, and that's where the world's attention was focused. Beating the British to the punch, Nazi Germany had launched its *Blitzkrieg* of Norway. In London, as is well known, the Chamberlain government was soon to topple, but what about Berlin? What was going on there, in the rapacious aggressor's nerve center?

As early as April 2, American radio correspondent William L. Shirer had reported from his base in Berlin: "Germany is now waiting to see what the Allies intend to do in stopping shipments of Swedish iron ore down the coast to the Reich. It's accepted here as a foregone conclusion that the British will go into Scandinavian territorial waters in order to halt this traffic. It's also accepted as a foregone conclusion here that the Germans will react."

As Shirer added in his entry for April 2 in his famous *Berlin Diary*, it was a puzzle. "S. whispers about Nazi troops being concentrated at the Baltic ports. But what can Germany do against the British navy?"

It was a question that still lingered on April 8. The British had announced their mining of Norwegian waters to stop the traffic in iron ore essential to the German war effort. Spokesmen in Berlin said, "Germany will know how to react." In his diary entry, Shirer once again asked, "But how?"

He had a partial answer the next morning. "Hitler this spring day has occupied a couple more countries. At dawn Nazi forces invaded the two neutral states of Denmark and Norway in order, as an official statement piously puts it, 'to protect their freedom and independence.' "

The news, Shirer added, was stupefying. "Copenhagen occupied this morning, Oslo this afternoon, Kristiansand this evening. All the great Norwegian ports, Narvik, Trondheim, Bergen, Stavanger, captured. How the Nazis got there—under the teeth of the British navy—is a complete mystery."

In Berlin on April 9, meanwhile, correspondents such as Shirer were treated to a boastful press conference featuring the German Foreign Minister, Joachim von Ribbentrop.

"We waited a half-hour. At eleven a.m. Ribbentrop strutted in, dressed in his flashy field-gray Foreign Office uniform and looking as if he owned the earth."

After a few preliminaries by his press chief, Ribbentrop "sprang up, snake-like," to accuse the Allies of plans to invade and create a threatening base in Scandinavia and to declare that Germany had occupied Denmark and Norway to protect them and "defend their true neutrality until the end of the war."

At the broadcast center for foreign correspondents, Shirer encountered "for the first time a swarm of censors." They warned him to be "careful" in what he reported. So far, it appeared the German operation had been a huge success. No resistance by the Danes, and in Norway a mere sputter expected to end by nightfall.

Later in the day, though, the picture began to change. "Apparently something has gone wrong with the Norwegian part of the affair," noted the Shirer diary. "The Norwegians were not supposed to fight, but apparently did—at least at one or two places. There are reports of German naval losses, but the Admiralty keeps mum. All the Danish and Norwegian correspondents were fished out of their beds at dawn this morning and locked up at the Kaiserhof. It was the first they knew that their countries had been protected."

Later, of course, it turned out that German naval losses had been significant. The fighting in Norway would last an entire two months, ending with full German control a month after the invasion of France and the Low Countries.

On April 18, meanwhile, Shirer heard an account, from another American correspondent, of Copenhagen's capitulation on April 9. German coal ships with troops hidden under the hatches had tied up in the neutral harbor two days before.

"At dawn (April 9) up came the hatches and the German soldiers piled out. The Royal Palace is but a short distance from the docks. Up the streets towards the palace marched the Nazi troops. The amazed Danes, going to work on their bicycles, could not believe their eyes. Many said afterwards they thought it was some film being shot." When some of the Danes didn't understand German orders to detour on side streets, "The Germans fired, killing a dozen or so."

In his April 19 entry, Shirer noted it was the eve of Hitler's 51st birthday. Propaganda chief Josef Goebbels was in full flower on the radio. But when Shirer passed the Hitlerian Chancellery that night, he noticed all of 75 persons "waiting outside for a glimpse of the leader."

"In other years on the eve of his birthday there were ten thousand." As Hitler again plunged into war, where were the German people?

From *Berlin Diary* by William L. Shirer
(Alfred A. Knopf, New York, 1941)

# ■ *"Intend To Fire Torpedo"*

Off Norway the morning of April 8, 1940, an Allied submarine and a disguised German transport played a deadly cat and mouse game that went on for hours—and could have upset an invasion.

The Polish *Orzel* (*Eagle*), assigned to the Royal Navy's 2nd Submarine Flotilla since escaping occupied Poland, opened the game as the "cat" in the affair. Submerged off Kristiansand, *Orzel* spotted an odd-looking passenger ship with no discernible flag showing and the name *Rio de Janeiro* emblazoned on her bows.

It was about 10:30 a.m., and she was pointed north, ploughing toward Bergen.

The British had noted a spurt of German air and naval activity in recent days, with Norway as the obvious target for fresh German aggression. But the British, in their compelling need to contain German expansionism, were willing themselves to violate Norway's neutrality. Just the night before they had laid three minefields off the Norwegian coast.

What the British didn't know in any great detail was the fact that six small task forces of German fighting ships and troop transports already were on their way to Norway under an overall plan calling for their arrival at various objectives at 4:30 the next morning.

*Orzel* had come across one of the German ships taking part in the surprise attack on Norway, although her identity was not immediately apparent. What *was* apparent upon closer look from *Orzel*'s periscope was the poorly painted-out port of registration—Hamburg, Germany.

A search of the Polish submarine's reference materials disclosed the disguised ship was a passenger liner of 9,800 tons normally sailing to South America. *Orzel*'s skipper Jan Grudzinski thought it all too suspicious to ignore—he surfaced nearby and messaged the *Rio*: "Stop engines. The Master with ship's papers is to report on board immediately."

The stranger, instead of replying, increased speed and turned toward Norway's territorial waters. *Orzel* quickly followed and let loose a burst of machine-gun fire that sent paint chips fluttering from the strange ship's sides.

She slowed up and lowered a boat after displaying a signal of acknowledgement. But the boat didn't really approach the Allied submarine. As the Poles realized the Germans were merely stalling, two Norwegian gunboats could be seen approaching the scene.

Undeterred, Grudzinski signalled anew: "Abandon ship immediately. Intend to fire torpedo in five minutes time."

By now it was 12:00. No response came from the German ship. No one could be seen on her decks. The boat lowered earlier still was making no attempt to reach the submarine.

At 12:05, true to his word, Grudzinski fired from his Number Two tube. Seconds later, the "fish" struck the *Rio* halfway down the hull from the bow.

As if on signal, "hundreds of soldiers in field-gray uniforms suddenly appeared on deck." Obviously, they had been cooped below decks, in hiding, to keep the co-opted passenger ship's true role as a troop transport secret. Now they burst into view in pathetic panic, some leaping into the deadly-cold water, others running about the decks aimlessly. The ship's lifeboats, unaccountably, remained unattended in their davits.

The *Orzel*, meanwhile, submerged to avoid an oncoming airplane, then stood watch for a short while by periscope. The gunboats from neutral Norway had reached the stricken ship and were taking on survivors, "unaware that the soldiers were on their way to invade their homeland."

When Grudzinski realized that the *Rio* was not about to sink, after all, he circled to the other side and sent another torpedo into her. This one completed the submarine's task; the onetime passenger liner went down almost immediately.

What was left in the chill seas was a horror scene, despite the best efforts of the Norwegian gunboat crews. Hundreds of bodies spotted the water, which was cold enough to kill in minutes. "They keep together with folds of uniform clutched tightly in a last spasmodic grasp," recalled one onlooker. "The one on the right is face downwards in the water . . . the faces of the two others, livid red and screwed up in a contortion of dread and fatigue, leaving a pitiful impression. Those two I shall never forget. They were both boys: capless, with yellow hair.''

Now, as *Orzel* departed, a Norwegian destroyer joined the scene. All told, 122 survivors were plucked from the water and taken ashore. There they provided the Norwegian government clear warning of the German attack—Hitler, they said, had sent them to protect Norway from a pending British invasion.

In Oslo, the Norwegian Cabinet didn't know what to do, although it ordered the coastal batteries on alert and imposed a blackout that night. In Berlin, the German General staff was afraid the vital surprise element of its invasion plan had been blown sky high. The next morning, Norway was invaded anyway, the Scandinavian country's resistance brave in places but overall spotty and uncoordinated. Despite fierce battles on land and sea over the next few weeks, Norway fell into German hands for the next five years.

In one of the first naval engagements marking the invasion of Norway April 9, German destroyers ordered two Norwegian coastal defense ships to surrender. They wouldn't, and the Germans promptly sank them. By the evening of April 9, the German *Wehrmacht* held every Norwegian port of any importance, the *Orzel*'s sinking of the troop-laden *Rio de Janeiro* notwithstanding.

From *Submarine Warriors* by Edwyn Gray
(Presidio Press, Novato, Calif., 1988)

# ■ *Landing With Piggyback Rider*

So much, during the Battle of Britain in the summer and early fall of 1940, was new, untested, as yet unrefined. Pilots of today, even of the later war years, would find some of the tales of baling wire and seat-of-the-pants flying nearly unbelievable.

Ken Haviland, an American-born RAF night-fighter pilot, was there, as one of Churchill's famous ''few.''

Night-flying had its problems. ''There was . . . the matter of lighting a runway on a grass field so you could see where to land. At first, in 1940, we were given lights that were self-contained in cans, battery operated. You laid them out and had to turn on each one, individually. The problem was that when there was an enemy intruder in the area, you had to go out and turn them off, and then when it was all clear, turn them on again. But in the dark you couldn't see to find them to turn on again! Finally, an engineer at our airfield laid out permanent runway lights, just like you see today. It was quite a stroke of genius."

Even in daylight, the improvised airfields of grass provided an occasional unsought thrill. "Originally, Fighter Command used ordinary grass fields that were mowed down for us. At one place, we had an auxiliary field about a mile or so from the main one, and there was a taxi-way mowed to connect the two—over a mile. At Digby, we operated with a Spitfire squadron at one end of the field and our squadron at the other. We had a scramble one day, and the Spitfires passed over us going in the other direction! In those days, we took off in formation, so things really got dangerous."

Radar was not yet perfected. And at night it was all too easy to visually misidentify other planes in the air. "It was especially bad when we flew the Mosquito, because it was a twin-engine fighter, and the Germans had the Messerschmitt 110, which was also twin-engined."

Even radar, however, could not always prove the identity case. "I was on the tail of an intruder once, and the radar operator on the ground told me it was friendly. I was ordered not to attack it. The German was able to get away. This was annoying because if I had shot him down, it would have been the first kill with a Mosquito."

Before obtaining the more advanced Mosquito, Haviland had to fly the Defiant, equipped with guns in a turret behind the pilot's seat. "That meant you had to shoot at the enemy when he was broadside of you. You had to pull up side-by-side, practically."

Such a maneuver obviously wasn't very practical. "I (once) managed to get alongside a Dornier, and my gunner started firing away at him, but he simply rolled over and slipped away. There was nothing I could do to catch him in the right position for a kill."

Overall, Haviland put in 1,600 hours of combat flying time by war's end and earned the Distinguished Flying Cross. It was after the Battle of Britain, of course, that he flew the Mosquito, often as a night-fighter pilot accompanying the big bombers in their raids on Germany. He later became a professor of aerospace engineering at the University of Virginia.

There, he might have had some difficulty explaining one more adventure from his "seat-of-the-pants" days in the air . . . explaining in aerodynamics terms the time he accomplished a piggyback landing of two airplanes at once!

Haviland and his trusty Mosquito had been "out" one night checking on German radar frequencies. Returning to base in the English countryside in the dark, he was alerted that there was an enemy intruder in the area . . .

"So we had to keep our lights off. I landed the airplane, but down on the runway, I found I couldn't control it. It wanted to swerve off to the side. Also, I couldn't throttle back, couldn't even cut the ignition on the port engine. Finally, the navigator turned the fuel shut-off and the engine stopped. I looked up above my head, and I thought it seemed unusually dark out. There was this strange object sticking into the canopy, too. Turns out it was the exhaust pipe of a Halifax bomber that had landed right on top of us!"

Possible? How could it happen?

"Well, he had no radio and had come in to land, too. He made a steeper approach than I had, and that was how we landed together. There he was, right on top of us! By the time we all stopped, his gear had collapsed, so we were bearing *his* weight, too."

And no one hurt? "We had trouble getting out of the Mosquito. The people outside on the runway thought we must be all dead, but we were arguing with the people from the Halifax. There was aviation gasoline showing in our tanks, which had been ripped open, and it's a wonder we didn't all get blown to pieces. The Mosquito was a total loss, as you might expect."

Haviland's entry for his logbook that day was somewhat understated: "Halifax landed on top of us. Bit of a mess."

From interview by Luther Y. Gore, *Military History* Magazine, October 1985

# ■ *Parachutist Draped On Wing*

The blitz was on, and in London Sunday, September 15 of 1940, was a bright and clear day. Anyone on the ground could look up and see the British fighters—*their* fighters—as they engaged waves of *Luftwaffe* bombers above.

For the German air force, it was a major effort, a peak in the storied Battle of Britain that contributed heavily to Hitler's ultimate decision against invasion of England. The bombing raids this Sunday morning were aimed at London, Portland and the Spitfire production facilities near Southampton.

Rising to defend London against Hermann Göring's Dorniers were 14 RAF fighter squadrons, and among them was a young man flying into his first combat, Sergeant R.T. Holmes of the 504 Hurricane Squadron based at Hendon.

He and his fellow Hurricane pilots first encountered cumulus clouds at 8,000 feet. "This was quite dicey," he later explained, "for we had only practiced formation flying in clouds in pairs, and to suddenly find 12 of us climbing through this bumpy stuff was quite a rare experience."

In short order, there would be even more of the *dicey*. Directed by radar, Holmes and his gang met the oncoming Dorniers at 17,000 feet. "I was tail-end Charlie, weaving above and consequently the last to attack."

In minutes, both the Dornier and the Hurricane formations had broken up, the Germans—most of them—turning for home, and the 504 Squadron reforming itself. "I spotted three Dorniers blazing a lone trail toward London. No one seemed to have noticed them, so I decided to give them a little attention."

As his idea of "a little attention," the intrepid Briton first attacked the two outside bombers, on each one's flank. "The first man belched oil all over my windscreen, blotting my vision entirely; but when the oil cleared, due to my overtaking speed, I saw his tail very close to my nose, and one of his airscrews stopped."

As related in the book *1940* by Laurence Thompson, Holmes "just grazed under his belly" and shot past below.

He now had a go at No. 2. "It was the second plane which caught fire at his wing root and from which came a parachutist who draped himself so artistically over my wing. I didn't give much for the chances of either of these machines getting home, but could not claim them destroyed, as I had not seen them crash." Mark them down as "probables."

But there still was the leader, who continued to press on for London. "One stern attack, without much apparent effect, left me low in ammo for we only had a total of 15 secs' firing. I thought a head-on attack might cool his ardor, and climbed up and past him to his left from my last breakaway."

At this point, Holmes became aware that his own engine sounded rough, his oil pressure had dropped and "there was oil bubbling up the inside of my windscreen—my own oil." He bore in for his head-on attack anyway, using up the last of his ammunition in the process.

"I knew the engine had had it anyway, so more in frustration than in hate I kept on and clipped one side of his fragile-looking twin tail with my port wing."

It seemed only a slight bump as the Dornier's tail "snapped off." In seconds, though, the Hurricane's own port wing dipped; the end of the wing tore away, and the British fighter spun out of control.

As Holmes struggled to free himself from the cockpit and bail out, the spinning fighter passed through the cloud layer—"and I knew I was halfway down already."

Finally extricating himself and dropping into the slip-stream, Holmes was hurled against his own aircraft's tail assembly; his right arm was rendered numb and useless. Plummeting earthward, he worked his left hand under his left armpit and pulled the ring. "There was a jerk so sickening that both my boots flew off my feet and then complete silence, and I said to myself in awe: 'It worked!' "

An instant later, wafting downward upon London, Holmes saw, just above the city's Victoria Station, "the front half of the Dornier floating lazily like an autumn leaf onto the station roof."

He, himself, landed safely enough, but with one more painful bump. "I hit a Chelsea rooftop myself, missed my grip, and rolled off into the dustbin."

About the time of the same *Luftwaffe* "peak," Hitler and Göring had a violent argument. *Luftwaffe* tactics changed (fewer daytime raids). The invasion of England was off—Russia, instead, would be "on." Intrepid young men like Sergeant R.T. Holmes, Churchill's famous "few," had saved their country from invasion.

From *1940* by Laurence Thompson (William Morrow and Company, New York, 1966)

# ■ Pet Spy In England

The German *Abwehr*, or military intelligence apparatus, was happy with the slim young man known as "Schmidt-Hansen," a native of the Danish Jutland. His face, wrote one of the *Abwehr*'s interviewers, was "fine and energetic, all his features and manners testifying to a good upbringing."

As further qualification, so far as the *Abwehr* was concerned, he had a good record as a pre-war Nazi in his native land. Finally, he spoke English.

In no time flat, Hansen was paired with a pro-Nazi Swede named Goesta Caroli, and on the night of September 3, 1940—at the height of the Battle of Britain—they stepped out of a black-painted Heinkel above the 13th-century cathedral of Salisbury, England.

Their parachutes floated them down into a grove outside of town, but young Hansen landed in a tree. Cutting himself loose from the chute's rigging, he then fell to the ground and broke an ankle.

They stuck together, found a doctor and had Hansen's ankle set in a cast. In three days, still apparently making his way to London to set up his spying base, Hansen radioed to his German superiors: "Roads blocked with refugees. Most of them look Jewish."

That pandering signal was the first of more than 1,000 that Hansen would be sending his superiors for nearly five wartime years spent as the elated *Abwehr*'s hottest spy in all England. As far as the *Abwehr* was concerned, "he was their pet, their pride, their miracle man," wrote Ladislas Farago in his 1971 bestseller *The Game of the Foxes*.

The broken ankle soon forgotten (and Caroli soon faded from view, too), Hansen may also have been the *Abwehr*'s most irreverent, wheedling, sulky or sentimental spy.

He thought nothing of filling the wartime airwaves with four-letter expletives when angered by his masters in Germany and their demands for specific information.

He complained quite freely: "You never let me know what you think of my work. An occasional pat on the back would be welcome. After all, I am only human."

He told the *Abwehr* he had struck up a relationship with a young woman who worked as a secretary at the Allied invasion headquarters in Norfolk house. Along with the tidbits of inside information he had gleaned from her, he once signaled his German headquarters: "Well, what do you think of Mary? Isn't she quite a gal?"

So outstanding was his work in the *Abwehr*'s eyes that in the sixth week he was awarded the Iron Cross First Class—"the first spy in the field to be awarded the coveted decoration," wrote Farago. Months later, an apparently sentimental Hansen came to his 1,000th signal to the *Abwehr*. "On the occasion of this, my one thousandth message," he radioed, " I beg you to convey to our *Führer* my humble greetings and ardent wishes for a speedy victorious termination of the war."

The intelligence service had, in the meantime, performed handsprings in response to the mercenary Hansen's demands for money.

In 1941 (before Britain was at war with Japan), Hansen met a Japanese military attaché on a bus in London one evening and was given his fellow "passenger's" copy of the London *Times* as the attaché rose to leave the bus. Pasted to the inside pages were eighty £50 notes.

"Won't be reporting for a couple of days," radioed Hansen later that day. "I'm getting drunk tonight."

As it turns out, the *Abwehr* should have wished he got drunk more often, fell under a bus or otherwise incapacitated himself. For Hansen, nearly from the moment he set broken foot on English soil, had been deftly "turned."

When Hansen broke his ankle landing in England by parachute, the *Abwehr* had contacted one of its other "best spies" in England to lead Hansen to a "safe" doctor. The go-between, though, had been suborned earlier by Britain's counterespionage agency, MI.5, and when the *Abwehr* radioed *him*, it was really "talking" to MI.5.

Hansen soon agreed to cooperate with his British captors, whereas the uncooperative Caroli spent the war under lock and key (hence his fading from *Abwehr* view). Hansen—and many other double-agents like him—represented a major intelligence coup—not for the *Abwehr*, but rather for MI.5.

From *The Game of the Foxes* by Ladislas Farago
(David McKay Company, Inc., New York, 1971)

# ■ Penalty Exacted For Coventry

"The truth is that we were not so ready, nor organized, for anything so terrific as this."

So wrote a clergyman after the *Luftwaffe*'s infamous raid on Coventry, England, on November 14, 1940, and *terrific* it was.

For 11 hours, dusk to dawn, the bombers came, 400 to 500 of them in waves. It was perfect flying weather.

To make matters worse for those on the ground, beneath the continuing cascade of incendiaries and high-explosive bombs, the city's water mains were knocked out by the first bomber waves. Coventry's firemen had little means for fighting the multitude of blazes springing up all around them.

The result, by morning, was devastation of an estimated 100 acres, with 1,000 homes destroyed and 32,000 damaged. In addition, 554 persons were reported killed.

"The German attack on Coventry has been described as probably the most concentrated and destructive on any British objective outside London throughout the war," said British journalist Laurence Thompson in his post-war book, *1940*.

The best-known "victim" of the Coventry raid was its cathedral, reduced during the "terrific" night to mere shards of its walls—and to its 15th-century spire.

The target at Coventry, said *Luftwaffe* General Albert Kesselring later, had been its arms factories. "Fire and smoke clouds made it impossible to aim accurately. The dispersion inevitable in any bombing is thus considerably increased and punishes adjacent areas in no wise intended as objectives."

Certainly, Coventry had been punished. "The situation seemed to justify German claims that Coventry had been knocked out of the war," added Thompson in his book. But not so. The city's armament production resumed at one-third capacity the day after the raid and in two months, it further seems, "it was back to normal."

The real punishment, though, was to be suffered by Germany itself. The "final lesson" of Coventry, wrote Thompson, "was learned not by the *Luftwaffe*, but by a British observer, the Deputy Chief of Air Staff, Air Vice-marshal A.T. Harris, who as Commander-in-Chief of Bomber Command did to Hamburg nearly three years later what the *Luftwaffe* had tried to do to Coventry."

The horrendous fire storm loosed at Hamburg took a staggering toll of 43,000 lives.

Even at that, production in Hamburg's factories and shipyards in a few months' time "was back to 80 percent normal."

In the interim, the British public and the country's wartime leadership debated the issue of bomb-raid reprisals against German cities. Winning out as official policy was retaliation, even though polls indicated that a sizable segment of British public was against it.

From *1940* by Laurence Thompson
(William Morrow and Company, New York, 1966)

# ■ *Patterns On A Kitchen Table*

Out of China in the spring of 1941 came the startling intelligence that the Japanese had a fighter plane that could outrace, outclimb and out-turn any aircraft in somnolent America's military arsenal. For some who were not so somnolent, even before Pearl Harbor, this was grim news indeed. One such man was U.S. Navy aviator John ("Jimmy") Smith Thach.

Apprised of the Zero's performance capabilities, Jimmy Thach hastily repaired, of all places, to his dining-room table with a box of ordinary kitchen matches.

"I decided that we had better do something about this airplane," he would later explain, "and I drew on my days on the football field and the basketball court. I know there that if you come up against somebody who is faster that you are, you have to trap him somehow so that he can't use his superiority, whatever that may be."

For nights on end in the months before his country was drawn into World War II, Navy pilot Thach spread out his matches on the dining room table to simulate aircraft formations. The next day, he and his squadron mates would try out his newly learned wrinkles.

He already thought the three-plane formation favored in Europe and the United States was unwieldy. In tight turning maneuvers, one wingman was likely to "slide" into the other. Thach experimented instead with a combat unit of four aircraft, divided into two pairs flying a wide formation. And from that arrangement of kitchen matches came the U.S. Navy's "Thach Weave," whereby each split pair keeps an eye on the other's tail and turns in, toward the oncoming enemy's path the moment he appears.

The idea was, "if any enemy came after one (pair), from above, ahead or astern, you might be able to confuse him by doing something he didn't expect." Further, the two aircraft "turning in" would have a quick shot at the on-coming Zeros. The turn itself, at the same time, would alert the second pair that they were under attack.

Thach and his squadron mates tried it out. His Lt. Cmdr. Edward ("Butch") O'Hare was to take four Navy fighters flying at full speed and attack Thach's own formation of planes flying at only half-speed. "So he made all sorts of attacks, quite a few of them from overhead, coming down this way and that. It looked like a pretty good thing to me. Every time he came in to shoot—you can tell when an airplane is in position to shoot—we just kept weaving back and forth."

When the Navy pilots landed, O'Hare (for whom Chicago's O'Hare Airport is named) was obviously excited. "Skipper," he said, "it really worked. It really worked. I couldn't make any attack without seeing the nose of one of your half-throttle planes pointed at me."

Explained Thach further: "You needed no communication. You were flying along watching the other two planes of your combat unit. They suddenly made a turn. You knew there was somebody on your tail and you had to turn in a hurry."

Then, a year later and six months after Pearl Harbor, came the Battle of Midway. Thach and his pitiful handful of fighters from the *Yorktown* accompanied the carrier's 12 torpedo planes for their near-suicidal attack on Japanese Admiral Chuichi Nagumo's Carrier Strike Force. As the Americans bore in for the attack, swarms of Zeros met them.

Thach radioed the leader of his unit's other two-plane section to spread out and weave. But his section leader's radio was out. With no reaction from that source, Thach then ordered his own wingman, Ram Dibb: "Pretend you are a section leader and move out far enough to weave."

The Zeros by this time had swooped in. "The air was just like a beehive and I wasn't sure at that moment that anything would work." But then . . . "my weave began to work! I got a good shot at two Zeros and burned them."

Thach, later a full admiral, didn't expect to come back from the landmark U.S. victory at Midway. But he did. So did his aerial maneuver, the Weave—soon to be passed on to U.S. fighter pilots worldwide. Fortunately for them and the country, Thach had been one of those individuals who was wide awake and prepared for war *before* the war.

From *The Pacific War Remembered*, edited by John T. Mason, Jr. (Naval Institute Press, Annapolis, Md., 1986)

# ■ *Saga Piled Upon Saga*

Not only triumph for one side, tragedy for the other, but often the totally unexpected attends so many wartime sagas of the sea. In the *Graf Spee* fight of December 1939, who, firstly, would have expected the lighter-gunned British cruisers *Ajax*, *Exeter* and *Achilles* to contain the monster that was before them—a modern, fully armed pocket battleship?

And then, secondarily, who expected the famous scuttling of the great German Goliath? Certainly not the crowds watching as the *Graf Spee* made ready, it seemed, to leave the neutral port of Montevideo for the wide seas—and the waiting British, with who-knew-how-many warships. But in mid-stream, as it were, the pocket battleship stopped full. "The great crowd immediately below us, denied their sight of a battle, was quite hushed. What was going to happen? Time passed in considerable speculation and suspense, but the truth, unlikely though it appeared was beginning to dawn on some of us."

So, afterwards, would recall the British naval attaché based in nearby Buenos Aires. "Exactly as the sun set behind her, a great volume of smoke billowed up—and an enormous flash was followed in due course by the boom of a large explosion. So the *Graf Spee* met her end."

Still, the unexpected here was caused by man, when often at sea, it is not. Take, for instance, the double saga of the *Jervis Bay* and the *San Demetrio*. The initial action belonged to the armed British merchantman *Jervis Bay*, whose 6-inch guns were the prime protection for an entire convoy of 37 home-bound ships when they were accosted in the North Atlantic by the powerful German pocket battleship *Scheer* in the autumn of 1940.

As the convoy's sole escort, *Jervis Bay* bravely charged forward, her smaller guns merely *popping* in vain. The sleek German wolfhound blinked in surprise at this seagoing mutt's effrontery, then savaged the pest with big 11-inch guns. The saving grace for the Allies was that *Jervis Bay*'s suicidal attack allowed the convoy to scatter while *Scheer* was momentarily busy at her kill. By the time *Jervis Bay* was dealt with, the *Scheer* could only catch up to and pummel five of the original 37. Those five did become victims of the raider, but 32 others did not. For his willing sacrifice, the *Jervis Bay*'s Captain, E.S.F. Fegen, received the Victoria Cross—posthumous, since he went down with his ship.

But the double saga was not yet over, since one of the five *Scheer* victims was to reappear—like a ghost, but a very solid ghost. After the tanker *San Demetrio* had been smashed and holed by the *Scheer*'s big shells, it seems, a handful of surviving crew abandoned their burning ship and its cargo of high-octane aviation fuel for the uncertainties of a lifeboat. As told by Richard Hough in his book *The Longest Battle: The War At Sea, 1939-45*, they survived their first night in the freezing North Atlantic latitudes and passed most of the next day without real incident—that is, unfortunately, without discovery or rescue.

Late in the afternoon, they came upon a drifting, burning ship. Rowing closer, they soon saw that it was their own, the *San Demetrio*, still afloat!

With nightfall upon them and the seas running high, they didn't quite dare to attempt re-boarding, but moved to the "weather side" for protection against the nasty elements and tried to stay close. By next morning, however, she was gone, practically—on the horizon and still blazing away. It would be a long haul to catch up to her again.

The night on the open water, though, had been "dreadful." The survivors determined that the very ship they had abandoned would be their only hope of salvation. "She was the only thing we could see in all the wide circle of ocean and she looked good," wrote Able Seaman Calum MacNeil later. "At least very warm. She might blow up at any time, but that was quick and painless death compared with this slow freezing and sickness, this forced labour of failing muscles."

Just as important, perhaps more, also noted MacNeil later, the *San Demetrio* was their own ship, "still floating in spite of what she had suffered." Not only was she home to the woebegone band in the lifeboat, but: "She was ours and had not failed us. She had looked for us and by some miracle had found us. We could not fail her."

The survivors did catch up and they did creep back aboard. The ship that they found upon re-boarding was a wreck—smashed and burned, flames still flaring, provisions destroyed, engine-room partially flooded, the dead—or their ashes—all about. But the survivors from the lifeboat somehow got the fire out. They got the engines going "after a superhuman effort of salvage." They turned (somehow again) for home. They did all this, plus take the tanker all the way to Glasgow, Scotland, "without charts, compass or steering," says Hough, in a manner "typical of the gallantry, determination and endurance of those who fought the Battle of the Atlantic."

*Graf Spee* had only been a start. *Jervis Bay* and *San Demetrio* were only continuation. The Atlantic, North and South, but mostly North, would remain a long, grueling saga of the war.

From *The Longest Battle: The War At Sea, 1939-1945*, by Richard Hough (William Morrow and Company, New York, 1986)

# ■ War Is 'Only Half Bad'

German tank gunner Karl Fuchs, a callow youth, was in on the big show—Hitler's invasion of the Soviet Union, June, 1941. "He was born in 1917 and as a youth grew up with the teachings of National Socialism," wrote his widow Helene Fuchs-Richardson many years later. "He was an impressionable young man and, like many of his contemporaries, was overwhelmed by the preaching of the party."

They had met as students at the University of Wurzburg, both studying education and planning to be teachers. "Karl's happy disposition, his sense of humor, his idealism, and his talent in music, especially in singing, made him a truly special person."

But the war came along, and soon Karl was writing home from the front, the later-to-be-dreaded Eastern Front. At first, things went swimmingly for the young Hitlerites and their middle-aged generals plunging into Soviet territory by storm and surprise.

To Helene, June 17, 1941, while on the move to the East—
*Our status at present here at this temporary base is still uncertain. No one knows what is going to happen to us but we feel that some kind of decision will be forthcoming in a matter of days—if not in a matter of hours. We all sense that something is about to happen. Don't worry about me . . .*

To his wife again, June 25, 1941, from Lithuania—
*We marched into Vilnius* (Vilna), *cheered on by the jubilant citizens. Yesterday I knocked off a Russian tank, as I had done two days ago! If I get in another attack, I'll receive my first battle stripes. War is half as bad as it sounds . . .*

Karl and his 7th Panzer Division were attached to 39th Panzer Corps, itself a part of *Panzergruppe 3* on the left wing of Army Group Center. His division forced its way into Vilna, Lithuania, on June 24 before turning toward Minsk in Russia proper.

To his wife from Russian territory, June 28, 1941—
*Up to now, all of the troops have had to accomplish quite a bit. The same goes for our machines and tanks. But, nevertheless, we're going to show those Bolshevik bums who's who around here! They fight like hired hands—not like soldiers, no matter if they are men, women or children on the front lines. They're all no better than a bunch of scoundrels . . .*

*The impressions that the battles have left on me will be with me forever. Believe me, dearest, when you see me again, you will face quite a different person, a person who has learned the harsh command: "I will survive!" You can't afford to be soft in war; otherwise you will die. No, you must be tough—indeed, you have to be pitiless and relentless. Don't I sound like a different person to you? Deep down in my heart, I remain a good person and my love for you and our son will never diminish. Never! This love will increase as will my longing for you. I kiss you and remain forever*

*Your Korri*

From *Sieg Heil! War Letters of Tank Gunner Karl Fuchs, 1937-1941*, compiled, edited and translated by Horst Fuchs Richardson (his son); historical commentary by Dennis Showalter (Archon Books, Shoe String Press, Hamden, Conn., 1987)

# ■ *A Farewell From Stalin*

The neophyte artillery officer who briefly spoke on the telephone with his father the day the Germans invaded their Soviet Union had been rated only "fair" in the fundamentals of Marxism-Leninism.

That, a short while before, had been at the Red Army's Artillery Academy. He earned a "fair" in tactics, as well. In shooting, artillery equipment and English, however, he earned a better grade: "good."

Yakov Dzhugashvili, in his late 30s, emerged a senior lieutenant. The commander of his 151st Training Section, according to the Soviet press agency *Novosti*, gave the aspiring officer a higher rating in an efficiency report—"showed himself well prepared during probationary period for the post of battery commander. Coped with his work well. Can be recommended for the next rank—captain."

But the commander's higher-ups decided that Yakov Dzhugashvili would need a year's experience commanding an artillery battery before he could be made a captain.

That was in March 1941, and fate—in the form of Nazi Germany's invasion June 22—would not grant him that added year of preparation.

On June 27, Yakov was in action for the first time, his battery a part of the 14th Armored Division's 14th Howitzer Artillery Regiment. On July 4, the German 3rd Panzer Division cut off Yakov's division. By July 16, among thousands like him, the fledgling officer had been captured near Vitebsk.

Interrogated by his captors, he allegedly explained details of his capture this way: "On July 12, our unit was surrounded and a heavy air bombardment followed. I decided to fight my way to our troops, but was hit and stunned. I would have shot myself if I had been able to."

In the same interrogation, he allegedly told his German captors they never could take Moscow—a prediction in which he was proven correct.

He and his famous father never had an easy relationship, it seems. Yakov's own autobiographical statement, written for an official dossier in 1939, had explained that he was born in Baku in 1903, "into the family of a professional revolutionary."

The Bolshevik Revolution of 1917, of course, had come along, and by 1939, Yakov could add, "Father is now at Party work in Moscow."

Somehow, in the alarm and confusion of June 22, 1941, the day of the German invasion, they managed a telephone connection and had a last conversation with each other. Allegedly, that is also what Yakov told his German interrogators.

What might Stalin have told his son on that day, in their last conversation? "As he learned that I was leaving for the front, he said, 'Go and fight.' "

Yakov, son of Stalin, did not survive his captivity. In fact, his fate surely ranks among the more tragic of the entire war.

According to Soviet historian Alexander Kolesnik's account for *Novosti*, it is not clear whether Yakov ever learned that his wife, Yulia Meltser, was thrown into prison for nearly two years after his capture.

But Yakov did hear, was stunned to hear, was "hardest hit" to hear, his father Stalin's statements that in the Red Army, "There are no prisoners of war, there are traitors."

Yakov consistently refused to cooperate in German attempts to use him for propaganda aimed at undermining the determination of Soviet troops to fight on against the Germans.

He survived a starvation camp where prisoners resorted to cannibalism. He joined an escape plot but was betrayed. Always, among POWs, he was a marked man—*Stalin's son*. He first was cajoled, then pressured, then threatened, in German efforts to "turn" him, Stalin's son, to use him for propaganda.

It was an added burden few could ever appreciate—*Stalin's son*.

A former POW once housed with him said: "His attitude to the Nazis was uncompromising. During checks he did not stand to attention, and in general (he) behaved defiantly and never saluted the German officers, for which he was often sent to the punishment cell."

Finally, he was transferred to the Sackenhausen death camp. On April 14, 1943, said another POW incarcerated with him, "Yakov refused to enter the barrack and ran instead to the no man's land."

The sentry who then shot him is quoted as saying that Yakov, Stalin's son, gripped the wires at the perimeter and shouted: "Hey, you are a soldier, so don't be a coward. Shoot me!"

With the report of the sentry's pistol, Yakov Dzhugashvili's last wish was granted. His death was instantaneous.

From *Military Bulletin,* July 1988, distributed by
*Novosti*, Soviet Press Agency

# ■ Fleet Of Moles

Nellie was her name, this dragon-like, earth-gobbling machine that was Winston Churchill's pet both in World War I and in World War II. Never mind that in the first of those wars she never was built, and in the second, her day already had passed. The fact is that for a time there really was a 77 ½-foot, 140-ton machine that slid through the earth like a giant slug and left a deep trench in her wake.

After pushing development of the tank in WWI with considerable foresight, Churchill next conceived of a fleet of mechanical "moles" like Nellie that would burrow trenches up to fixed defenses during the night. At that point, the infantry following the mechanical monster's track would spring to the attack against a thoroughly startled enemy.

In the stalemated trench warfare of WWI, such a fleet would have been very useful indeed. But the mechanical state of the art was not yet on line.

When World War II came along, with the long "Phony War" following the German invasion of Poland in September 1939, Churchill again proposed his mole concept, in the expectation of another trench stalemate on the great continent lying across the English Channel. Such mechanical moles would be most useful in approaching Hitler's static West Wall, it seemed reasonable to conclude at first.

But the German blitzkrieg unleashed against France and the Low Countries in May 1940 forever dashed the concept of static defenses withstanding the new, highly mechanized weapons of war. Nonetheless, while assuming the post of Prime Minister, Churchill insisted that England would have her Nellie.

Apparently for the first time, the full and detailed story of the Churchillian project, a well-kept secret during the war, appeared in a book-like "paper" published in 1988 by the Society for Lincolnshire (England) History and Archaeology as 'Nellie': The History of Churchill's Lincoln-Built Trenching Machine, by John T. Turner.

A press release from the historical group explained that Churchill's initial hope was to avoid "the trench warfare and horrific casualties of the First World War." The highly mobile tank warfare that Nazi Germany introduced in Poland, and then employed to perfection in the conquest of France, rendered Churchill's mole-machine unnecessary. But a handful were built anyway, and

"Nellie was a masterpiece of heavy engineering, the biggest machine of its kind ever built, and it worked."

As might be imagined, creation of such a huge self-propelled, trench-digging machine at a time of national emergency and carefully husbanded resources was a mind-boggling feat—"a tale of a challenge accepted, wrestled with and overcome against terrific odds."

Flinging away the loose dirt as it travelled, the fantastic machine "was to travel at .5 mph through no-man's land at night, cutting a trench six feet wide and six feet deep for infantry to follow and penetrate enemy lines."

Fairly successful in field trials, the original Nellie carried a three-man crew. They were the pilot, seated in a topside conning tower with a slit window for visibility; a driver seated below, facing the rear and *driving* totally blind; and the unfortunate engineer, trapped in a mechanical cubicle full of oil fumes and deafening engine noise (from two 600-horsepower engines).

The machine, visited by Churchill in person during its field trials, consisted of a plough-and-cutting section in front and the propel section in the back. Like a very slow-moving submarine, it could dig into the earth, nose first, find its proper level and then proceed on the chosen course (more or less). Steering, though, was a major problem, and tree roots tended to stop Nellie in her self-made tracks.

In the end, Nellie never was sent to the Continent, and she died a dinosaur's unlamented death. Only six of the giant machines were completed.

"On Churchill's instructions," writes author Turner, "they were to be kept serviced and ready in case a need for them arose." It never did, and "all but one were reduced to scrap shortly after the end of the war." The one remaining machine, apparently the original pilot, was consigned to like fate in the early 1950s—once Churchill was out of office.

And so vanished the last of Churchill's once-farsighted mole-machines—"and much that might have been learnt has been lost forever."

# ◼ *Mount Your Tanks!*

By July 9, 1941, the power-laden Army Group Center had sealed the Minsk Pocket, having overrun 21 Soviet rifle divisions and 14 tank brigades, taken 300,000 prisoners and accounted for 2,600 tanks and 1,500 guns of the Red Army. By now, too, Karl Fuchs was both a tank commander and a platoon leader in his 25th Panzer Regiment, 7th Panzer Division.

To his wife on July 5, 1941—

*My darling wife! My dear boy* (their infant son)

*We have fought in battle many days now and we have defeated the enemy wherever we have encountered him. Let me tell you that Russia is nothing but misery, poverty and depravity! This is Bolshevism!*

*It is late in the evening now and quite dark already. We only wait for our expected orders: Mount your tanks! Start your engines! Move out! Maadi* (a nickname), *if you were only here and could see me—tanned by the sun, dusty, dirty, with eyes as clear as a falcon!*

*Our losses have been minimal and our success is great. This war will be over soon, because we are fighting against only fragmented opposition . . .*

As time went on, so did the letters from the Eastern Front. On September 22: The countryside, like its people "seems eternally gray and monotonous." Everywhere, nothing but poverty and "wretched misfortune."

Terrible conditions for the fighting men of the Reich, too. Mud, rain, with "time and space . . . suspended." But, once the battle is over, peace will reign for Germany and all Europe. The men at the front are convinced, and so should be the people back home. Children in school should be so taught.

As October began, Karl's tank outfit was a part of the German drive on Moscow itself. The foolish Russians hadn't expected the Germans to risk the on-coming Russian winter! *The Last Hour of Bolshevism is near and that means that Old England's destruction is imminent.*

By October 15, snow, pure and white, on the ground. Now, in fact, there is a grudging respect for the Russian winter. *What all of us fear most now is the snow and the accompanying cold temperatures, but we'll get used to it.*

His friend Roland just died of wounds. Why did he have to die now, the end seemingly in sight? But . . . no time to "bemoan his fate." Rather, it's time for the invading Germans to think of revenge for their dead comrades. They can expect to "roll on," since after the great victories thus far, the Russians can hardly offer major opposition.

In early November—yes, it would be nice to buy and send him some woolen clothing items. Can't wait to get home, naturally. By November 11, temperatures in his area of operations reflected a "gripping cold" unlike anything Germany itself would experience.

On November 12, he wrote his mother that he and his comrades might not be able to return by the end of the year, or even early in the next year, 1942. He would be thinking of home and family when Christmas came. Still, disappointment must be endured, sacrifices must be made. It is a struggle for the future of the German people. *You at home must always keep in mind what would have happened if these hordes had overrun our Fatherland. The horror of this is unthinkable!*

On December 2, came the first official letter. Karl had been killed on the field of battle—*his heroic death occurred when he was fighting bravely for a greater Germany in the front lines during a heavy battle with Russian tanks.*

Karl's company commander, a Lieutenant Reinhardt, said he had been buried in "a dignified resting place." It was near Kiln, north of Moscow, which the Germans at the very peak of their invasion never quite reached. And so, Karl Fuchs, absorbed, swallowed up and forever a part of the same eternally gray and monotonous countryside he held in such obvious contempt.

From *Sieg Heil! War Letters of Tank Gunner Karl Fuchs,1937-1941*, compiled, edited and translated by Horst Fuchs Richardson (his son); historical commentary by Dennis Showalter (Archon Books, Shoe String Press, Hamden, Conn., 1987)

# ■ Faith, Hope *And* Charity

"This morning," wrote Italian Foreign Minister Galeazzo Ciano on November 9, 1941, "Mussolini was depressed and indignant." And well he might have been, since the night before an Italian convoy bound for embattled Libya had been roughly accosted by the Royal Navy.

The disposition of the convoy had been seven merchantmen under the protection of no less than two cruisers and ten destroyers. The ration of nearly two warships for each supply-laden merchant ship was planned with the expectation that otherwise British "wolves" would appear among the Italian "sheep."

As Count Ciano noted, the wolves appeared anyway. "An engagement occurred, the results of which are inexplicable. All, I mean all, our ships were sunk (the merchantmen, that is) and one or maybe two or three destroyers. The British returned to base having slaughtered us."

The "lair" of the wolves so upsetting to Mussolini that morning was a mere island in the Mediterranean no bigger, overall, than Greater London. An island only 60 miles from Sicily and half-an-hour's flight time from Italian airfields. An island lying nearly athwart the vital supply line to Italian and German armies in North Africa—a beleaguered outpost that soon would prove most depressing not only to Mussolini, but also to Hitler and his "Desert Fox," Erwin Rommel.

The island was Malta, a fulcrum of war and battle for many centuries even before the advent of World War II. Once allied with Rome against Carthage, it also had sustained capture by the ancient Byzantines, the Arabs and the Normans. As refuge for the Knights of St. John in 1565, it withstood its famous siege by vastly superior Turkish forces. Next to come along was Napoleon, who seized the island base while on his way to invade Egypt in 1798. The British then blockaded Malta, landed their troops and eventually gained control of the island.

By the time of World War II, Malta was a British crown colony. Its 75 square miles of land held a population of about 280,000. It boasted its old fortifications of the Turkish siege, an undeveloped British fleet base, and not much else in the way of defenses or war-making capability. Its chief defense at first were three old Gladiator biplanes that were called, appropriately, *Faith, Hope* and *Charity*.

And in the days ahead, Malta would undergo one of the most furious sieges by air ever unloosed upon a single territory. First, it was the Italian Air Force, and then the mighty German *Luftwaffe*. With Malta's key position recognized by all the warring parties, the RAF moved in many more aircraft (including Spitfires), while the Royal Navy staged subs and surface ships from the island.

The result was crucial interdiction of the supply line to the Axis forces in North Africa—their eventual disintegration was due in large part to Malta's denial of vital supplies. But Malta, too, had to be supplied. It had to survive under the fury of just about daily air strikes.

With its population living what one writer called "a troglodytic existence in caves," Malta by May of 1942 had endured 2,470 air raids. Its RAF fighters and bombers flew from six airfields constantly holed with bomb craters—fighter pilots might fly four or five sorties a day for weeks at a time.

By the time the war moved up the map into southern Europe in 1943, the RAF had lost nearly 1,000 aircraft staged from Malta—but the Germans and Italians combined had lost an estimated 1,400 in related combat.

British convoys to the gallant island also took a terrible beating. Launched from both Gibraltar and Alexandria, Egypt, one double convoy of 17 ships succeeded in docking just two of them at Malta. Another convoy, Operation Pedestal's 14 ships, landed five at Malta.

There was a moment, probably an inspired moment, when Hitler and Mussolini seriously considered seizing Malta. When Tobruk fell to Rommel in June 1942, however, they all too recklessly gave up the idea—Malta remained a thorn in the side to the end of the *Afrika Korps*' days in Africa.

In the meantime, Malta had earned Britain's George Cross, the highest British award for heroism of civilians. The award always went to individuals, but in Malta's case, a unique one, it was bestowed collectively to the entire island population.

From *Military History* Magazine, October 1988

# ■ *A Date To Mark*

*Yesterday, December 7, 1941, a date which will live in world history, the United States of America was simultaneously and deliberately attacked by naval and air forces of . . .*

Crippled man, crippled fleet.

At Pearl Harbor in Hawaii, rescue and repair parties were just beginning their grim work. Farther around the globe, Japanese forces now were assaulting Malaya, Hong Kong, Guam, the Philippines, Wake Island, Midway . . .

In Washington, the polio-crippled Commander-in-Chief thought the better of the opening line in his draft speech. *Simultaneously*, at the stroke of a pen, became the more suitable *suddenly*. Emphatic dashes took the place of the two mid-sentence commas. The prosaic *in world history* was changed, too. Set off by the helpful dashes, President Franklin D. Roosevelt's war message to the Congress of the United States now would open with its famous, ringing reference point for posterity: "a date which will live in infamy."

Thirty-three minutes after FDR delivered his "Day of Infamy" speech, Congress with but one dissenting vote approved a resolution declaring war on Japan.

The Senate vote was 82 to 0, and the House count 388 to 1, the single nay on December 8, 1941, being that of Rep. Jeannette Rankin, D-Montana, who had been one of the few members of Congress voting against war with Germany in 1917. While she had had some support in those World War I days, her *no* vote this time stirred boos and hisses. There was no debate over this war resolution.

America this time was angry. The country was unified in shock and outrage.

*I ask the Congress to declare that since the unprovoked and dastardly attack by Japan on Sunday, December 7, a state of war has existed between the United States and the Japanese empire.*

Roosevelt had hardly to ask.

His speech broadcast live by radio, he appeared at a joint session of the House and Senate. The Cabinet and the Supreme Court were on attentive hand, as well. Millions listened in home, office, factory or military post.

And so on a Sunday morning of 1941, the separate, even somewhat limited wars that had been raging in Europe and Asia became one.

With the attack on Pearl Harbor, a hesitant, still somewhat isolationist United States at last was pulled, headlong, into the vortex of violence and destruction. And not only America—in a week's time after Pearl Harbor, three dozen nations populated by one half of the planet's inhabitants were officially at war.

They call it World War II. In its scope, in its impact on very nearly all peoples of the earth, it really was the *first* world war. No conflict like it had ever taken place before, and none since.

Its worldwide spread might soon have happened anyway—some other way—but in fact the way it did happen was with the attack on Pearl Harbor.

"There were loud cheers as each plane rose into the air," recalled Mitsuo Fuchida, commander of the carrier-based air armada that struck Pearl Harbor. "After circling the fleet formation, we set course due south for Pearl Harbor."

Under Fuchida's command, he later said, were 49 level bombers, 40 torpedo planes, 51 dive-bombers and 43 fighters. That was only the first wave, though. Soon, "our second wave of 171 planes swept in." (Fuchida's numbers are at slight variance with those of U.S. sources.)

And *sweep* they did.

Surprised, caught barely awake that Sunday morning, was an American fleet of 70 combat vessels (94 to 96 ships in all). Eight battleships were in port, seven of them neatly lined up as the famous "Battleship Row." Fortunately, for America, the Pacific Fleet's carriers were gone . . . at sea.

It took less than two hours for the Japanese to sink or to cripple seven of the battleships, three cruisers, three destroyers, while also destroying 188 aircraft at nearby fields like Wheeler, Hickam, Bellows . . . and leaving 2,403 Americans dead, another 1,178 wounded.

"But there are still many targets which should be hit," Fuchida argued when he returned to his carrier. His urging of another attack on Pearl Harbor was overruled.

"Immediately, flag signals were hoisted, and our ships headed northwest at high speed."

From *Military History* Magazine, December 1986

## ■ *Footnote To Pearl Harbor*

Not everyone gets to be an historical footnote, and for young Japanese Ensign Kasuo Sakamaki on Pearl Harbor Day, that distinction came the hard way. Sakamaki in fact began the day in footnote status. He began the day in the water, and not in the air.

Not swimming in the water, exactly, but piloting one of the five midget submarines the Japanese launched against the U.S. Pacific Fleet on December 7, 1941, in concert with their surprise air attack on the American naval base in the Hawaiian Islands.

The midget subs did not have quite the success of the air armada for which the surprise attack chiefly is known. All five of the two-man craft were lost, and none struck a target with the three torpedoes thought to have been fired.

As a second, but grim footnote reference for Sakamaki, he apparently was the only one of the ten Japanese crewmen to survive the attack by the flotilla of midget subs.

It was, naturally, an experience he never would forget.

His "mother" submarine, the *I.24*, had surfaced off the harbor entrance to Pearl the evening of December 6. "We could see the stars twinkling," said Sakamaki many years later. "There were so many lights visible from the shore. I listened to music from a Honolulu radio station."

Strapped onto the deck of his mother boat was a 75-foot metal tube packing two 18-inch torpedoes. Sakamaki and his crewman, Petty Officer Kiyoshi Inagaki, were supposed to climb into it shortly after midnight, make for Pearl Harbor—seven miles away—and sink the battleship *Pennsylvania* at her moorings.

The plan was foiled from the start—Sakamaki's midget sub wouldn't steer properly and bucked the running seas "like a wild horse," he recalled. "Every time I started the engines, the nose popped up to the surface. So for three hours Inagaki and I carried heavy lead ballast from the stern to the bow. This exhausted us."

Finally on course and running beneath the water's surface, Sakamaki raised his periscope for a quick glimpse of his surroundings, only to see two American patrol boats so close, "I could see the seamen running on the deck." In the depth-charging that followed, the midget's torpedo-launching gear was wrecked and both crewmen suffered minor injuries.

But they escaped. "I made up my mind to enter the harbor and dash into a battleship and explode the torpedoes that way."

Sakamaki's midget banged into a coral reef instead, popped to the surface in full view of an American destroyer, then—at his direction—backed into deeper waters. They would wait for dark that night—December 7—and try again to enter the harbor. "By this time, the bad air and gas in the sub and the tension had almost killed us."

They couldn't, after repeated attempts, manage to penetrate the harbor that night. They decided to save their tiny boat for future attacks against Japan's new enemies by keeping the planned rendezvous with their mother boat off Lanai Island, southeast of Pearl. "At dawn on December 8, we surfaced off what we thought was

Lanai," recalled Sakamaki later, "but it turned out we were near the northeast coast of Oahu Island—way off course."

They then became grounded on another coral reef, firmly stuck this time. "We set the sub on fire and jumped overboard. I was so exhausted I was unable to swim, so I just floated on my back. Inagaki tried to swim to shore and I learned later that he drowned."

The exhausted Sakamaki, meanwhile, fell unconscious, even while he was floating in the water. "And the next thing I remember was being picked up on the beach by an American Army sergeant."

That would have been near Bellows Field, and the American Sergeant was David Abuki. Both men then became footnotes, since Sakamaki instantly qualified as the first Japanese combatant taken prisoner by the Americans in World War II, and Abuki as his captor.

"Pretty short war," said Sakamaki years later, by then the chief of exports for Toyota Motor Co., Ltd., Japan's largest auto-maker. "The Pearl Harbor attack started World War II for me—and ended it."

From the *Associated Press*

# ■ *Bird Named* Swoose

As Boeing's No. 40-3097, she may not be all that well remembered. Under the name combining concept of both swan and goose, however, she still is a legend—the indestructible, ubiquitous and amazing *Swoose*.

Her story begins in a production lot of 42 Boeing B-17Ds turned out before the war began. It continues as No. 40-3097 crosses the Pacific in original form and alights in the Philippines. Eight hours after Pearl Harbor, as is well known, the Japanese wiped out the B-17s that were parked at Clark Field.

Only airplane rubble was left behind, with not a single one of the vaunted Flying Forts left in flyable shape, but from such rubble—and the determined genius of its ground-crew keepers—emerged patched-together, Phoenix-like creatures of the air that again *would* fly.

Writer-historian John H. Mitchell of Springfield, Missouri, says the 19th Bombardment Group's No. 3097 was *not* one of the planes rebuilt from scrap parts at Clark Field—"she wasn't even at Clark when the attack occurred." Luckier than her mates at Clark, she had been flown to the U.S. air field at Del Monte on Mindanao Island just before the Japanese attack.

Nor was Clark knocked completely out of action. "None of our bombers was left flyable, but by heroic efforts, finding a wing of one and a rudder from another, a tailplane from a ruined fuselage, and such engines as remained whole, and putting these odd parts together on fuselages less damaged than others, our men assembled a very few bombers," notes a Smithsonian publication. "It was from such Phoenix-like resurrections that the *Swoose* came into being."

But not quite yet . . . for all these new creations, the war had only begun—none was to fly home into safe retirement. Not by any means. In the days and weeks to follow the Clark Field attack, they flew against the invading Japanese in the Philippines, in the Dutch East Indies, in the respective nearby islands. And one by one, they fell to the enemy until one day in Australia, along about March 1942, the body of a badly damaged No. 3097 was married to the tail ("only a stabilizer" and perhaps a few more spare parts, says Mitchell) of a previously wounded Flying Fort, with not only a hybrid resulting but its christening as the *Swoose*! "Even with this new tail, the other parts were so pieced together and battle-scarred that the airplane little resembled the beautiful Flying Fortress that had landed in the Philippines a few months before," says the Smithsonian account.

An amateur artist went to work and placed a strange looking bird as insignia on the creation's fuselage, helpfully adding the guarantee: "It flies."

And actually, she did . . . continually and consistently. Not only in her time based in Australia, but also for months—even years!—afterwards. The *Swoose* in fact became the command plane for Lt. Gen. George H. Brett, for a time commander of Douglas MacArthur's air forces (Brett's own plane had been shot up in a Japanese strafing attack).

Not only did the *Swoose* carry Brett about the southwest Pacific, but she carried him all the way back to Washington when he was reassigned; she later flew him up and down the Western Hemisphere on flights to Central and South America. She flew on, in fact, throughout all of World War II and finished her career with a total of 4,000 hours of in-air time.

On the way to Washington from Australia, incidentally, the patched-together *Swoose* "established new speed records between Australia and Hawaii, and from there to San Francisco."

Later, the *Swoose* was headed for a post-war meltdown into scrap, but Mayor Fletcher Bowron of Los Angeles managed to save her for display as a war memorial. His city then, in 1949, turned her over to the Smithsonian's National Air Museum for permanent safekeeping. As befitting the *Swoose*, she flew all the way east under her own power. Indeed, with her wartime pilot Frank Kurtz at the controls and many of her crew aboard, she was greeted by crowds of onlookers at various stops along the way— her final flight one of proud acclaim.

From John H. Mitchell and *The National Aeronautical Collections* by Paul E. Garber, head curator and historian, National Air Museum, Smithsonian Institution (*The Smithsonian Institution*, Washington, D.C., 10th edition, 1965)

# ■ *Chennault Strikes Back*

In Washington late in 1941, the skeptics were many. Chinese Ambassador T.V. Soong sent Claire Chennault a cable citing unsettling reports to the U.S. War Department that "your group cannot be ready before February 1942 and will not last two weeks in combat."

Back in Burma, where he was training his American Volunteer Group (AVG), Chennault did his usual slow burn at thoughts of untutored bureaucratic meddling. Still, he merely replied that his fighter pilots would be ready by the end of November and continued his unorthodox training methods. The setting was Toungoo, 170 miles north of Rangoon, a damp, sweltering place. The methodology, all Chennault, was loose, relaxed discipline on the ground (open shirts, weekly "gripe" sessions) and tight discipline in the air (meaning, learn to fight the Japanese Chennault's way).

In China, the Japanese still were rampaging. It only was a matter of time before they turned south for Burma—after Thailand surrendered October 8, the Japanese placed bombers and fighters on Thai airfields along 300 miles of the Burmese border. Hanoi,

Indochina, occupied since 1940, was another staging base for Japanese air power. The target surely would be the long Burma Road, beginning at Rangoon and ending at Kunming, China, as the only overland supply route for the hard-pressed Chinese.

Chennault's American volunteers, most of them from a military background, were not *all* fighter pilots by training. More than half had flown bombers, torpedo planes, even commercial air liners instead. Those with fighter training, in fact, had to *un*learn their standard American lessons and adhere to Chennault's insistence upon teamwork and hit-and-run tactics. They had to realize that, on the one hand, the Japanese were no second-raters in the air, but on the other hand they tended to fly by the book, undeviating from predetermined tactics.

"The object of our tactics is to break up their formation and make them fight according to our style," Chennault told his flyers. "Once the Japanese are forced to deviate from their plan they are in trouble. Their rigid air discipline can be used as a powerful weapon against them."

Chennault acknowledged that the AVG's P-40B had a better top speed than Japanese fighters such as the Zero, a faster dive and heavier firepower, but he stressed the more unhappy points that the Japanese aircraft boasted a higher rate of climb, a higher ceiling and a superior maneuverability. "They can turn on a dime and climb almost straight up. If they can get you into a turning combat, they are deadly."

Most difficult for the naturally combative pilots to accept was Chennault's radical precept of dive, make a pass, shoot and break away—it smacked of running away, a court-martial offense for the British RAF stationed in a nearby Rangoon and a firing-squad offense in the Chinese Air Force, despite Chennault's influence there. But Chennault had too few planes and qualified pilots to squander in dog-fight heroics reminiscent of the Lafayette Escadrille or the Flying Circus of World War I days. Chennault wanted his men to live and fight another day.

With patience maddening to some of his men, he insisted upon training, training and more training, across the Burmese border, while Chinese cities and military targets absorbed almost daily pastings by the Japanese air force.

By the time of Pearl Harbor, however, he was just about ready. And in the days immediately after December 7, 1941, he posted one AVG squadron outside of Rangoon, under RAF operational control, while moving his other two squadrons to Kunming, with himself in command. The second move came right after the Japanese bombed Kunming on December 18; at dawn on the 19th, his P-40s were on patrol over the key city.

Chennault's other "secret weapon" now came into play, the early warning network he had developed in China—"people, telephone and telegraph lines and many hundreds of portable radio sets." At the sight of Japanese aircraft, they were to pass along instant warning, and as the alerts built up, the path of the enemy could be calculated in advance.

On the morning of December 20, Chennault was alerted by telephone that watchers in Yunnan Province had spotted 10 twin-engine bombers cross the provincial border at Laokay, headed northwest. "Their probable objective is Kunming."

In response, Chennault threw up 24 of his AVG's P-40s, all emblazoned with shark-like teeth painted on either side of their sleek nose. Four of them were to make the actual intercept; another four would fly a combat air patrol at high altitude over Kunming, and the remaining 16 would stand by, on the ground, at an auxiliary strip west of the city.

Soon, 60 miles to the southeast, Jack Newkirk's four-plane intercept flight found the bombers. So confident were the Japanese of air superiority that they hadn't even provided their bombers with a fighter escort. The American volunteers came down on the bombers from above, their .50 calibers and .30 calibers spitting.

The bombers immediately jettisoned their deadly loads and turned for home. Newkirk, his guns jammed, did likewise after one diving pass, along with two of his fellow pilots. A fourth, Ed Rector, came out of his power drive, recovered, and went after the bombers. From the auxiliary field to the west of Kunming, meanwhile, the P-40s on standby took to the air, also in pursuit of the Japanese Mitsubishis. The swarming P-40s soon caught up, and before the raiders could reach the Indochina border, six of the original 10 had gone down. Of the four still in the air, only one managed to reach home base. Chennault's AVG had lost one plane—Rector's gas gave out and he had to crash-land in a rice paddy.

The jubilant Chinese press responded to the aerial victory with banner headlines throughout the country—and a nickname for the American volunteers, the "Flying Tigers!" The Japanese, in the meantime, didn't attempt to bomb Kunming for another 16 months, "and when they did, they brought along a 30-fighter escort."

Meanwhile, Rangoon and Burma finally had come under the Japanese gun, and here again the AVG fliers distinguished themselves. On December 23, for instance, 54 Mitsubishis, 12 Nakakima type-97 fighters and 8 Zeros struck at Rangoon. Fifteen AVG P-40s joined the RAF in defending the city, the Americans split into two free-wheeling groups. Two AVG pilots bagged five enemy aircraft each as the Flying Tigers accounted for a confirmed total of 25 Japanese bombers and fighters (while losing two men and three planes). The RAF, with 18 Brewsters in the air, claimed seven enemy downed (while losing five pilots and 11 planes.)

Christmas Day at Rangoon was a repeat performance, as the Japanese struck with 81 bombers and 42 fighters as escort. In battle lasting an hour and a half, the 12 serviceable P-40s flown by the Flying Tigers accounted for another "15 bombers and nine fighters." With bravado typical of the AVG volunteers, Squadron Leader Arvid Olson radioed Chennault in Kunming: "Could put entire Jap force out of commission with whole group here."

In the 10 weeks before Rangoon finally fell, "the AVG with never more than 20 planes that could fly and sometimes as few as five, met the Imperial Japanese Air Force on 31 occasions and chalked up the incredible score of 217 confirmed victories and 43 probables." The cost to the "Tigers" was five men killed, one taken prisoner, 16 P-40s lost in combat.

Winston Churchill weighed in with the message: "The victories of these Americans over the rice paddies of Burma are comparable in character if not in scope with those won by the RAF over the hop fields of Kent in the Battle of Britain."

Overall, before its absorption into the U.S. Army Air Forces in China in July 1942 (also under Chennault's command), the AVG in seven months of almost constant combat knocked down 299 Japanese aircraft, to 32 AVG planes downed, 10 pilots lost in action, 9 in accidents. Clearly, Chennault's painstaking and unorthodox training, coupled with his vital knowledge of the enemy, had paid off.

From *Chennault and the Flying Tigers* by Anna Chennault
(Paul S. Eriksson, Inc., New York, 1963)

# ■ Disorderly Ran The Two Ships

Cecil Brown was standing on the flag deck of the mighty battle cruiser *Repulse* when the first of the Japanese bombers approached. "Strung in a line," they were "clearly visible in the brilliant sunlit sky."

They flew the length of the British warship with no *apparent* harm done. Their estimated altitude was 10,000 feet. But around Brown, "our antiaircraft guns were screaming constantly."

The harm had been done. In the intervening seconds, their bombs had been on the way. "Just when the planes were passing over, one bomb hit the water beside where I was standing, so close to the ship that we were drenched from the waterspout." Worse, though, and simultaneously, a second bomb struck the catapult deck, "penetrating the ship and exploding below in a marine's mess and hangar."

Half a mile away, the *Prince of Wales*, as a battleship even more mighty than *Repulse*, also was under attack from the air. Both capital ships and their escorting destroyers were "throwing everything they have into the air."

Until this moment in time, in history, two notions had prevailed among the leading Western military circles. First, that air power would wilt before ship power. The second, a contradiction, that somehow there was not all that much to fear from the steadily rampaging Japanese of the Far East.

The scene that CBS newsman Cecil Brown witnessed aboard the *Repulse* on December 10, 1941, three days after Pearl Harbor, erased both impressions so dramatically that Prime Minister Winston Churchill reported to the House of Commons, "In my whole experience I do not remember any naval blow so heavy and painful."

The revolution in naval warfare was painfully evident even to those aboard the two stricken ships. Within 24 hours—his report delayed only by the necessity of rescue from the sea—Brown was explaining in his cable to CBS in New York that the Japanese attack succeeded "because of, first, a determined air torpedo attack and, second, the skill and efficiency of the Japanese bomber operations."

For Brown and others aboard the *Repulse*, the *key* word, the really devastating blow, had been *torpedo*. By his account, the bomb-wounded *Repulse* managed to elude any hits during two torpedo-bomber runs. At 12:20 p.m., however, a third wave was approaching. "Stand by for barrage," barked the ship's public address system.

Brown watched as a plane circled, then approached the port side at 300 or 400 yards. "It's coming closer, head on, and I see a torpedo drop. It's streaking for us. A watcher shouts, 'Stand by for torpedo,' and the tin fish is streaking directly for us. Someone says, 'This one got us.' "

It had. It struck Brown's side of the ship 20 yards astern of where he was standing. "It felt like the ship had crashed into a well-rooted dock. It threw me four feet across the deck, but I did not feel any explosion. Just a very great jar."

The ship listed and took a second torpedo hit on its starboard side. "That the *Repulse* was doomed was immediately apparent."

It still seemed unbelievable. "It was most difficult to realize I must leave the ship. It seemed so incredible that the *Repulse* could or should go down."

But she did, and Brown found himself in the water along with the hundreds of surviving British seamen.

From that uncertain vantage point, he not only saw the cruiser's end, but also that of the *Prince of Wales*. "Swimming about a mile away, lying on top of a small stool, I saw the bow of the *Wales*." When the battleship gasped her last, the suction was so great, "it ripped off the life belt of one officer more than fifty feet away."

A Japanese airman's eyewitness report was blunt and short: "Our formations of bombers fell on the two capital ships amidst antiaircraft fire from the enemy. Our torpedoes hit their mark with incandescent glow flashing and dark smoke columns. In disorderly wakes ran the *Prince of Wales* and the *Repulse*, and in a moment they turned into columns of fire, going to the bottom."

Two views, same revolution in naval warfare.

From *World War II* Magazine, January 1989

# ■ *Tale Of A Stowaway*

Few had it as tough during the war as Charlie Mott, who went to war *before* the war (for the United States), as a gung-ho pilot with Claire Chennault's Flying Tigers in China and Burma.

Mott had been a fighter pilot in the U.S. Navy, but he resigned his commission and risked his future Navy opportunities to join Chennault's volunteers.

He then was shot down over Japanese-held territory in Burma. He had been strafing a Japanese air strip.

He bailed out, but his luck was tough. "Hitting the silk" at low altitude, he broke an arm, a leg and his pelvis when he reached the ground with battering impact. The Japanese who then captured him were totally unsympathetic.

"The Japs threw him into a truck that had no suspension and slammed him around for four days over rutted tracks. The Japs did not set his fractured bones."

He was thrown into a dungeon-like prison cell in Bangkok, Thailand, where he mustered the strength and fortitude to set his own arm and leg. He simply had to live with the pelvis.

Eventually recovered, he was placed "in charge of trucks supplying food to British POWs working on the infamous Burma-Siam railroad." In all, he was a POW until 1945.

But now came unexpected problems—the bureaucracy of the war's victorious Allies! "At the end of the war, Charlie was a civilian. He was not eligible for repatriation by any government. He borrowed enough money to get from Bangkok to India."

Even back home in America shortly after the war, Charlie was a veteran without real veteran status. "As a civilian, Charlie got no POW pay, no demobilization benefits, no medical benefits, no GI Bill of Rights, and no credit on his Navy time for more than three years in the CBI (China-Burma-India Theater) as a Flying Tiger and POW."

Undeterred (though many would have been), he subsequently rejoined the Navy, still as a fighter pilot. He put in his years qualifying him for retirement with full benefits, after serving with distinction, and that, *almost*, is the end of the story.

*Almost*, since we haven't yet said how he got home from India in his stateless-like, post-war status. And that was by further demonstration of the fortitude and resourcefulness that had carried him through his wartime ordeal.

When even the American repatriation authorities in India clung to their red tape and refused to allow him to sail home on an officially sanctioned ship, Charlie Mott simply "stowed away on a U.S. troop transport."

From Hugh Crumpler's "How's Your CBI IQ" column
in *Ex-CBI Roundup*, April 1989

# ■ MacArthur's Extended Escape

If he got through to Australia, Douglas MacArthur had promised Jonathan Wainwright back at embattled Corregidor, he would "come back as soon as I can with as much as I can." With a Japanese cruiser cutting ahead of the MacArthur party's PT boats in Philippine waters just a day later, however, no one could be sure that MacArthur would be going anyplace.

In the Japanese homeland, Tokyo Rose had been talking of a public execution of the 62-year-old American general once he was captured. That implied chilling personal grief, too—with him on Navy Lieutenant John Bulkeley's PT Boat 41 were the general's wife Jean, their four-year-old son Arthur and a Cantonese nanny named Ah Cheu.

The party that had left Corregidor and the Bataan Peninsula the evening before—aboard four PT boats of Bulkeley's Motor Torpedo Boat Squadron 3—also included 12 Army officers, a master sergeant familiar with secure radio codes and two ranking Navy officers.

Left behind to harsh fate at the hands of the invading Japanese were 20 or so generals and thousands of fighting men, both American and Filipino. President Franklin D. Roosevelt had ordered MacArthur to leave "The Rock," as Corregidor was called. Uncomfortable with the idea of abandoning his men, MacArthur briefly considered resigning from the U.S. Army and joining the defenders of Bataan as a "volunteer" private.

But reason prevailed—if he could get out, his experience, his expertise and his prestige in the Far East would be needed when America was ready to fight back in strength. Then, too, and unlike most of the service personnel still in the Philippines, he had his family with him.

The projected escape from certain capture, likely torture and possible death would not be easily accomplished in waters or skies so dominated by the Japanese. Their engine noise covered by artillery barrages from the Corregidor fortress, the PT boats had shoved off at dusk the evening of March 11, 1942. Speedy, but small and frail, they headed into unusually rough seas that rattled and shook the passengers all night—the MacArthurs were deathly ill with seasickness until the party stopped for quick rest at a midpoint in the dash for Mindanao Island, territory still held by American and Filipino forces. Signal fires on the way had indicated their run for freedom was known to the enemy.

66

Now, after the voyage was resumed in broad daylight (in just two PT boats), a sailor aboard Bulkeley's 41 Boat called out: "Sail ho!"

It was a Japanese cruiser cutting westward across their path. Bulkeley called for stop-engines, and for more than 10 suspense-filled minutes the low-slung boat wallowed among the white caps at dead stop.

The cruiser, to everyone's great relief, passed on without noticing the two small boats in the white-capped seas. Later in the afternoon, the party repeated the hair-raising performance upon encountering a Japanese destroyer. That night, passing off occupied Negros Island, the rumble of the PT-boat engines stirred up fresh trouble—a searchlight that stabbed the inky blackness. But it was pointed upwards, into the sky. The Japanese manning a coastal battery apparently thought it was aircraft they had heard. The PTs crept on by.

The seas this night were rough again, and aboard both boats the landlubbers once more were deathly ill.

Towards morning, MacArthur left his mattress, unable to sleep, and awoke his aide Sidney L. Huff. "I just want to talk," he said. For the next couple of hours, as Bulkeley's boat hurtled through the night, "the General was sitting on the mattress talking about what he had gone through in the last four years or so." He "choked up as he expressed his chagrin at being ordered to leave Corregidor." And he vowed to recapture the Philippines in such terms that Huff could see "he meant it, and he was already planning how he would do it."

At 6:30 a.m., dawn, Cagayan Point's light appeared on the horizon—Bulkeley had hit his navigational nail on the head, on time. He and his equally nerveless crewmen had run the rough seas for 35 hours since leaving Corregidor two days before.

For MacArthur and family, however, the escape from Corregidor and the Philippines was not yet over—they were still in the Philippines!

As it turned out, too, the B-17s that would be their next conveyance were not yet "in" from Australia. Guarded by elements of the 25,000 Americans and Filipinos still fighting the invading Japanese on Mindanao, the MacArthurs spent the night at the Del Monte plantation at Cagayan, despite reports that the Japanese were rushing from Davao to Del Monte—the news of MacArthur's arrival having quickly spread across the embattled island.

MacArthur's wait for the rescue planes lasted, in fact, for four days, during which the Americans often had to "dodge" raiding Japanese planes. In Australia, American commanders were having trouble finding three airworthy Flying Forts.

By MacArthur's own account years later, four B-17s had been dispatched for the pick-up, but one crashed, two others never reached their destination, and a fourth had been sent back to Australia, rejected for being "dangerously decrepit." An angered MacArthur, says biographer William Manchester, then radioed his demand for the "three best planes in the United States or Hawaii."

In Washington, Henry Stimson, Secretary of War, called MacArthur's "rather imperative command" to FDR's attention, but the message did produce results. Two newer B-17s finally appeared at Del Monte on the Monday night following the Wednesday-evening leavetaking at Corregidor's North Dock. A third plane had turned back due to engine trouble.

Overloaded, the two B-17s took off the same night, their passengers packed in like sardines, even over the bomb bays. As MacArthur's lead plane roared down the torch-lit runway, one engine faltered, but it caught again at last moment. The Flying Fortress struggled aloft for the five-hour flight to Darwin on Australia's lightly defended northern rim.

The two bombers had to fly over newly occupied Japanese territory—the Indies, Timor, northern New Guinea—but they evaded searching Japanese fighters. Air turbulence over the Celebes Sea made some of the passengers sick all over again. Then, approaching Darwin, the Flying Forts were shunted away—the Japanese were hitting Darwin from the air.

The B-17s landed at Batchelor Field, 50 miles away, and as the party stiffly climbed from their aircraft, MacArthur said: "It was close, but that's the way it is in war. You win or lose, live or die—and the difference is just an eyelash."

If MacArthur were relieved to have reached Australia safely, his wife and son also pulled from the fiery end awaiting Corregidor, he was shocked to find few forces and no immediate buildup underway in Australia to mount a counteroffensive against the Japanese. His first inkling came at remote Batchelor Field, where he hailed an American officer and asked about the "buildup."

The other man didn't know what MacArthur was talking about. "So far as I know, Sir, there are very few troops here."

Startled, MacArthur told his chief of staff, Richard Sutherland, "Surely, he is wrong."

And for the moment, the MacArthurs still were a long way from their destination of Melbourne. They were, in fact, in a remote, hardly defended war zone under intermittent attack from the rampaging Japanese.

The MacArthurs didn't want to fly again, but the nearest train station, Alice Springs, was 1,000 miles away. MacArthur would have driven there, rather than fly, but young Arthur was ill and was being fed intravenously—he must be moved much more quickly.

As a result, they flew to Alice Springs, an air raid starting behind them just as they left Batchelor Field. At Alice Springs, they landed one day after the weekly train had pulled out. A "special train" ordered up for the visitors in this "Wild West" town consisted of a locomotive with a huge cowcatcher up front, two wooden coaches and a red caboose. It took 70 hours to make the 1,000 added miles to Adelaide, from which a modern, well-appointed train finally would whisk the MacArthurs on to Melbourne.

On the *dinkum* Alice Springs train's long wooden benches, however, MacArthur did sink into his first deep sleep in weeks.

At Adelaide, MacArthur encountered his first welcoming crowd, replete with reporters. By now more fully apprised that no avenging army awaited his command in Melbourne, that America's first focus would be the war in Europe, the outraged MacArthur prepared himself by scratching a few words on the back of an envelope. He made his appearance then and spoke his few words, explaining that he had been ordered to leave Corregidor for the purpose of organizing the American offensive against Japan, against the occupiers of the Philippines.

His last words were deliberate and all MacArthur: "I came through and I shall return."

The American Office of War Information subsequently asked him to change the last three words to read "we" instead of "I." But MacArthur refused. To him, it was his sacred pledge to the Philippines he had left behind. *I shall return.*

From *Sea Wolf: A Biography of John D. Bulkeley, USN* by William B. Breuer (Presidio Press, Novato, Calif., 1989) and *American Caesar: Douglas MacArthur, 1880-1964* by William Manchester (Little, Brown and Company, Boston, Mass., 1978)

# ■ Long Odyssey Into War

For RAF pilot Arthur Murland Gill and members of his Number 84 Squadron in Egypt, simply reaching the war's new theater of operations against the Japanese in the Far East was a storybook odyssey of survival. This was early in 1942, with the Japanese swarming into Malaya and soon to threaten Singapore and its great British naval base.

Gill and his aircrews flew out of Egypt January 13, 1942, aboard 24 three-seater Blenheim medium bombers—"of which three fell by the wayside on the way out." The ground crews and other support personnel were to be shipped east aboard an old transport ship named the *Yoma*.

The squadron made its way across Palestine, Iraq and the Persian Gulf, then to Karachi, Bombay and Calcutta on the great subcontinent of India, across the Bay of Bengal and into Burma. The next stop would be Sumatra, Indonesia, just south of the besieged Malay Peninsula.

"We did Burma to Sumatra in one hop," explains war veteran Gill, "and we were running out of fuel by the time we got there."

Worse, the RAF pilots didn't know where to land. "It was getting dusk when we arrived at the latitude and the longitude marked on the map, and there was no airfield! And so we flew on down the coast of Sumatra, one aircraft ran out of fuel and ditched in a paddy field, and the rest of us turned back."

The hope now was to reach Sabang Island, known to have a tiny 300-yard strip. "Then suddenly one of the rear-gunners shouted 'Windsock!' and we did a circle 'round and there was the airfield, which was nowhere near where we had been told it was."

Moving on to Medan for operations against the Japanese, Gill and his men spent the next three weeks striking at targets in Thailand, Malaya and Sumatra for the most part.

"On one occasion," notes Gill, "my aircraft was out of service and so I borrowed a short-nose Blenheim from Number 97 Squadron and dropped my bombs and flew back to Singapore that night—and found no lights to mark the runway! No lights there at all to get us down. We only knew it was the airfield because it was dark compared with the rest of the town, which was brilliantly lit. So eventually we landed over the palm trees and in complete darkness."

In the process, Gill ran his plane into a gaping bomb crater "and bent it badly," as he recalls.

He caught a ride back to Sumatra and resumed the war.

Shortly, though, the Japanese were threatening the base at Medan, and the squadron was ordered to transfer out of Java.

Since Gill didn't have a plane to call his own, he was ordered to remain behind, destroy ammunition and supplies and find a way out on his own.

"I was in charge of the rearguard and 'Good Luck!' "

He and his ground personnel commandeered a Dutch truck for a 13-hour land journey to the coast through mountains, valleys and torrential rains. "We arrived the next morning about 0800 at the extreme southern tip of Sumatra just about as the last ship out was casting off."

That last ship, it turned out, was the familiar old *Yoma*, the same ship that had carried Gill's ground crews east from distant Egypt.

From interview by Peter Smith, *Military History* Magazine, June 1988

# ■ Blind Leading The Blind

After Pearl Harbor, many were the lame and the halt who felt America's patriotic fervor and tried to "join up."

Nearly everybody has heard tales of the youngsters and oldsters who bamboozled the system and sneaked their way into the nation's fighting forces by hook or by crook.

It took a young opthamalogist, however, himself a volunteer, to run across a nearly blind man who had "conned" the system and made it into the U.S. Army.

Dr. Albert E. Meisenbach, Jr. was stationed at the base hospital at Sheppard Field, Wichita Falls, Texas, before his deployment in mid-summer 1942 as flight surgeon for a photo reconnaissance outfit stationed in the Southwest Pacific combat zone. In the Army, the eye specialist had more general medical duties, of course. He was sent to Sheppard to equip the new Eye, Ear, Nose and Throat (EENT) Department and for a time was Chief of the EENT, of Orthopedic and of Genito-Urinary Services (plus Athletic Officer). Various kinds of surgery became a part of his routine.

He was on more familiar ground one day when he spotted a soldier groping his way down a hospital hallway. "I observed a GI holding onto the guide rail as he made his way down the hall."

His curiosity aroused, Meisenbach stopped the young man to ask why he was feeling his way along like that. "Imagine my amazement when he told me he was nearly blind!"

And it was no joke. "I took him to the clinic to confirm this and was shocked to find that he had less than 20/20 vision in both eyes." Nor was the young man's condition anything sudden—he was a practiced reader of Braille.

How could such an obvious 4-F slip into uniform? Meisenbach, naturally, asked the question.

The answer was that the otherwise fit man before him had memorized all the various eye charts used in the U.S. Army physical at the time. "All I had to do was to get the officer to name the top letter and I would recite the entire chart to him."

And why? What could a nearly blind man accomplish in the Army? "I knew that many men would be blinded as a result of the conflict, and because of my knowledge of Braille, I know that I can help."

> From *Memoirs of a Flight Surgeon Serving in the South Pacific During World War II* by A.E. Meisenbach, Jr., M.D., Dallas, Texas, 1988

# ■ *Tokyo's Psychological Shock*

On the ground in Tokyo during Doolittle's famous raid of April 18, 1942—

Father Bruno Bitter, Roman Catholic priest, noticed the alarm sounded at about noon. "Most of the people did not believe it, thinking it was just another drill." In fact, there had been a drill and practice alert that very morning—it was just ending when Jimmy Doolittle's carrier-launched, U.S. Army B-25s appeared in the skies over Tokyo and environs.

"But when they learned it was a real raid, nobody could hold them back to go outside, to climb the roofs or the chimneys to get a better view. In other words, it was a thrill rather than a frightening event."

The American planners had not counted on devastating material damage, but they were hoping that the raid from the U.S. carrier *Hornet* would demonstrate Japan's own vulnerability and thus sap the nation's morale . . . that the raid would achieve *some* psychological inroad. That effect apparently did seep in.

Toshiko Matsumura, 13 at the time, was not immediately aware of the raid—it was a few days before she overheard her elders in Tokyo's suburbs "discussing it in hushed tones." What she heard, the gradual effect, indeed was undermining.

"My people had always placed emphasis on spiritual strength and the medieval belief that Japan would never be attacked. As children we had been taught to believe what the emperor and his advisors told us. It was a severe psychological shock to even the most ardent believer when it was officially announced that we had been attacked. We finally began to realize that all we were told was not true—that the government had lied when it said we were invulnerable. We then began to doubt that we were also invincible."

Under "confinement to quarters" in the American Embassy, interned U.S. Ambassador Joseph C. Grew was winding up a meeting with a visitor, the Swiss Minister, ". . . and just as he was leaving before lunch, we heard a lot of planes overhead and saw five or six large fires burning in different directions with great volumes of smoke."

Grew told their reaction in his diary. "At first we thought it was only maneuvers, but soon became aware that it was the first big raid on Japan by American bombers . . ." They saw one of the twin-engine U.S. Army Air Corps bombers, "apparently losing altitude and flying very low, just over the tops of the buildings to the west." They thought it would crash, but then realized the pilot was flying low to avoid fighters and flak.

To the east, they saw another plane, closely followed by "a whole line of black puffs of smoke, indicating antiaircraft explosions." Since it didn't look like a bomber, "we are inclined to believe that the Japanese batteries lost their heads and fired on their own pursuit planes."

It was an exciting day for the Allied noncombatants interned in Tokyo. "We were all very happy and proud in the Embassy, and the British told us later that they drank toasts all day to the American flyers.''

Elsewhere in Tokyo, meanwhile, Vice Admiral Matome Ugaki, chief of staff for the Combined Fleet, already was at lunch when he received word of the astounding attack. He also kept a diary: ''I did not know what was happening, and all I could do was order a pursuit to the east.''

He ordered his Third Submarine Fleet ''to attack,'' but none of the Japanese forces attempting to react was able to locate the fast-retiring carrier *Hornet* and her escorts. Jimmy Doolittle's brave B-25s, in the meantime, were headed for the China coast in hopes of finding sanctuary beyond a wide belt of Japanese-occupied territory. In the days ahead, there would be vigorous and cruel response by the Japanese in China, but for now Ugaki felt humiliated. ''It is regrettable that I missed my chance three or four times,'' he wrote in his diary of April 18, 1942. ''It had always been my motto not to allow Tokyo or the homeland to be attacked from the air, but today my pride has been deeply hurt and my spirits are low as today I gave the enemy his glory.''

From *The Doolittle Raid: America's Daring First Strike Against Japan*, by Carroll V. Glines (Orion Books, New York, 1988)

# ■ *Tragedy At Sea*

*Kuru* and *Armidale*, patrol vessel and corvette, were running for Timor off Australia's northwest coast when Japanese aircraft found them out. It was high noon, December 1, 1942, and aboard the speedy *Kuru*, Lieutenant J.A. Grant had the formula to avoid more than 200 bombs dropped by an estimated 44 enemy aircraft.

Essentially, he watched the bombing pattern develop, wave after wave, then skittered out of the way as the deadly things fell toward his craft:

''Their first attack was line abreast—I ran at right angles to their flight until I saw their bombs release. I then turned towards them at fullest speed and the bombs landed across our wake.''

As other waves came at him, in a number of different formations, Grant continued to make last-minute turns that allowed sticks of bombs to fall behind, to either side, but never *on* the *Kuru*. The *Armidale* was not nearly so fortunate.

The unlucky *Armidale*, carrying 66 troops in addition to her crew, was struck shortly after 3 p.m. by two torpedoes and one bomb; she sank, it is said, in just three to four minutes. Most of the troops, about two-thirds of them, apparently were killed when the first torpedo hit.

The attackers machine-gunned the survivors, and one of them struck back. He was Ordinary Seaman Ted Sheehan, a "loader member of the aft oerliken gun." As later related by another survivor: "When the order 'abandon ship' was given, he made for the side, only to be hit twice by the bullets of an attacking Zero. None of us will ever know what made him do it, but he went back to his gun, strapped himself in and brought down a Jap fighter, still firing as he disappeared beneath the waves."

In the silence that followed the departure of the attacking airplanes, the *Armidale*'s surviving complement had the ship's motor boat, a Carley float, a makeshift raft and a whaler for their conveyances at sea, 120 kilometers off Timor Island. The whaler was so shot full of holes that it was underwater, kept from slipping away by lines to empty oil drums. Many of the survivors clinging to these uncertain props were wounded.

When no search planes had appeared by noon of the next day, the corvette's commander, Lieut. Cmdr. D.H. Richards, decided he must take *some* action—the motor boat must split off and seek help.

Since the only other navigator in the stranded group was badly wounded, Richards would have to go with the motor boat. Going with him would be six still able men and 13 wounded. Those left with the raft and whaler agreed to the decision, and soon they were left alone in the Sea of Timor.

Richards and his company had to proceed alternately by rowing, sailing and motoring, since their fuel supply was low. They wended to the south, and after two days, a searching Hudson plane came across them. Two days after that an Australian corvette sent to pick them up finally reached them.

Back on the raft, survival had been a struggle from the time the motor boat disappeared over the horizon. The night that followed was a sleepless one. "Every now and then the raft would break up," wrote Ordinary Seaman R.M. Caro later, "and we would have to swim around in the dark hunting up the bits and pieces, and lash them together again.''

After a blazing hot day in the sun, it was the same the next night. One of the survivors disappeared under the waves.

The next day, the stranded crewmen busied themselves raising the whaler and plugging its holes as best they could with bits of clothing and canvas. With unceasing baling, it was barely serviceable. Fortunately, the seas were calm.

By the day after, with still no sign of rescue, the senior officer remaining, Lieutenant L.G. Palmer, decided the whaler also must go and seek help. He would try for Bathurst Island and take 23 men with him. Twenty-seven sailors and Sub-Lieutenant James Buckland would be left behind on the unsteady raft. A terrible choice must be made, since only the 23 could go. ''The whole thing was very grim, believe me, as we left them that Saturday morning, and one does not have to use much imagination to see again the expressions on the faces of those chaps who were left behind,'' added Seaman Caro in his subsequent account.

Two more days now passed, both for the raft's complement and for the men in the whaler. Another searching Hudson now found the raft. It and two additional Hudsons dropped supplies before they had to take leave; their crewmen reported ''30 to 40 men (sic)'' clinging to ''raft and wreckage.'' In response to the find, a Catalina ''Flying Boat'' flew into Darwin and the next morning, December 8, again located the raft party in the area cited by the Hudson crews. The Catalina crew spotted only 17 survivors, however.

The Catalina dropped food, water, blankets, life preservers, sun helmets, whiskey and an aircraft marine distress signal, according to the Catalina's No. 11 Squadron diary. ''All appeared in fair condition but have little clothing,'' said the official account.

The same Catalina, moving on, then found the whaler. It dropped supplies, along with a note saying, ''Your captain (Richards) is safe, we have found the raft, dropped them food and water, and now we are returning to Darwin to send out a ship for you.''

The men of the whaler were ''very happy,'' said Caro. ''The raft we had left was found and our own worries were over.''

It would have been better, of course, if the Catalina had landed and taken aboard some of the castaways, from raft or whaler, but the seas had become too rough. Now, both groups had to survive one more night, this time in worsening weather and roughening seas, before help could reach them.

The next morning, the corvette *Kalgoorlie* came up beside the whaler and rescued Caro and company. Others, both Hudsons and ships, set out for the raft's location, but . . . it was nowhere to be seen. Four more days of intensive search turned up nothing. Neither the raft, nor any of its 17 or so survivors ever was seen again.

It was a saga with bitter ending—a Board of Enquiry endorsing the various command officers involved; pleas for help and recriminations from families never convinced, sometimes for months and years, that their loved one really had been lost at sea.

One mother wrote that other survivors reported her son was alive and well when last seen on the raft. No wounds. "I felt sure they must have drifted ashore," she wrote.

A year later, she wrote again, in search of peace of mind. "Grant's brother was killed in action in New Guinea a few weeks ago, and it is more than I can bear not to know something of Grant." She never would, though.

From *The Shadow's Edge: Australia's Northern War* by
Alan Powell (Melbourne University Press, 1988,
distributed in the United States by *ISBS*, 5602 N.E.
Hassalo St., Portland, Or., 97213-3640)

# ■ *Rendezvous For Faithful Companion*

Two to four p.m. on the banks of the embattled Tenaru River on Guadalcanal, and the tanks are advancing. It is August 21, 1942, just days since the U.S. Marines landed.

First, much shooting, and then the tanks. Four tanks. "No gun of ours can oppose them."

One of them stopped, however, apparently disabled. After a pause, the other three continued. As they drew closer, their paths diverged somewhat. The number seemingly aimed at Japanese Sergeant Okada's hiding place became two.

On they came as he, lying on the sandy soil, "made like dead."

The first one was not deliberately aiming at him. It was moving very slowly, inexorably. But right at him. "My body was stuck in the sand and I felt two or three pressures on my back. It passed over me! What a surprising! I am still alive!"

It may be that the root of a nearby coconut tree had created a pocket protecting his body. But . . . no time to think it through, for now here came the second tank.

Near Okada, it mysteriously stopped. The crew is looking for signs of enemy life, he thought. Silent, he slowly pulled the key from his grenade in case they did see him . . . but, no, in moments the second tank ground forward again. He felt the pressure of its treads pushing sand onto him. It was so close.

In minutes, the American tanks had moved on. The battle zone in short time was silent, not even any wounded groaning. Around Sergeant Okada, nearly everyone was dead. "Only two men left alive. I and Sergeant Kuragane. He was in deep hole only meters from me. He said that tank passed, though on him, he only got slight bruise because of deep 'octopus trap' in hole he was safe. We talked to each other of course."

They talked about how to escape their predicament. They would have to wait for dark, and then make their way through the lines. If they could.

In short time, their predicament worsened with the arrival of three more tanks and "hundreds of soldiers advancing toward here and shooting at random." Okada thought, "I will be killed, never could be alive this time."

The roar of engines was deafening, and Okada heard the enemy's voices. He continued to play dead while the men of the 1st Battalion, 1st Marines, passed by and stopped, along with the tanks, a hundred meters beyond him. For some reason, they did not examine him to see if he were really dead.

By now, night had fallen. "We, Okada and Kuragane, were left alone in enemy's domain!" They decided to start out about midnight, when their enemy probably would be sleeping.

That decision made, Okada fell into a coma-like stupor that lasted until he felt Kuragane shaking him awake at midnight. To their dismay, the moon was high in the sky and the American Marines and their tanks were shooting "at something." Why would they be shooting at midnight? Okada found it very perplexing.

But the two Japanese must make their escape anyway. They split up, and Kuragane went first, "running like a cat." Minutes later, Okada heard machine-gun fire. No doubt, Kuragane had been killed. They wouldn't be meeting, as planned, at another river a mile to the east.

Now, it was Okada's turn, but he wouldn't take Kuragane's route. He would try the sea, since the river emptied into the sea a short distance away. If he could just swim 200 meters eastward, he would be safe, with his own.

Parched with thirst, he crawled for 30 meters in the dark and reached the water line, where he drank the salt-laden seawater. Then he walked out in the water until it reached his neck, but the wind and tide kept him from making any headway to the east. "I still carried my helmet and sword. I abandoned them all. I wanted to go back to the beach, but too dangerous, so I crawled in the sea—maybe 20 meters from the shore. This way I could advance. Finally, I crawled out of the water at about 300 meters east from the Tenaru. It seems safe to me."

There was no sign of the Americans as Okada entered the foliage lining the beach. Recklessly, he plunged into the jungle and ran at full speed for his appointed meeting place with Kuragane. He was not there. Okada thought, "He was killed for sure." But still Okada "returned towards enemy area twice," dangerous as it was, since "it is disgrace for me to escape before he does."

And still Okada didn't retreat to his own lines somewhere behind him. "I crawled about and once more approached enemy's line, but no avail."

He then finished the night resting by the riverside. At sunrise, he was trapped again because of an airplane in the sky that was shooting at something on the ground. "So I remained there until sunset."

Two days after the ordeal began, on the afternoon of August 23, Okada finally emerged from the Guadalcanal jungle to rejoin his forces at Taivu. There, he found "ten or more" fellow survivors of the fighting on the banks of the Tenaru. There, too, he found Kuragane, safe and well.

Kuragane, it seems, had reached their river rendezvous point after easily passing through the American lines. He waited about an hour for Okada, then heard shooting and thought that meant the worst. "Both thought that the other was not alive," summarizes Okada, who was evacuated from Guadalcanal on October 5, 1942, with "heavy illness," never to return to battle but forever the faithful companion.

From "The Okada Memories of the Tenaru (Ilu)," *Guadalcanal Echoes*, The Guadalcanal Campaign Veterans, July 1986

# ■ Hunt For Tall, Limping Man

For the 61-year-old, five-star general held prisoner in Germany's Konigstein fortress atop a 150-foot cliff, escaping his immediate confines would be difficult enough. Beyond that feat, however, he still would have to elude his pursuers and somehow make his way out of the country itself.

Henri Honoré Giraud's native France, just next door to the west, would be no safe haven, either. Its upper half had been occupied by the German *Wehrmacht* for the past two years, while the collaborationist Vichy administration of Henri Pétain governed the bottom half of France.

Giraud, though, was not a man easily deterred—he had proven that during World War I, when he had escaped from a German prison camp in Belgium while still recovering from the wounds of battle.

In the war that followed two decades later, he was captured again, caught in a forward machine-gun post while inspecting the front the very day, May 10, 1940, the Germany of Adolf Hitler launched its offensive against France and the Low Countries.

By April 17, 1942, Henri Giraud was ready to make his attempt at leaving Konigstein. He previously had woven a rope of twine from packages sent by friends and relatives. But it wouldn't hold his 200-pound weight. Communicating by code in personal letters, he had made his needs known at home. As a result, an innocent-looking ham had been the conveyance of a 150-foot coil of copper wire hidden inside.

Giraud was allowed to use a balcony above the cliff-face and a sentry circuit at the top. The morning of April 17, he secured his copper-strengthened rope to the balustrade, waited for the sentry to pass by, then started his trip down the steep cliff, hand over hand. Even gloved, his hands were rubbed raw, but he reached the bottom safely and hurried into some trees nearby, out of sight.

Temporarily free, he was still in great danger of recapture, if only because he was so easy to spot. He was tall, six feet; he sported a fierce mustache; he walked with a permanent limp from his WWI injuries. Moreover, for the moment, he had only a secreted Tyrolean hat as a civilian garment. His military raincoat might pass casual inspection, but underneath he still had on his informal French general's uniform of blue.

Aware of such drawbacks, Giraud had made his plans carefully. Boning up on his German-speaking capability, he had studied a map of his immediate area—and through his letter code he had made certain arrangements.

First, shaving off the mustache, he made his way to nearby Bad Schandau, and there he met a contact carrying a suitcase full of Giraud's own civilian clothing and a raft of false papers, plus that all-important commodity, money. Without speaking, they boarded the first train to stop at the town, then met in a bathroom.

From then on, his clothes changed, the distinguished-looking Giraud could look and act the part of the industrialist that his false papers said he was. The next step in Giraud's escape would be carried out all on his own, however—having done his part, the contact disappeared from the scene.

But where could the hare find sanctuary? For Giraud, even disguised, to approach a guarded frontier and attempt to cross into France would be sheer madness. Every border guard would be on the lookout for such a ranking escapee with a tell-tale limp. On the other hand, Giraud was still in the enemy camp; there was no sanctuary for him in Nazi Germany, the most vicious and suspicious of police states.

His solution was risky but simple: for now, until the immediate furor faded a bit, he would ride the trains.

For days, he did just that, on occasion just barely outwitting the Gestapo men aboard the trains or in the railroad stations. He once entered the occupied half of France but was stymied trying to reach the Vichy provinces to the south—the Germans were challenging any man close to Giraud's height.

He resumed his train travel, back into Germany, and now made for the Swiss border. That, too, was tightly closed, but one night Giraud left the rails and climbed a mountain trail that allowed him to slip into neutral Switzerland on foot.

He could have stayed on there, but duty still called, and Giraud was determined to reach unoccupied France. A concerted plan involving a brace of cars fooled the Gestapo and enabled him to make the dangerous dash.

But now Nazi Germany called on the Pétain administration to surrender the escapee—the old Marshal of France bravely refused, while Giraud went to ground again to avoid Gestapo assassination squads.

Giraud, a public hero to the French but still a hunted man, would not really be free until just before the Allied invasion of North Africa in early November 1942. Even then, to join the Free French and their Anglo-American Allies, he had to escape one

more time. On this occasion, working with British agents sent into southern France, he was spirited to a waiting submarine that
then carried him safely across the Mediterranean to join his compatriots fighting the long but ultimately victorious war against
Hitler's Germany.

Giraud, in the unfolding of that great drama, reestablished the
French Army and became its commander-in-chief, although he
never got along with Charles de Gaulle and finally retired in April
of 1944, a year before the war in Europe ended. He died a free
man in 1949, his beloved France by then also free once again.

> From Frederick C. Painton in *True Stories of Great
> Escapes* (The Reader's Digest Association, Pleasant-
> ville, N.Y., 1977)

# ■ *High Drama At Sea*

For U.S. Navy Ensign Gerhart S. Suppiger, Jr., convoy duty
in May of 1942 did not begin auspiciously. First, one of his nine
gun crewmen was hospitalized after he injured his hand carrying
a box of supplies. Next, the captain of their merchantman, the
SS *Santa Elisa*, went ashore, too ill to carry on.

Then, after *largely* uneventful days crossing the dangerous
North Atlantic (one near-collision in the fog and two U-boats sunk
by escorts), the *Santa Elisa* laid up for 46 wearisome days at
Newport, England, twice on-loading, then off-loading various war
cargo.

Clearly, larger events were in store for the young ensign and
the men of his U.S. Navy Armed Guard—those often forgotten,
unsung sailors who manned the few guns aboard merchant ships
against enemies ranging from commerce raiders to U-boats and
aircraft. (Nearly 145,000 navy men performed this high-risk duty
aboard 6,236 ships during World War II, with 1,810 lost, or one
out of every 185 men setting sail.)

Finally, her armament significantly boosted, the *Elisa* joined
a convoy of 12 cargo ships and two tankers escorted by a virtual
armada—two battleships, eight cruisers, five carriers, a flotilla
of destroyers. The *Elisa* had become a part of the Royal Navy's

Operation Pedestal, with embattled Malta in the Mediterranean as destination.

The *Elisa* left port in Scotland to join the Pedestal convoy on August 2, 1942. Eight days later, the convoy safely passed through the Straits of Gibraltar (with one aircraft carrier peeling off there), and at 9 the next morning Pedestal's ordeal began.

The action opened with two bombing attacks 30 minutes apart. One of the cargo ships went down. At 10:30, one of the aircraft carriers was struck by three torpedoes. "She sank in seven minutes."

The convoy proceeded as its escorts accounted for two enemy submarines. That evening, though, fresh waves of German aircraft damaged a destroyer and sank two more of the merchant ships. The *Elisa* sailed on.

The next day, August 12, was a continual nightmare—action stations all day long. Wave after wave of Stuka dive-bombers, Junkers and Heinkel bombers struck, along with Italian torpedo planes. Another Royal Navy carrier was hit and left behind enveloped in smoke and fire. Of the escorts, all but two cruisers and a "few destroyers" stayed behind, too. Intelligence had reported the Italian fleet might sally forth to engage the British battle fleet.

As the diminished convoy pressed on, the air and submarine attacks continued. One of the two remaining cruisers, HMS *Manchester*, went down. At 8 p.m., another freighter was sunk by dive-bombers. The hour of 9 o'clock brought "the most concentrated attack of all." Three more merchantmen went down, with "sticks" of bombs narrowly missing the *Elisa*, and not for the first time.

At this point, the convoy remnants scattered, and after two near-collisions in the dark, the *Elisa* had a choice between sailing alone past coastal batteries and an Italian E-boat base, or chancing a known mine field to the west. "We decided to risk the mine field instead of the others," wrote Suppiger in his later report.

At 3:30 the next morning, however, a speedy E-boat found the *Elisa* anyway. In an exchange of machine-gun fire, it was driven off, but then a second E-boat appeared, and this one soon was able to launch torpedoes. At 5:05 a.m., "there was a terrific flash and explosion forward."

With the ship "burning furiously," the crew took to the sea. Survivors were rescued about two hours later by a destroyer. At 7:30 a.m., a new wave of dive-bombers dropped from the sky and sank the *Elisa*.

Upon finally reaching Malta two days later, the Americans learned that five of the original 14 merchant ships had run the gauntlet. While Ensign Suppiger's contingent and others had lost their ships, a vitally needed few vessels had survived one of the entire war's most difficult convoy operations.

Not all Armed Guard duty would be so hazardous (on a good day), but the danger was constant enough to produce a high casualty rate for such a small percentage of the U.S. Navy's 3.4 million sailors of the WWII era.

Nonetheless, "we aim to deliver" was the Armed Guard's motto, and in more ways than one, they did.

From *The Pointer and the Plane Shooter,* USN Armed
Guard WWII Veterans, December 1988

# ■ *Romance Amid Society's Ruins*

He was 17 and she was 16, both from the same corner of Poland near the Russian border, Walter and Olga. For forced labor in Germany, each family in the conquered territory must give up one. That one would go.

He was the oldest, and she was the oldest, so each volunteered to go rather than allow a younger brother or sister to be *used* in that way.

They had not known each other before, and on the train from Dubno they didn't meet. It was a long trip, 12 days, tightly packed into freight cars, standing only, no sleep, guards with machine guns. The train passed though Walter's own town, and there, somehow, were his father, his mother, his younger brother, waving. Last time he ever saw them, waving goodbye.

In Cologne, the camp was quartered in an old theatre, girls on one side, boys on the other, boards in between.

They walked to work in a column, four miles. Their factory made engines, motors for subs, trucks, jeep-like vehicles. 40,000 working in three shifts. All kinds of displaced, drafted, POW peoples—Russians, Hungarians, French, Yugoslav, Poles like Walter and Olga.

They arrived June 9, 1942, and stayed until war's end, 1945. Olga for a time was placed out as a nanny, was sent to Aachen for a short time, then was a blueprints courier in the big factory, *running* from one section to another, "morning to night."

They met, finally, in one of the interminable camp lines for food and drink. Walter wanted his ersatz coffee ("Some grass in a big bag and dump it in hot water"), and there she was, in the line. He got next to her and said: "That would be a nice pair, you and me."

And so they courted—on food lines, in the column marching to work, in a communal washroom outside the separate toilets for men and women. "You come from work, you are going on lines," she says. "It's dark, so people will sneak with each other."

Actually, she had been "going" with his friend, but that was nothing serious. "He was funny, his friend, he played harmonica and we would all have this fun. Then Walter came and he grab me from behind, he lifted me up and he turned me towards him, like face to face. He said, 'Don't you think we would match together?' So we were joking from that time and having this little going out and sneaking here and there."

After a while, Walter wrote Olga's father for permission, and her father wrote back and said, "I think you are old enough and God bless you."

In the camp, in the war, though, Olga was telling Walter they must not think too much about the future, they must first survive, and they couldn't get married just then.

In January, 1944, Olga's father wrote rather cryptically that at home all of the fences have been taken down, "meaning the ghettos." And the trees are down. Just bare ground. And remember the woods where she used to go for mushrooms? "The letter penetrates something. I said, 'Oh, my goodness, the Jewish people were all killed.' "

At the camp, at the factory, in Cologne, one thing and another, alarms, scary moments, always the deprivations, but they both survived. They were, at end, liberated by the advancing Americans.

Finally, it was time, but for the wedding she had no dress. She made one for herself, but now she had no shoes. A German gave her a pair of men's shoes, his son's, very large. But Walter went to a Russian camp and swapped a pocket watch from home for a pair of women's shoes.

They were married along with very many other couples—30 people standing about the altar, and when they reached the part about the ring, no ring. They borrowed another couple's ring.

They came to America, "because the Russians took over there (Poland)." They have lived in Southwick, 90 miles from Boston, a married couple, ever since. He began to work in a paper mill upon their arrival and never left. Walter and Olga. Decades gone by. On their kitchen wall a frame around the words, "*Boze Blogoslaw Naz Dom,*" which means "God Bless Our Home." Walter and Olga Nowak, Southwick, Mass.

From "*The Good War,*" *An Oral History of World War Two,* Studs Terkel (Pantheon Books, a division of Random House, Inc., New York, 1984)

# ■ *Hitler's Bathwater Purloined*

Even "good" Germans who despised the Hitler regime had "black sheep" in their families totally enamoured of the man who led Germany into a devastating war. In Gertrud Breier's case, the "black sheep" were her great aunt Lina and her husband Gustave.

"Gustave was an officer with the military court, who was always wearing his uniform." Great Aunt Lina, though, went a bit further.

She traveled one time to Bad Godesberg, "where Hitler and his big shots would frequently stay for a cure."

Aunt Lina then paid a chambermaid at the hotel that Hitler frequented to obtain some of the *Führer*'s bathwater. Aunt Lina provided a small bottle for the chore, and the chambermaid complied. Aunt Lina returned home with her prize, presumably never known to Hitler.

"For years to come, the dirty water was kept in her vitrine for everyone to admire. What a nut she was."

In an obverse way, Lina's son Richard may have outdone his own mother. "He was full of pep and resented his parents. He usually got satisfaction when he could embarrass them."

He achieved that end one day when he managed to raise a chamber pot on a flag pole. "Sure enough, up there, right under the eagle with the swastika, was the chamber pot."

When Cousin Richard was identified as the perpetrator, he was punished by his undoubtedly furious mother, "and he had to apologize openly." At least he wasn't shot—his mother, at the end of the war, was. She died still a fanatical Nazi. "The day the American troops moved into the suburbs of Frankenthal, that stupid Lina took the Nazi flag, saluted and screamed at a group of soldiers. One shot was fired and Lina with her flag in her hand fell to the ground. A neighbor, who had watched it from a small window in his basement, told us it looked as if she wanted to fight those soldiers off."

Son Richard survived both the war and parents who "almost destroyed everything good" in him. "He was a very kind soul. Years later, after the war, he married a very nice girl and let his then-senile father live with them."

From The Governess by Gertrud Breier (Vantage Press,<br>New York, 1988)

# ■ *Intelligence War*

With the British at Bletchley Park leading the way, the Allies had achieved solid breakthroughs in their decoding assault upon the German coding machine called Enigma—but then the U-boat fleet came up with its all-but-indecipherable SHARK radio traffic.

SHARK, it seemed, also utilized the Enigma machines, several of them by now in British hands, but the Enigma put into play by the U-boats in 1942 contained four internal rotors rather than the standard three.

That simple-sounding addition of a single "cog" multiplied the possible variables by a geometrically multiple factor. If, as first seemed the case, the decoders and *their* machines could not cope with SHARK, what was needed would be a SHARK-modified Enigma from a U-boat, or relevant documents showing how the new system worked. But how to lay Allied hands on such closely guarded material belonging to the enemy?

The breakthrough came in unexpectedly poignant fashion and at high cost.

In the Mediterranean on October 30, 1942, a Sunderland flying boat on patrol off Port Said came across a U-boat skimming the surface 70 miles north of the Nile delta.

Alerted by radio, British destroyers converged and after 16 hours of hunting and depth-charging finally brought the now-submerged U-559 to the surface. Under fire from the British *Petard*, the German crew abandoned the submarine. Unknown to the British, but a suspected possibility, the Germans had opened the boat's seacocks in order to scuttle her and keep out of British hands.

As the U-boat crew swam for a *Petard* whaleboat, Royal Navy Lieutenant Tony Fasson and Able Seaman Colin Grazier leaped into the water, naked, and swam the opposite direction—to the submarine. They were after the U-boat's coding equipment and documents.

By the time they reached the U-boat's conning tower, it barely protruded from the waves, but they climbed down inside anyway and made their way to the radio room.

Although the sub was empty, they soon had company—a ship's canteen assistant named Tommy Brown, who, without orders, also decided to board the stricken U-boat. The fact that Tommy Brown was only 16 and had lied about his age to join his country's navy was not very well known at the time.

In the radio room, the three found an intelligence bonanza—one of the new four-rotor SHARK machines and documents revealing its encoding keys.

Grabbing those materials by the armful, the older two men handed them to the teenager, who stationed himself by the hatch and then transferred the precious cargo to a whaler pulled alongside.

But the U-boat all this time literally was sinking. At last moment, Tommy Brown got off, but not the two brave sailors still inside. They went down, two Englishmen, with the German U-boat to a joint grave beneath the sea.

While the intelligence experts subsequently and happily seized upon the prize haul, the two men lost were awarded Britain's George Cross for their bravery (posthumous). So was Tommy Brown, at 16 its youngest recipient ever.

His age, though, was to be his undoing. He was discharged as too young for the Royal Navy and returned home to North Shields. There, two years later, he died the hero's death just barely missed off Port Said in 1942—still a victim of war, he died attempting to rescue a younger sister trapped by fire in their slum tenement, the fire caused by a German air raid.

From *The Sigint Secrets: The Signals Intelligence War, 1900 to Today* by Nigel West (William Morrow and Company, Inc., New York, 1988)

# ■ *Brave* Trigger's *Last Patrol*

Normally a bright-colored tropical fish, *Trigger* in World War II also meant a U.S. submarine—the little (by today's standards) sub *that could*, to hear it from the underwater boat's official U.S. Naval History. For instance, as *Trigger* nosed into the submarine base at Pearl Harbor before her first war patrol, "she was a neophyte, a trifle self-conscious and perhaps apologetic to slip her trim form into the berth of her illustrious sisters."

Pickings were slim on *Trigger's* first war patrol, but never mind, for more was to come. The doughty sub found a very real contact in enemy waters west of Japan soon enough, in October of 1942. She encountered a freighter that tried to ram; she averted the collision and managed to place a torpedo in the enemy ship. Threatened by a patrol vessel, *Trigger* then had to scurry below.

Resurfacing later, she went after the wounded freighter again. As she closed, however, "Several large puffs of smoke billowed over the ship, and then nothing was seen." Adds the official (but colorful) history: "The Jap freighter was not designed to submerge, but encouraged by enough torpedoes, she exceeded the designer's expectations on this occasion."

Like other American subs early in the war, *Trigger* experienced the frustration of torpedoes that didn't work. On October 17, she maneuvered into perfect firing position upon another freighter and sent three torpedoes "straight and true for the target." Nothing happened—they were duds. "The skipper could be forgiven if he slammed his cap on the deck."

Just three days later, though, *Trigger* scored two hits on a tanker, then dove to avoid another ramming attempt. "The tanker churned right overhead, dropping a depth charge as she passed. It was her last pass, for *Trigger* had already thrown the lucky pair. A violent eruption; silence from the vessel's screws; the crackling noise of a ship breaking up; a clear horizon. That is how a ship is lost. That is how this one went down."

Returning to Pearl from her second war patrol, "*Trigger* could hold her head higher now." On her third sortie, she scored often, in one case upon an on-rushing Japanese destroyer. "With her bow turned up like an old shoe, the destroyer sank on an even keel."

*Trigger's* fourth war patrol produced 13 contacts with enemy ships, but various untoward factors held the sub's score to one ship apparently sunk, another damaged. After replenishment at

Pearl in April of 1943, *Trigger* would begin her fifth patrol. Thus, "It was the slender snout of a seasoned veteran that pushed the water aside on her way out."

Off Tokyo in June, *Trigger* spotted a brand new aircraft carrier and two escorting destroyers coming right at her. She ducked under and held her breath while one destroyer passed overhead; then came the sound of the carrier's heavy screws. "The crisp orders to fire were repeated six times, and each time a swish responded that sent a deadly torpedo on its way. Four solid detonations echoed back . . . and the carrier's screws stopped."

A fast look showed the giant ship drifting and at a list—"Little white-clad forms scurried madly about the decks." But that same periscope peek showed the destroyers racing furiously toward *Trigger*. And now it was her turn for a beating, a pounding by depth charge that blanked the lights and knocked crewmen off their feet. "The heavy sides of the submarine squeezed in with each reverberating shock . . . The temperatures soared, the humidity hit the saturation point and the men worked to the point of exhaustion controlling the flooding . . . from the tortured sea valves and fittings."

But *Trigger* survived. Survived, surfaced well after midnight and moved on. "Fresh, cool air never felt so good and the men knew the grateful feeling of returning from the shadow of death."

On her sixth patrol, *Trigger* came across two unescorted freighters in the East China Sea. She unleashed her torpedoes at the biggest of the two, but once again frustration—"two duds thumping the ship's side with nothing more accomplished than putting the Japs on alert."

But now a big show lay ahead—a six-ship convoy that *Trigger* chose to attack from the surface and in the dark of night. Her first six torpedoes struck two tankers, with spectacular result. Flames shot 500 feet into the air and illuminated the surrounding sea. "Crew members in white uniforms were sprinting forward on her (the first tanker's) decks ahead of the rapidly spreading flames." A freighter beyond the tankers was also hit, broke in half beneath the stack and disappeared below the surface.

In more than three hours of battle with the convoy, *Trigger* struck a third tanker and a second freighter. In all, four ships were sunk, one was left damaged.

As *Trigger* departed, a glow flared up. It was one of the tankers blowing up. "Huge fires billowed into the air and the bow, bridge and stern of the tanker were incandescent. The hull of the first tanker disappeared and the place where she had been was still burning fiercely with flames lashing up 50 to 100 feet.''

And so it went, one successful war patrol after another, as 1943 faded into 1944 for the now-veteran, sea-going fighter *Trigger*. By now, she and her crew had earned the three presidential unit citations. Even the proud *Trigger*, though, would find April 8 of 1944 a trifle trying.

Sailing her ninth patrol, she encountered a large convoy—ships in four columns—guarded by ''a terrific escort force.'' Indomitable, *Trigger* worked her way among the ships and was about to loose 10 torpedoes for ''a mass killing'' when a destroyer suddenly loomed not 50 yards away, on a collision course. *Trigger* avoided the ramming, saw a clear lane and fired four torpedoes down the enemy's path, then was trapped by four of the escorts. ''As one tried to ram, the second followed him up with depth charges and the other two were lined up on either quarter. Just then, two hits were heard on a huge, heavily loaded tanker and two more hits were heard on a ship elsewhere in the convoy.''

*Trigger*, of course, couldn't stay for a look at the damage inflicted. She instead ''plunged to the depths to take the inevitable working over by the Japanese destroyers.'' And now came *Trigger's* worst moment yet. Six ''very close'' depth charges shook her badly. Worse, the submarine hunters would hound her for the next 17 hours as she lay silent in the deep, her steel hull ''buckled in and out.'' In addition, her pipes and bulkheads ''vibrated like guitar strings.'' Locker doors sprung open. The heat and humidity drenched the shoes and socks of the crew members with sweat. ''Lack of oxygen in the air and the nervous strain of the unrelenting depth charges brought some to the verge of collapse.''

But *Trigger* at last emerged, made temporary repairs ''by mustering spare parts and baling wire,'' then joined her sister sub *Tang* for further hunting of their own. They found a convoy off Palau. *Trigger* crept to within 2,600 yards and had four ships lined up in her sights as an overlapping mass. With six of her ''fish'' fired, four made hits. ''One of the closer ships blew up from an explosion on her after parts and one of the far ships was seen straight up and down with her course set for the bottom.'' The others milled about in a state of confusion ''that was not unpleasant to see.''

Three destroyers gathered close to exchange blinker signals. ''*Trigger* decided to add a little more confusion to their conference with torpedoes. A cloud of smoke shot into the air where the middle destroyer had been . . . The last thing heard . . . was her load of depth charges erupting in rapid-fire order way down below.''

After major overhaul in San Francisco, *Trigger* continued her one-sub war against the Japanese with a 10th, then an 11th war patrol. By now it was 1945, the end of that war only months away. *Trigger* out on her own for a 12th patrol, was supposed to join her sister *Tirante*.

The day came when *Tirante* arrived on station and called out by radio for *Trigger*. But . . . no reply. ''Silence was the only answer—a silence that has never been broken; a silence that told a wordless story.''

*Trigger*, brave *Trigger*, was gone.

From U.S. Navy files

# ■ *Romance Of A Courier's Mission*

A young American lieutenant in England was overjoyed by his new orders late in 1942. He was to take a train from London to Glasgow within 48 hours, and from there proceed by shipboard back to the United States. With any luck, he'd be home for Christmas!

It sounded too good to be true. There was, in fact, one slight complication. Like many other officers returning Stateside, he could do the Army a great favor by serving as a courier of secret documents bound for Washington. Not only a favor, but in fact, he *would* so serve. Orders.

To Jerome Chodorov, it didn't sound all that bad. In fact, he was mildly thrilled by the idea. He soon conjured up an image of himself ''as an important War Department character, bearing a slim manila envelope containing plans for the opening of the second front.''

The rude shock came when he reported to an Air Intelligence office to pick up his ''slim manila envelope.'' The major in charge instead indicated not one or two, but eight ''huge and bulging'' mail sacks on the floor nearby, easily weighing 100 pounds apiece. Each one was fastened shut with a combination lock, and Chodorov had to sign papers stating that all eight were his responsibility until he turned them over to some other officer in New York. "They were not to be out of my sight unless they were put behind the bolted doors of a government vault."

When the young lieutenant, a technical specialist with no real officer training, asked the major how one man could bully such a shipment from one place to another, the major "made it plain that this should be no problem at all for an officer of the Army of the United States."

He then got busy with a phone call while Chodorov contemplated his first hurdle—moving the eight bags down two flights of stairs to an Army bus on the street below that was loading for the run to the Euston railroad station. The newly appointed courier also had his own tightly stuffed Valpak, gas mask and helmet to lug from bus to train to ship across-the-Atlantic.

Chodorov knew very well that London teemed with enlisted men whom he presumably could commandeer as helpers in his vital task . . . but he also knew he was not a regular officer used to grabbing men off the street and barking peremptory orders. "I was certain that if I attempted to order an enlisted man around, he would laugh in my face, and the whole foolish masquerade would be over."

Indeed, as he personally hauled the sacks from the busy major's office, one by one, and dragged them down the stairs and onto the bus below, he spotted a Marine sergeant and said, "Oh, Sergeant, would you mind giving me a hand with this bag?"

The non-com displayed "amused tolerance" and said, "Sorry, Lieutenant, but I'm on duty right now." He disappeared, with Chodorov's worst fears fully confirmed.

As the neophyte officer slumped wearily in his bus seat minutes later, still sweating from his exertions, he thought happily of being with his wife by Christmas. Happily . . . until he realized he still had to get the eight bags off the bus and into the big station and aboard the right train, all in a few minutes' time!

He had a captive audience of enlisted men aboard the bus, but when he announced his need for their help, a corporal quickly begged off with the excuse he was being shipped home because of back problems. In seconds, the others "unanimously declared themselves to be medical cases, too."

A pitying sergeant and a meek private, however, did help out, and after much trevail, Chodorov at last found himself squished into a train compartment with his eight bags and personal luggage.

At last, he thought, he could relax for a while. The train would be a good 12 hours reaching Glasgow. At last . . . except that he hadn't eaten since morning, and even if there were a diner on the train, he couldn't leave the bags unattended. He did have a couple of candy bars and a bottle of Scotch with him. The combination was, to say the least, somewhat acidic.

De-training at Glasgow the next morning, no long-term solution to his problems yet to be found, Chodorov spotted a wondrous sight—a *second* lieutenant, leading a group of enlisted men. "Scotch and desperation gave my voice a power and resonance theretofore unsuspected. 'Lieutenant!' I snapped. 'I need eight men to carry some courier mail!' "

Unbelievably, it worked. Minutes later, "a squad of sullen soldiers was following me down the platform, carrying my bags and muttering about breakfast."

They left *first* lieutenant Chodorov and his sacks on the deck of the tender that would carry him to his ship. Progress! The courier was not even remorseful that he had discarded his gas mask and helmet on the train.

He was learning the ropes, the means of survival . . . except that when they announced sandwiches and hot coffee for sale in the tender's saloon, he had to stay on deck with his eight bags, "faint and shivering" in the Scottish winter.

Rebelling a second time, he darted into the crowded saloon, "clawed" his way to the counter, grabbed coffee and sandwich, then retreated back to his outdoor perch on the deck. No harm done. The bags were still there.

Ahead, though, loomed the big ship, a converted liner, that would cross the Atlantic. On the tender, most of the personnel appeared to be officers; the few enlisted men in view appeared to be real invalid cases. How to get the bags off the tender and onto the big ship?

"The instant we had made fast and a gangplank had been lowered, I shouldered full colonels aside and dashed aboard in search of aid." If he didn't hurry, of course, the tender might pull away with his unguarded bags till aboard.

Fortunately, he found a cooperative ship's officer and a gang of Italian POWs. They got the bags aboard in short order. A harried purser then agreed to place them in a locked strong room. Chodorov was ecstatic—"I practically danced to my cabin." He didn't care that the small cabin contained 14 wooden bunks. He was a free man.

He took a bath and an hour later turned out on deck, whistling.

The whistle died when he saw another tender alongside loaded with sacks just like his and saw them being fed into a chute leading, as he soon ascertained, into the same strongroom that held his bags. "The likelihood of my ever being able to separate my bags from the others in the confusion of the New York pier at landing time struck me as negligible. Court-martial and ruin, I now felt certain, lay ahead."

The passage across was stormy, and the big ship didn't reach New York until December 26. He had missed Christmas, and of course his nerves were in a state. "From the river I could see the West Side apartment house my wife was living in, and I mused sadly on whether I would be able to elude the agents of the dread CID—the Army's secret Counter Intelligence Division—long enough to have a few moments with her."

At the pier, Chodorov found a "towering pile" of mail sacks in "his" strong room, just as he had feared. But the gods of war now smiled upon him. As the city's longshoremen entered to take the mail bags ashore, he asserted himself once more, "assuring them that the course of the war rested on their efforts." They dragged aside the only sacks with the locks, just eight. *His* eight. In 30 minutes, he was on the pier, ready to turn them over—mission fully accomplished.

From *The Lighter Side of the Battle* compiled by John W. Hazard. (H & G Books, Shepherdstown, Md., 1988) and *The New Yorker* Magazine, Nov. 22, 1947

# ■ *Non-Swimmer's Worst Nightmare*

Off northern New Guinea in October 1942, the Australian coastal vessel *Alacrity* was carrying the men of the U.S. Army's 22nd Portable Hospital to a forward position near the vicious fighting at Buna when about 20 Japanese aircraft zoomed in to the attack. On board a nearly defenseless ship loaded with ammunition, half a mile from the beach and under bombing and strafing attack was no place to be if you couldn't swim.

Medic William Vana was such a man, and his first exposure to combat conditions was an unforgettable, searing experience. "The planes were so low that we could see the pilot sitting in the cockpit. Everyone started jumping overboard at this time. The 20 other planes came back and joined in the fun. Then all hell broke loose. The planes started strafing and dropping bombs, and what a racket! I don't think I ever heard as much noise before. The water was full of men swimming and yelling for help or praying."

The *Alacrity* was towing a barge full of added supplies and soldiers, while behind were three more coastal vessels carrying troops and supplies. "I heard a loud explosion and looked behind and saw the last ship blow up. At this time I didn't know what to do. I couldn't swim and there were no life boats."

Vana was not alone in his predicament—"there were about 20 of us still on board and all in the same fix as me."

Vana's first reaction was to fight back. He ran to a nearby machine-gun mount, "and let loose." He had never fired a machine gun before, but he got this one going and "sprayed the sky" until the ammo ran out." A buddy ran to another machine gun and did the same.

The planes kept attacking—strafing the swimmers in the water now. Vana, not knowing what to do, was "running around all over." An attempt to loosen an assault boat lashed to the deck failed; it was too heavy for him and a couple of other men to handle. "There were wounded and killed lying all over."

Vana ran back to the stern and yelled at the men there: "What the hell are we going to do? And how the hell are we going to get to shore?"

The two remaining ships of the small convoy were now on fire, and so was Vana's own vessel. "We expected at any minute for it to blow up, as there were tons of ammunition on board."

One of the men suggested tossing their packs overboard and using them for support in the water. "So I threw mine overboard and started taking my clothes off. I think that was the fastest I ever got undressed. I had my fatigues on, leggings, shoes, and underwear, and in no time I was standing naked on deck. I had on a pair of socks and these were the only clothes I had on. I, for some reason, grabbed a handkerchief and tried to tie it around my watch—and at the same time grabbed a pack of cigarettes. I must have been in a daze, as all at once I wondered what the hell I was trying to do. I threw these down and went to jump overboard. I looked for my pack and couldn't find it anyplace. The damn thing must have sunk!"

Frantic, Vana was about to go over the side anyway, "sink or swim," but he happened to see that up near the bow of his burning coastal vessel someone had gotten the assault boat into the water after all. "I ran through a hail of bullets to the bow and jumped overboard. I hit the water and at the same time grabbed onto the assault boat. I was afraid if I was to go down I'd never come up."

In the boat were eight or ten men, including Vana's buddy Herb Grew, while three or four more men were in the water alongside, hanging on. Vana climbed aboard and took an oar; someone else had found a paddle, and together they tried to move the assault boat away from the *Alacrity* and toward the shore, half a mile away.

We managed to get about 20 or 25 feet from the ship and seemed to be getting on pretty good. There were cries of help and prayers filling the air. All at once we heard a plane diving near us and we all looked up—here came a plane straight at us. We could see the tracers coming from it and they seemed to be coming straight at us. We all thought our time was up. We all got excited and the next thing I knew I was in the water. At first I didn't know what to do—then something told me to keep my head above water and try to get to shore. At this time two chaps who were in the boat with us grabbed onto me—they said they couldn't swim and started to pull me down with them. I yelled to them to let me loose as I couldn't swim either. I then started kicking and finally they let me loose. I saw Herb Grew at this time. He looked at me but didn't say a word. I guess he knew his time was up—and he died like a real soldier. He was fully clothed and went straight down. I had all I could do to save myself—so I was unable to help him or anyone else. The planes were still strafing and bombing and I started in towards shore. My arms and legs were moving like hell. I knew if my head were to go under I'd never come up—so I held my head up the best I could. Then I started yelling for help and praying. The air was full of chaps yelling for someone to help them. I hope to never hear anything like it again—and not being able to help them—but it was everybody for himself. Whenever a bomb would explode in the water, I'd get tossed around and get a mouthful of salt water. After a while my arms and legs began to get tired. My socks felt like they were full of cement. I was tiring out fast and just managed to keep afloat. I knew I couldn't last much longer, and the shoreline seemed to be getting farther away. I spotted a rowboat on shore and yelled for someone to come out in it. I and everyone else all had the same idea. Everyone was yelling for someone to come out and save us. Two men came out of the jungle and started pushing the boat in the water. I yelled to them to hurry up, as I couldn't last much longer. I was the nearest to shore, so they headed for me. The planes at this time decided they had had enough fun— or else that some of our planes might come—so they left us. I kept yelling at the two men in the boat to hurry. I was about 200 yards from shore by this time and could hardly move my arms and legs.

Hauled into the rowboat by the two "Aussies" manning it, Vana recovered a bit and helped them in rescuing others from the water. Soon they had 25 men in the tiny boat and another five hanging onto its sides as it pulled for the beach.

A few feet away, some of the men jumped out and staggered onto the sand. Some onlooking soldiers ran forward to help. "The first thing I did was drop to my knees and thank God for bringing me through safe and sound. I was naked except for my socks, which I took off and threw away. All I had saved were my ring and watch, which had stopped. The watch stopped at 6:57 p.m. That meant I was on board ship for almost half an hour before going over the side."

While the rowboat went out again to hunt for survivors—and attempt to haul in the barge—the medics left on the beach didn't know if the enemy was in the jungle right behind, or where. "Then our ship started to burn almost all over and the ammunition started to go off. Shell after shell went off and we hit the ground. There was a log lying down the beach, so we made for it. We scooped out a hole to lie in."

A couple of "infantry boys" then told the newly arrived medical corpsmen that the front line was two miles up ahead. In the hours that immediately followed, the 22nd Portable Hospital set up shop with what little equipment was left and began treating the wounded from the air attack—including its own personnel. "Someone had found some flashlights and they (the doctors) were using these to see by. The place was full of blood-soaked uniforms and bandages. The doctors were extracting bullets and shrapnel from the boys. All the doctors did a wonderful job with the little medical equipment they had.''

With the sky often lighted by the exploding ammunition, the 22nd Portable Hospital did its work through the night. Only its CO, Major Parker Hardin, had on any clothes at all—a pair of shorts. In the morning, the medics faced the task of sending the seriously wounded miles to the rear for real hospital care and of treating the wounded coming in from the fighting ahead, and all subject to intermittent bombing and strafing attacks by the Japanese.

In the meantime, they scrounged or made up what clothing they could—one man cut up a blanket to fashion a pair of shorts. Vana, who was awarded the Bronze Star for his action on the machine gun, went barefoot for many days.

From first-person account by William H. Vana, *World War II* Magazine, September 1990

# ■ *Sniper Duel In Stalingrad*

With a debris-strewn no-man's-land between them, two hunters stalked each other in the way of ancient and fierce tribesmen.

Their jungle, though, was the ruined cityscape of Stalingrad in the fall of 1942, a terrain littered with rubble, charred tank shells and the stanchions of collapsed buildings. The Germanic tribe and the Soviet tribe had each chosen a champion to go forth and slay the champion of the other.

Around them the war still raged, but for these two the city might as well have been a vacuum, with no one else present. Never mind the crash and thump of heavy arms or the patter of the light stuff on the nearby streets—theirs was a personal duel, to the death.

The search of these two snipers, each for the other, was intense, requiring full concentration.

The Soviet champion, one Vassili Zaitsev, had arrived first. With the German juggernaut stalled in the streets of the city next to the Volga, the great battle had degenerated into a struggle for every intersection or shattered building. Short of men and supplies, the Soviets made fortresses of the rubble piles and husks of buildings; they channeled the German panzers into chosen routes registered for devastating artillery fire, while their small arms erupted from every tumble-down cellar and cranny of the ruined city.

Stalingrad had become a great and deadly proving ground for snipers, for the sharpshooters of both sides. Russian or German, they had been finding their targets with cruel regularity.

Sometimes the shot from nowhere even struck down civilians. In one residential area of Stalingrad early in the months-long battle, Mrs. Katrina Karmanova watched from a trench as a family of four suddenly appeared and raced toward the river.

But a German sniper had seen them, too. As he went into action, the son, the father and the mother all went down, one by one. Last was a small girl, who halted uncertainly by her mother's body. Soldiers in Mrs. Karmanova's trench yelled at her—"Run! Run!" Finally, the stunned child did. The sniper let her go.

Later in the battle, it was a German officer's turn. Late in October, the German 16th Panzer Division was trying to subdue Soviets holed up in the shattered suburb of Rynok. A captain named Mues led his battalion through a difficult obstacle course of bunkers, pillboxes, stationary tanks and trenches, all fiercely defended.

He and his men had reached the banks of the Volga and turned north, in hopes of linking up in the center of Rynok with other German units. Aggressive as a combat leader, courageous, loved by his men, Mues had no idea that in the fog and light snow he was being tracked by a Soviet sniper. But he was, and an instant later, he was down, fatally shot in the head.

The men who gathered around him cried. Some collapsed. The news of his death demoralized much of his battle-hardened battalion.

In still another instance, it was the German marksmen who scored a small victory. In a guttered workers' district, 11 Germans from Combat Group Engelke dashed into the ground floor of an industrial building and set up a radio post. Only then did they discover that on a floor above them were several Russian troops, trapped by the Germans below.

The Germans calculated it would be too costly to storm them by the only stairway, and they also ruled out using the noisy freight elevator. As in the city-wide battle outside, it was a stalemate. The two groups passed one night in their shared building, then a second one, with only brief exchanges of satchel charges and automatic-weapons fire that produced no definitive results for either side.

In the hours following the second night, however, German snipers quietly took up positions across the street. They could see the Russians through the upstairs windows. The Germans on the first floor heard the shots outside and the screams above.

After a long silence, the Germans fearfully mounted the stairs and found their enemy—seven Russians, all fatally wounded by the snipers.

When the Siberian sharpshooter Zaitsev arrived in Stalingrad, both to conduct his sniping and to teach others, he already was a marksman widely ballyhooed in the Soviet press for his many combat "kills." The Germans also had seen the breathless stories, and they knew Soviet sniper tactics all too well by now. In Stalingrad especially, the sniper war was taking a dreadful toll among the German infantry.

Deciding to fight fire with fire, they called in their own champion of the telescopic rifle sight, a Major Konings who soon arrived from Germany proper and began to prowl the debris that once was Stalingrad. His particular mission was to find and kill the Great Zaitsev.

A careless prisoner then revealed the "supersniper's" presence to the Russians, and Zaitsev set out to find Konings before Konings found him.

For days the two scoured the jumbled ruins of the city, edging along the no-man's-land that lay between the opposing forces. Fellow snipers also searched on behalf of their respective champions.

The German had the advantage of knowing something about his opponent's habits and technique from captured documents and press clippings. Zaitsev, on the other hand, had killed many a German sniper, but he had no idea of Konings' favored tactics such as camouflage, deceptions or shooting techniques,

Except for the prisoner's tale, Zaitsev couldn't even be sure the German ace was "in town." But then someone, a real expert, shot down two Soviet snipers with single shots, one right after the other. Konings definitely was there.

Soon after, Zaitsev and his spotter, Nikolai Kulikov, found a prime position in the ruins between Mamaev Hill and the Red October Plant. They settled in and studied the rough ground opposite for any artificial change from its carefully memorized contours of the past weeks.

Toward the end of the first day, they saw a German helmet moving in a distant trench. It made a tempting sniper's target, an easy shot for a marksman like Zaitsev, but he held back. It could be a trick intended to lure his fire and thus reveal his position.

The next morning, the two Russians took up their hidden position again. For hours, they waited and watched. Directly ahead of them was a tank hulk to the left and a pillbox to the right. In between was an innocuous pile of rubble—bricks—and a sheet of metal.

The day passed uneventfully for the pair, and with the darkness of night they withdrew again. The hunt was still on.

The next morning, a political commissar named Danilov insisted upon going with them. The war raged loudly throughout all Stalingrad as the trio occupied Zaitsev's chosen position, again facing the tank at left, pillbox at right.

In a short time, however, Danilov rashly exposed himself. Incredibly, he rose and shouted: "There he is. I'll point him out to you."

A shot rang out, and Danilov slumped down. As Zaitsev noted with grim satisfaction, he was only wounded in the shoulder. The hidden shooter across the way wouldn't be that bad a shot. No, he wanted to draw out any companions helping the foolish Danilov.

It was a ruse worthy of Konings himself, and now, with his binoculars, Zaitsev studied the debris before him even more intently. Others carried away the wounded Comrade. Kulikov stayed by Zaitsev's side.

The tank they could dismiss outright. Too exposed, too obvious. The pillbox wasn't likely since its gun slot was sealed off. That left the rubble and sheet of metal. And the more Zaitsev stared at the spot, the more artificially arranged it began to look.

But how to be sure?

Zaitsev took a glove, raised it on the end of a stick. His opponent bit—with the crack of a rifle, a bullet whistled through the glove.

Now, the Russian champ was positive. So was his spotter. "There's our viper," hissed Kulikov.

But now was not the time to act, with Konings surely on guard after the glove trick. Slithering and crawling away, the two Russians instead mapped out their strategy for the morn, then retired again for the night.

The next day found them settled still within view of the sheet metal and bricks, but at a new point in the arc of terrain facing the German ace's suspected position. This time, Zaitsev had selected a point that by late afternoon would place the bright sun at his back—in the German's face. In the morning, though, the Russians fired an errant, aimless shot, to get their quarry's attention . . . make him wonder.

During the long hours that followed, the Russians kept their rifles down to avoid any bright reflection revealing exactly where they were. The single aimless shot no doubt gave the German a fair idea—he still would be wondering, tense, what caused it.

By late afternoon, the sun had crawled behind the Russian pair; they now were clothed in a shadow.

Zaitsev intently watched the spot where the hidden sniper would be himself watching, in their direction, toward the source of the mysterious shot. And he would be facing the sun; its bright rays then were likely to . . . and they did!

Zaitsev saw the telltale reflection from glass. By plan, Kulikov raised a tempting helmet. The expected shot came. Play-acting, Kulikov screamed and briefly jerked into view, as if shot.

Reflexively, the shooter stirred, raised his head to see his results.

The next shot was Zaitsev's. Just one, between the eyes. The historical accounts say it really was Konings.

The duel was over. The war went on.

From *Enemy at the Gates: The Battle for Stalingrad* by William Craig (Reader's Digest Books, New York, N.Y., 1973)

# ■ *Ship's Piano Purloined*

While Chaplain Paul J. Redmond of the U.S. 4th Marine Raider Battalion was ashore at Espirito Santo in the New Hebrides celebrating Mass at a surprisingly convenient and tarp-covered altar, the skipper of the transport ship *President Polk* was still fuming and fretting over the mysterious disappearance of his piano.

Here was a twain which, like East and West, might never meet. Since the Marine Raiders had just debarked from his ship, though, the skipper wasted no time in going ashore and planting himself before the battalion's Lt. Col. James Roosevelt (yes, FDR's Marine Corps son) to demand satisfaction.

The *Polk*, after all, carried very few pianos as a rule. Just one, in fact. And it was the apple of the skipper's eye.

But Roosevelt explained quite logically that no object so large and unwieldy as a piano could have become mixed up with the Raiders' fighting gear. Unimpressed, the skipper "threatened dire repercussions" if the piano were not immediately found and returned to its accustomed place aboard ship.

As the search then began, a few hardy men wisely kept their mouths shut. Only years later, in the veterans' newsletter *The Raider Patch*, did the full story come out. For instance, Weston A. Hartman's account of the piano leaving the ship while the officer-of-the-deck was diverted to an unloading "problem" elsewhere.

When the coast was clear, wrote Marine veteran Hartman, he and a few others in 2nd Lt. Thomas J. O'Connor's company rolled the heavily wrapped piano across the main deck to the port gangway, but then had a bit of difficulty easing it onto the gangway. "We finally had to turn it upside down. The piano played an unwritten symphony all the way down."

Below a lighter was waiting—this was a well-planned operation, meticulous in detail. The lighter headed immediately for the beach, where "a Raider Recon truck was waiting."

Also waiting was another helping hand, Harold P. Hart, posted on the beach with 32 others to guard the off-loaded Raider gear. Sometime before, he had been asked "to leave an open spot right off the beach for a 'Special off-load.' "

And then, "precisely on the hour, here comes an unloading barge from the *President Polk* with one huge object well-covered and escorted by several Raiders."

Hart watched admiringly as the Recon truck quickly backed up to the barge and took on the "mysterious object." The entire operation was "short and sweet," and Hart certainly would ask no questions. If it came from the *Polk*, "I was all for it—they had treated us like hogs aboard." In fact, "When we left the ship, we lifted everything that was loose, and if it wasn't loose, we loosed it."

And where was the piano going after its trip ashore? Enter again the chaplain, Father Paul J. Redmond, whose innocent remark some days before had been that it would be nice to have a piano for Mass.

The Raider "padre" then became *aware*, one might say, that the piano had made its way ashore. But he asked the men *not* to compromise *his* conscience by telling him where it was.

Ashore also, he had wasted no time in saying Mass for the island natives in the local chapel. The altar he found there "was very convenient in size and height—covered with a tarp, which should have made me suspicious, but didn't." His altar cloth, covering all, furthered the masquerade as the search went on, with the irate skipper now threatening to contact Washington.

When Roosevelt first asked Father Redmond to return the piano, "I truthfully told him I did not know where it was." Now, on direct order from Roosevelt, the chaplain exerted greater efforts on his own. "I made inquiries and *honestly*, much to my surprise, I had been saying Holy Mass on stolen property!"

The piano was returned, but "with regret." Aboard ship, meanwhile, Marine Captain Donald Floyd, emerging from sick bay and ready to disembark, was startled when the Navy insisted on searching his gear before allowing him to leave the ship. "When I asked the reason for this unwarranted action, they wouldn't tell me, but I remember somebody saying 'Roosevelt and his Thousand Thieves.' "

From *Guadalcanal Echoes,* July 1988, The Guadacanal Campaign Veterans, with credits to *The Raider Patch,* USMCR Raider veterans, for piecing together the full story.

# ■ *Kilroy Really* Was

In the midst of all the savagery of war, of its long tedium and its outbursts of lethal action, there was that one mysterious name that always seemed to get there first—Kilroy.

Shattered walls, crates of ammo, crude road signs . . . nearly any object that confronted the American GI, world-wide, bore that mark: "Kilroy was here."

Painted or chalked, the Kilroy message greeted probably millions in every corner of the globe.

And not only the message, but a drawing of a snoop-nosed fellow with beady eyes hanging onto a fence, peering over it—right at you.

No one will ever know the number of fighting men who *thought* they were the first to reach some important objective, only to find that "Kilroy" had beaten them to it. "Kilroy was here."

Kilroy, of course, had many helpers, and why not? A little humor in the midst of such carnage and destruction could be a rare positive element, a balm helpful to one's sanity.

There was something about the legendary Kilroy, too, that was uniquely American. Somehow, it strains the imagination to think of the French, the British, the Russians or the Chinese indulging in like whimsy on such grand scale. The Aussies? Yes, maybe the irreverent Aussies, but surely no one else.

In any case, Kilroy was a "movement" that spread like wildfire. All over the world, previously pristine surfaces blossomed with the Kilroy message. He was everywhere.

Even a murder victim in London was left, strangled, near a message scrawled on her apartment wall that Kilroy had been there, a pathetic aberration that really had nothing to do with the Kilroy phenomenon. The killer, it turned out, was a mental patient living next door—a man named Kilroy. Apparently unaware of the world-wide Kilroy joke, he couldn't understand why it took the police so long to track him down. He had left his name, hadn't he? The police, somewhat naturally, had been thinking in terms of a disturbed American GI.

But who, or what, was Kilroy himself? The original Kilroy?

The theories and the claims were many. After the war, it was time to get serious and ascertain the true facts. The Transit Company of America became a prime vehicle, establishing a contest with a prize for the man who could make the claim and back it up with irrefutable proof.

Jim Kilroy, a former Boston City Councilman, Massachusetts state legislator and shipyard supervisor, heard about the contest and joined more than 40 other Kilroys vying for recognition as the "real McCoy."

His story (as one by one other Kilroys were eliminated) was fairly simple but convincing. His shipyard job in Quincy, at the Fore River Shipyard, had required him to check the number of rivets driven into place on a given work shift. He would check them off with a slash in chalk as he went, but the riveters would come along later and erase his mark. It seems they were paid on a piece-work basis, and if the rivets could be counted more than once, they would be paid twice over.

When management caught on and complained to rivets-checker Kilroy, he began adding the message "Kilroy was here" as he counted off blocks of rivets done.

For some reason, that stopped the riveters from wiping out his work.

Meanwhile, as the newly built ships left their ways at Fore River Shipyard, the Kilroy scrawl often was still visible on beams and other surfaces requiring rivets. GIs on their way overseas saw the chalked message—and took it with them wherever they went to war.

Jim Kilroy's claim was corroborated by his fellow workers from the shipyard, and he won the Transit Company prize, a trolley car. Strange to say, the man whose name somehow shot ahead of nearly every mud-slogging GI overseas was himself never there in person.

What he and his morale-boosting message had done for the war effort, though, was a good deal more than simply make sure his ships had tight rivets in the right places. (And now to find the inspired wag who added that famous, long-nosed caricature that soon popped up alongside the Kilroy message throughout the world of the 1940s!)

From Richard W. O'Donnell in *Naval History* Magazine, Winter 1989

# ■ *A Square Balloon's Contribution*

A square balloon? The Goodyear people couldn't quite understand—who would want a square balloon? But the emissary from the squash court in Chicago was quite firm. He provided very exact specs, and they said, okay, one square balloon of rubberized cloth coming up.

About two months later, Goodyear Tire and Rubber Company faithfully delivered the square balloon to that odd address—a squash court under the west stands of the University of Chicago's Alonzo Stagg Stadium.

Once unfolded, the big rubberized square neatly matched the squash court's dimensions—as planned. But erecting the balloon thing in place was a tricky chore. The scientists attempting to manhandle it into place couldn't see its top. That was when Enrico Fermi, the Italian emigré and Nobel-prize-winning physicist, mounted a rolling scaffold with a raiseable platform. Hoisted on high, he shouted his directions to those below—for some time after, they fondly called him "Admiral."

Indeed, theirs in late 1942 was wartime work, vital work to complete a fantastic project before the enemy might do the same.

With the balloon assembled, they then began to build their pile. "They planned their pile even as they built it. They were to give it the shape of a sphere of about 26 feet in diameter, supported by a square frame, hence the square balloon."

A more crucial reason for the square balloon, though, was the ceiling. As the world now knows, none of this had ever been done before—no blueprints to follow, no schematic drawings, just theory. And no time to fool around.

The ceiling *should* be high enough, according to theory, but the margin for possible error (or unknown factors such as undetected impurities) was admittedly narrow. If the ceiling were not high enough for their pile to do its expected job, they could improve the pile's efficiency by creating a vacuum around it. An earlier experiment at Columbia University with a "canned pile" had "indicated that such an aim might be attained by removing air from the pores of the graphite." At Chicago, they could, if necessary, enclose their pile in the square balloon and pump out all the air inside.

But that would be decided later. For now, the pile began to grow. Its supports were blocks of wood. Next came bricks of graphite. They left a black powder everywhere, on everyone, the floor black and "slippery as a dance floor."

In six weeks, it was done. It would not be a sphere after all, but instead remained flat at the top. It also did not reach the ceiling. No vacuum appeared necessary, either.

On the morning of December 2, 1942, three young men waited on top of the pile as the "suicide squad." If things got out of control, they were to flood the pile with a neutralizing cadmium solution, since cadmium absorbs, extinguishes, neutrons.

"Suicide squad" was a sort of joke, but who knew, really?

Key personnel and witnesses watched from a balcony at the north end of the squash court. Physicist George Weil was stationed on the floor by one of the cadmium rods inserted into the pile. His would be the last to be withdrawn.

Quite unnecessarily for his small audience of fellow scientists, Fermi explained and instructed step by step.

At the beginning: "The pile is not performing because inside it there are rods of cadmium which absorb neutrons. One single rod is sufficient to prevent a chain reaction. So our first step will be to pull out of the pile all control rods, but the one that George Weil will man."

A pen on a graph device would trace a line showing the intensity of the radiation, then level off. "When the pile chain-reacts, the pen will trace a line that will go up and up and that will not tend to level off."

And so it was, for hours—interrupted, prosaically enough, for a lunch break. With all the rods pulled out but Weil's, he extracted his by pre-determined steps. Even the first time, the radiation measurably increased. "The counters stepped up their clicking; the pen went up and stopped where Fermi had said it would." And each time after that, the same.

By 3:30 p.m., after many such small steps, they had reached the crucial one. Fermi told Weil to pull out his rod by another foot. Turning to the onlookers in the balcony, Fermi said: "This will do it. Now the pile will chain react."

Again, the pen traced its line, and this time there was no leveling off. "A chain reaction was taking place in the pile."

The suicide squad atop the pile tensed, "ready with their liquid cadmium: this was the moment."

But all went well. In the pile—not only of graphite but also layers of uranium and uranium oxide—the first self-sustaining nuclear reaction created by man had taken place.

Later that day, anxious higher-ups in the Manhattan Project who were overseeing the development of an atomic bomb received word from the Fermi group in Chicago.

The carefully phrased word was: "The Italian Navigator has reached the New World."

The question that came back was: "And how did he find the natives?"

Answer: "Very friendly."

From *Atoms in the Family* by Laura Fermi
(University of Chicago Press, 1954)

# ■ Start Of The 'Mush' Morton Legend

Lieutenant Commander Dudley ("Mush") Morton of the U.S. Navy's submarine service would become a legendary figure of the Pacific War, and he showed why on his very first war patrol as skipper of the boat *Wahoo*.

His initial assignment as the submarine slipped away from Brisbane, Australia, on January 16, 1943, was merely to provide reconnaissance of the Japanese facilities and ships at Wewak, an anchorage on the northern coast of New Guinea.

As events would demonstrate, reconnaissance meant one thing to the Navy planners and quite another to the aggressive Kentuckian at the helm, once described as "built like a bear and playful as a cub."

As the patrol began, the happy-go-lucky Morton was undismayed by the absence of Wewak from the Navy's official charts. A speck in the vast Pacific, it simply wasn't shown.

Pure chance came to the rescue: a motor machinist's mate aboard the *Wahoo* had bought a high school atlas while ashore in Australia. Perusing a map of New Guinea, he happened across Wewak and showed it to one of the boat's officers, who of course brought it to Morton's attention. With the help of a Graflex camera, the submariners blew up the map section to match the undetailed Navy charts in scale, then set course for the enemy harbor.

Now coming into play was Morton's conception of harbor reconnaissance—still risky in the absence of elementary navigational information such as water depth, position of reefs and like details. His conception was *not* to stand outside the harbor and look things over through the periscope. "Hell, no," he said, "the only way you can reconnoiter a harbor is to go right inside it and see what's there."

Which is why, on January 24, the submerged *Wahoo* was to be found picking its way through the channel between two islands at the entrance to Wewak's harbor with the aid of the boat's echo sounder. Inside the enemy "chicken coop," however, the underwater hunter found few chickens—at first. Only a tug and two patrol boats could be seen through the *Wahoo*'s periscope. None was worth an attack revealing the sub's presence and expending its precious torpedoes.

The skipper and crew were disappointed to find so little after their blind sojourn of the nine-mile passage into the inner harbor at maddeningly slow and careful speed.

Soon, however, the masts of a larger vessel could be seen above and behind a screen of palm trees—moving.

"Mush" Morton and his crew discovered that a reef barred a closer approach; the *Wahoo* turned and followed the reef to its end, turned again and headed toward the mysterious ship. At 6,000 yards, they raised periscope for a real look at their quarry and found, for a submarine, the worst of all adversaries—a destroyer!

Worse yet, it was broad daylight and in the clear, shallow waters of the harbor the *Wahoo* had been seen. The Japanese warship already was up to speed and maneuvering, first toward open water beyond the harbor, then, after four torpedoes launched by the *Wahoo* missed, straight toward the sub itself. The intent was obvious: ramming!

This was serious. The *Wahoo* quickly fired another "fish" at 1,800 yards, "down the throat," or head-on at the charging destroyer.

—Missed. Ran wide of the difficult, bow-on target.

The next one, though, launched at last possible moment, set off on a true track. The *Wahoo* crash-dived, and all aboard steeled themselves for the certain depth-charge attack that would follow if the boat's last fish also missed. In these shallow waters, of course, any submarine would be a dead duck.

Instead, there came a heavy explosion, then . . . nothing.

After a time, Morton cautiously rose to periscope level and raised his viewing device. What he saw was most gratifying for any submarine skipper—a rare sight at that. The enemy destroyer had been broken in two, with the bow end fast sinking.

The Japanese aboard the stern section saw their tormentor and opened fire, but that half of the warship also went down in minutes. No survivors.

His "reconnaissance" finished, "Mush" Morton set sail for the rest of his war patrol, his first as a submarine commander. Thus began a legend that would inspire and excite American submariners throughout the Pacific during World War II. First war patrol. First enemy vessel encountered, a destroyer. Destroyer sunk.

From *Submarine Warriors* by Edwyn Gray
(Presidio Press, Novato, Calif., 1988)

# ■ Plea Of The White Rose

Hans and Sophie Scholl, brother and sister, were students at a university during the war. Committed Christians, they sent a shower of their anti-Hitler Leaflets of the White Rose from the upper floors of the university's main building into the inner court-yard below.

"We must attack evil where it is most powerful, and it is most powerful in the power of Hitler," exhorted their leaflet.

They were caught and executed by guillotine. Sophie went to her death, "as if she were looking into the sun," said associates. Sophie, 22, had to hobble forward to her death on crutches, since the Gestapo interrogators had broken her leg.

Hans, about the same age, had been tortured, too. But he faced his frightening death "without hatred, with everything, everything below him."

They issued their appeal to fellow students shortly after the German surrender at Stalingrad, early 1943. Their school was Munich University, in the city where Hitler had his political start. His power had snuffed out their protest . . . but the leaflets, it is said, "went from hand to hand in thousands of copies through all of Germany."

> From *Germans Against Hitler: July 20, 1944*
> (English edition; Press And Information Office,
> Government of West Germany, 1964)

# ■ Soothed Into Agreement

Beyond his untrammeled power, the fear he instilled, the rages, Hitler had yet another weapon at his disposal when he treated with his generals (or anyone else). "Hitler had a magnetic, and indeed hypnotic personality," recalled the young panzer general who developed the tactics for the Battle of the Bulge, Hasso von Manteuffel. "This had a very marked effect on people who went to see him with the intention of putting forward their views on any matter. They would begin to argue their point, but would gradually find themselves succumbing to his personality, and in the end would often agree to the opposite of what they intended."

Manteuffel was one of those also familiar with Hitler's flair for intimidating his generals with obscure facts and figures, but in Manteuffel's view Hitler himself would fall prey to their mesmerizing effect.

Hitler, he said, "had a tendency to intoxicate himself with figures and quantities." He did use them against others: "When one was discussing a problem with him, he would repeatedly pick up the telephone, ask to be put through to some departmental chief, and inquire—'How many so and so have we got?' Then he would turn to the man who was arguing with him, quote the number, and say: 'There you are'—as if that settled the problem. He was too ready to accept paper figures, without asking if the numbers stated were available in reality. It was always the same, whatever the subject might be—tanks, aircraft, rifles, shovels."

From *The Other Side of the Hill* by B.H. Liddell Hart
(Cassell and Company, Ltd., London, 1948)

# ■ *Brothers To The End*

The wartime careers of the two Stilinovich brothers of Hibbing, Minnesota, were closely matched until the fearful night of St. Patrick's Day, 1943.

Joseph Anthony Stilinovich, 20, and his younger brother William Joseph, 18, both joined the U.S. Navy on November 17, 1942. Both were sent to the Great Lakes for their training, and both then were assigned to the Navy's Armed Guard Center in Brooklyn, New York.

The Armed Guards were those brave men who manned the few guns aboard the merchant ships plying submarine-infested waters around the globe with vital war supplies for the troops or Allies overseas.

The two brothers were separated, though, in their ship assignments. Joseph went aboard the SS *Harry Luckenbach*, which had a crew of 54 and 26 Armed Guards. William drew the SS *Irene DuPont*, crew of 49 and Armed Guards, 26 again.

They were aboard separate ships, but in the same convoy setting out across the North Atlantic. The convoy was designated HX-229, out of New York.

The waiting German U-boats struck the night of March 17, 1943—St. Patrick's Day. Both the *Luckenbach* and the *DuPont* were hit with two torpedoes. Both ships went down, the *Luckenbach* in four minutes, the *DuPont* the following afternoon, after a second submarine attack.

Both stricken ships got off lifeboats, but only one, the *DuPont*, would have survivors to be accounted for later.

The *Luckenbach* launched three lifeboats, and three or four escort vessels spotted them in the water. In the confusion and turmoil of the U-boat attack, however, the onlookers lost track of the lifeboats. No survivors were picked up—no one from the *Luckenbach* was ever seen again, including Joseph Stilinovich.

Aboard the *DuPont*, brother William had reached a lifeboat being lowered down the side, but it capsized. He wound up in a lifeboat holding eight others—and no oars. They drifted past a ship and someone on deck shouted that they would be rescued. But they drifted away. Nearby, another ship was burning brightly.

The abandoned *DuPont* remained afloat the next day. An escorting British corvette tried to sink her with shelling and a depth charge, but to no avail. Then, in the afternoon, the German U-91 came across the *DuPont* and sank her.

William Stilinovich and his lifeboat companions were picked up by a British destroyer. Of the *DuPont*'s 49 crew, 26 Armed Guard and 9 passengers, 13 had been lost.

William Stilinovich had survived and would continue to sail—aboard two more merchant ships—throughout the war, in all its theaters, before his discharge in early 1946.

The Stilinovich brothers are in the *History of the United States Navy Armed Guard Veterans of World War II*, where it says that Joseph's "life ended in the waters of the Atlantic, but he will always be remembered by Armed Guard brother William Stilinovich."

From *The Pointer and the Plane Shooter*, December, 1988, USN Armed Guard World War II Veterans

# ■ *Young Man Whittling*

A U.S. Army private caught up in the Tunisian campaign in the spring of 1943 came across a young German soldier in rough North African terrain near Beja. The German had not noticed the American's approach.

They were 20 feet apart, and the young German harmlessly was whittling a piece of wood.

The American, lying behind a nearby bush, couldn't bring himself simply to shoot. He wondered, "Why should I kill him?"

But, failing that, what *was* he to do? If he spoke, the German would spring to action, and the shooting would start.

The American thought seriously of throwing a rock or moving his bush to end the impasse. It just "didn't seem fair . . . to up and shoot him."

As the private later told doctors in the U.S. Army's 15th Evacuation Hospital near Beja, the dilemma had been "resolved" by another "Jerry."

The second German, a "patrol," came along, spotted the hesitating young GI and shot him. He had arrived in the hospital tents with gunshot wounds of the thigh and the shoulder.

But *his* wounding was not the end of the story. "Made me so . . . mad I just used all my strength and shot both of them—the boy whittling had grabbed his gun and I know I killed him."

From *A Surgeon's Diary* by Frank W. Peyton, M.D.
(Self-published, 1988, Lafayette, Ind.)

# ■ *Death Of Leslie Howard*

Winston Churchill thought it was because of him. A Roman Catholic priest was called off the airplane by an urgent telephone call that later could not be traced to *anyone*. Passengers who stayed on board had spoken of unsettling premonitions. British actor Leslie Howard, for one, had gone to neutral Portugal and Spain with "a queer feeling about this whole trip."

The KLM airliner, a DC-3 called *Ibis*, took off from Portella airport outside Lisbon, Portugal, at 9:35 a.m., June 1, 1943, with 13 passengers on board. Leslie Howard was the only famous personage aboard, and he was accompanied by his friend and business associate Arthur Chenhall, a *heavy-set man who smoked cigars*.

Their fellow passengers included Reuters correspondent Kenneth Stonehouse; Jewish-relief activist Wilfred Israel; Ivan Sharp,

115

a mining engineer negotiating vital tungsten imports for embattled Britain; Tyrrel Shervington, Lisbon manager for Shell Oil; two other men, three women, and two children.

Dora Rowe, a nanny, would have been aboard with her young charge, Derek Partridge, son of a Foreign Office official, but they were "bumped" at the last minute to make room for actor Howard and his associate, Chenhall.

Father A.S. Holmes, vice president of the Roman Catholic English College, also would have been aboard except for the mysterious phone call to KLM informing him that "he was to report immediately at either the British Embassy or the Papal Nunciature."

The airliner wouldn't wait, and, as he returned to the terminal, the priest paused momentarily to watch *Ibis* roll down the runway and then take off, "Holmes hurried away to make his inquiries, but at neither the Embassy nor the Nunciature could anyone be found who had made the telephone call that had so urgently taken him off the plane. Nor could the switchboard operators remember one being made. He rang the airport again, but they could only repeat the message they had already given him."

Until that same spring, by tacit agreement of the warring parties, the civil air service between Britain and Lisbon had been allowed to fly its daily flights unhindered. Then, a week before Leslie Howard flew into Portugal for a round of lectures on his films and *Hamlet*, as well as on film distribution business of his own, the same *Ibis* had been attacked off Cape Corunna by six to eight German Ju 88s, but after some hits, it eluded them in a cloud bank and flew on to Portugal. That was on April 19, and until then, KLM, or the Royal Dutch Airline, had been flying the route for the British BOAC, undisturbed, for three years. "It had carried over 5,000 passengers between the UK and Portugal without loss and almost without incident."

Even after the April 19 attack, the daytime flights had continued without further incident. Leslie Howard, who played Ashley in *Gone with the Wind*, was nervous about his pending trip to Iberia, in part to "show the flag," but he went anyway. In fact, he told one friend, "Well—what the hell—you know I'm a fatalist anyway."

To his wife, Ruth, however, he acknowledged his "queer feeling" about the trip to Portugal and Franco's Spain, the latter neutral, but a near-ally to Nazi Germany.

Before the return trip June 1, both fellow passengers Stonehouse and Shervington were apparently nervous. Shervington of Shell

Oil dreamt that the plane was shot down with him on board. And journalist Stonehouse told a friend: "I'm not normally frightened but somehow I feel bad about this air-trip. I wish I could go to sleep here and wake up at some English airfield."

As their *Ibis* lifted off from Lisbon the morning of June 1, the crews of eight German Junkers prepared to take off from the *Luftwaffe* base of Kerlin-Bastard outside of Bordeaux, France, for a roving mission over the Bay of Biscay. What orders the commander of the Junkers wing may have given to the flight leader are not known. The German Atlantic archives vaguely refer to air-sea rescue and U-boat protection, but there is no evidence to support such activities that particular day.

Whatever the case, the German fighter-bombers and the civilian KLM *Ibis* were soon flying on intersecting pathways through the air.

In spy-infested Lisbon, there was no secrecy to the airliner's departure. Adjoining German *Lufthansa* personnel could see the crew and passengers board the KLM plane. Among those on board, who might have incurred German wrath? In Berlin's view, British actor Howard was a propagandist and possible intelligence agent (his most recent films had been distinctly anti-German, anti-Nazi). There is evidence that the Germans considered Shervington a British agent. Israel's Zionist activities and work in rescuing Jews from Nazi genocide certainly made him no friend to the Hitler regime. Altogether, none of the passengers *was* a friend.

Churchill, at the time, was in North Africa following his recent consultations in Washington. He was due to fly back to England very shortly. (He did, on June 6.)

In his history of World War II, Volume IV, *The Hinge of Fate,* he wrote that German agents apparently mistook a *heavy-set man* at the Lisbon airport for him, *cigar* and all. "The German agents therefore signalled that I was on board . . . Although these passenger planes had plied unmolested for many months between Portugal and England, a German war plane was instantly ordered out, and the defenseless aircraft was ruthlessly shot down."

As Churchill also said, but more accurately, it was "difficult to understand how anyone could imagine that with all the resources of Great Britain at my disposal I should have booked passage in an unarmed and unescorted plane from Lisbon and flown home in broad daylight."

Leslie Howard's son, Ronald Howard, agrees that such a scenario would have seemed improbable "even to the dimmest German mind."

The German *staffel* of Ju 88s soon met the *Ibis* over the Bay of Biscay, and with six of the eight planes attacking the defenseless civil airliner, shot it down into the sea. All aboard were killed— not a trace of them was ever found. *Why* has been a mystery ever since.

The *why* part "nagged" at Howard's son for many years, he acknowledged in his book, *In Search of My Father*. In reconstructing the last four years of his father Leslie's life, especially the circumstances of his fateful Iberian trip in 1943, Ronald Howard says he "sought a motive for murder—for murder I believe it was—of all those who died that day in *Ibis*."

But after extensive research, with findings of his own, and with review of what others had found before him, "I am still no nearer a positive solution." The missing piece of the puzzle may be the orders given to the flight leader by his wing commander, Major Alfred Hemm. But after the war, he could not be found. Nearly all in the Ju 88 air crews had been killed during the war.

As for Churchill's mistaken-identity theory, that doesn't seem likely even by the most elastic of interpretations, since the first announcement of the shooting came from Berlin itself—with the added specifics that the passengers killed included Stonehouse, Leslie Howard, and his *heavy-set, cigar-smoking* associate, Chenhall.

From *In Search of My Father* by Ronald Howard
(St. Martin's Press, New York; William Kimber
& Co., Ltd., London, 1981)

# ■ *Shipmates To The End*

Ted and Paul were shipmates aboard the U.S. light cruiser *Helena*, pals who shared the same fire-director tub, and before any engagement with the enemy in the South Pacific, Paul would say to Ted, "You protect my back and I'll protect yours."

And for Ted, "it was always comforting to know that Paul was at my back."

When the *Helena* was torpedoed shortly after 2 a.m., July 6, 1943, in the Battle of Kula Gulf, however, the two shipmates were briefly separated in the tumult and confusion of a ship going down. Ted Blahnik, in recent years president of the Guadalcanal Campaign Veterans and editor of their *Guadalcanal Echoes*, remembers the sequence of events very clearly.

At 2:04 a.m., speed 25 knots, the first Japanese Long Lance torpedo struck their cruiser. The blast tore off the forward end of the ship so completely that a torrent of water, a cascade, poured through the ship and even came over Ted's director shield two decks above the main deck. With him in the director tub at the moment were his buddy Paul—Paul Foster—and two young officers.

As the initial burst of water receded, Ted went to the port side of their tub and looked over the side. "I glanced down toward the water just in time to see the unmistakable tracks of two more torpedoes streaking amidships. Time, 0207. Two more thunderous explosions rocked the ship and broke her back."

That was it . . . the *Helena* was fatally stricken and soon would be going down. The men from the director tub worked their way down to the main deck and prepared to join those abandoning ship. People were jumping into the water, throwing rafts over the side, sliding down lines. This was the expected. The unexpected, though, was that before leaving one way or another, many of the men turned to salute the flag, just like before hitting the gangway for liberty. *Salute the flag.*

Whether for instinctive discipline or love of ship, they did it. "It would be most difficult to describe my feelings as I, too, turned and faced the bravely waving battle flag. As I saluted, I thought, 'Good-bye, old girl.' Melodramatic? Yes!"

Over the side and into the water, Ted Blahnik and the men in his vicinity made haste to move away from the sinking ship and her suction. In 20 minutes, she was apparently gone. "A lady to the end. No fires, no internal explosions."

Paul no longer was with Ted; they had become separated, and now neither was there to protect the other's back. In the black night, on the oil-coated water, however, American destroyers were moving about, dark and silent, as they picked up survivors. After a while, they received orders to "clear the area." As they departed, Ted was among those men left to float "aimlessly during the rest of the night." He was wearing a Mae West but was afraid it would become waterlogged.

"What daylight would bring, we didn't know. We did know, through a briefing the previous night, that we were in enemy territory."

Dawn brought a totally unexpected sight—"I saw the bow of our ship sticking straight up out of the water not more than a few hundred yards away. It may sound corny, but I couldn't help but feel that she was still valiantly trying to protect her crew of survivors."

Ted now made his way to the upraised bow, slipped on an inflatable life belt in place of the Mae West—and found many of his shipmates clustered in the water around the bow of their ship. Among them was his buddy, Paul. Naturally, the two friends were very happy to see each other.

Among the other sailors, though, were men with injuries. One had broken bones that grated with every ripple of the water. "His cries of pain were heartrending to all of us." And inside the ship? If any were still alive, "Their world, inside the ship, was slowly filling with water and their time was running out."

There was nothing the men treading water outside could do.

Late in the day, an American B-24 spotted the sunken cruiser and her survivors. The aircrew dropped two rafts, and the injured were tenderly hoisted onto one of them. Ted and Paul took turns inflating the second raft by handpump, then, with others, began taking turns paddling or sliding back into the water to make room for someone else. There was land visible in the distance, but the ocean current took the raft and its men where it wanted.

During the next night, some men simply disappeared—"drifted off into the night." Ted and Paul still were there, but after a second night aboard or alongside the raft, they and two other sailors decided to strike out on their own and reach the tantalizing island shores near them by swimming and dog-paddling. "By now the number of men in and around the raft had greatly decreased."

What may not be apparent to those never caught in such circumstance is the fast-building disorientation. "It would seem that physical and mental properties wouldn't leave you so soon, but the two days without food or water were taking their toll. What was before an effort to swim to shore became more a matter of drifting and hoping."

So, Ted wasn't really surprised, or even dismayed—not just then—when sometime on that third day Paul called over to him. "I'm going below," said Paul. On board ship, it was something they said a thousand times. "That would simply mean that he was going to go below decks." Here, it meant something else, but here both men by now were delirious. Perhaps Paul really thought he was going below decks. In any case, "He took off his life jacket and went 'below.' "

As for Ted, well, he didn't quite realize. "In retrospect, you might ask, How could you lose a shipmate and close friend of more than two years and not give it another thought? Answer: My own mind was beginning to wander. A female voice called to me and asked, 'Why don't you stop at the gas station and have a Coke?' And I answered by saying, 'I can't seem to get there, can you help me?' "

Ted's ethereal female then said no, she had to go to Paris, but he could meet her there that night. "I replied weakly, 'Okay,' and she was gone."

Meanwhile, Ted could make out the sand on the beach that lay ahead! His thirst was "overpowering." He shouted either for help or maybe it was "water" . . . and passed out.

"When I came to, a native outrigger canoe was alongside and a native was brandishing a long knife over my head demanding, 'American or Jap?' Luckily for Ted Blahnik, it was the Americans that the knife-brandishing native seemed to like best. In mere moments, " He hoisted me into the canoe and we headed for the beach."

From Ted Blahnik in *Guadalcanal Echoes*, January 1988,
The Guadalcanal Campaign Veterans

# ■ Stalingrad's 'White Rose'

If statues could only speak, the memorial sculpture of a comely young woman in the Soviet Union's Donetsk region would tell a Shakespearean tale of triumph and tragedy, romance and bitter, *hemlockian* revenge.

Lydia Litvak, a Muscovite born in 1921, had been flying for four years when Nazi Germany launched its massive invasion of the Soviet Union in June of 1941. She answered the call for female pilots from the reeling Soviet Air Force and won appointment to the all-female 586th Fighter Air Regiment. After brief emergency training, she and her companion flyers of the Russian Yak-1 found themselves based at Saratov on the Volga River, just north of Stalingrad . . . just as Hitler launched his second summer offensive in May 1942. By September, the major battleground would be Stalingrad.

By that time, too, the USSR's standard, all-male fighter ranks had been so depleted by combat with the *Luftwaffe* that women were allowed to fight alongside the men. "Lydia, was one of the chosen few, now being assigned to the Soviet 73rd Fighter Air Regiment."

She was not guaranteed instant acceptance, however, especially in the 73rd, which had earned itself special "free hunter" status allowing its aircrews to range far and wide in search of opportune targets, rather than sit on the ground awaiting alerts to scramble and intercept oncoming German forces. "On her first day of duty, Lydia suffered the humiliation of standing helplessly by her assigned Yak fighter and watching a strange male pilot climb aboard and zoom off into the skies."

Lydia had spent months of air-combat duty defending Stalingrad from German bombers, but that apparently didn't count with the 73rd's CO, who had no intention of sending her out with any of his elite "free hunters." Enter, then, the CO's best friend, a future Hero of the Soviet Union with many "kills" to his credit, one Alexei Salomaten. Let Lydia fly at least one patrol as his own wingman, argued Salomaten, and then see if she should stay in the unit or be transferred out. The CO agreed, and off they went the next day.

First, though, Alexei told her to simply follow close behind and duplicate his "every maneuver," rather than worry about protecting him. On their patrol, they went through violent maneuvers; Lydia heard gunfire, and occasionally glimpsed other aircraft in the sky with them. But she concentrated entirely on following her new-found friend.

"Upon landing, the young woman was surprised to learn that her leader had assisted another Russian pilot in shooting down an Me 109. Nevertheless, the beaming Alexei praised her skill in sticking with him, then reported his satisfaction with her wingman performance to their commander. Lydia thereafter fought with the 'free hunters' throughout the rest of the battle of Stalingrad."

Not only *fought*, but soon became known, to German and Russian alike, as the "White Rose of Stalingrad"—for the flowery emblem painted on the nose of her fighter, by now a Yak-9. As her "kills" mounted, they were signified by smaller roses painted on her plane. By the end of 1942, Lydia had shot down three enemy fighters and three transports. She, herself, had gone unscathed, as had Alexei—by now not only her partner in the air, but her constant companion and lover on the ground.

With the collapse of the German Sixth Army's assault upon Stalingrad in early 1943, their 73rd Fighter Air Regiment was transferred to the Donbass region. There, while scoring her ninth downed enemy plane, Lydia herself was wounded and forced to make a wheels-up landing in her damaged Yak-9. She recovered, though, and returned to duty in the unusual and prestigious role of a flight commander in the still mostly male outfit.

Known as "Lilya" to her friends, Lydia Litvak would score a total of 12 enemy "kills" as the Soviet Union's leading female ace of the war, but not without personal tragedy. "One day, Alexei took a new replacement pilot aloft to teach him the latest techniques of winning a dogfight against a German. Far below, Lydia watched the graceful aerial duel when, to her horror, tragedy struck. Alexei suddenly lost airspeed in a particularly sharp turn and spun into the earth. The young blonde neither cried out nor shed a tear during the entire episode, but her face was a twisted mask of anguish."

With Alexei gone, Lydia threw herself into one combat after another with "an almost obsessional desire to defeat the Germans." There was no shortage of opportunity in the spring and summer of 1943, and one duel matched her against a *Luftwaffe* ace with more than 20 "kills" of his own. They fought for 15 minutes before the Me 109 went sailing to the earth below in flames (the pilot managed to bail out first).

As a fateful day in August approached, Lydia herself escaped two close calls: in one case, she again had to make an emergency landing in a damaged plane and in the other she had to bail out of a burning Yak-9.

Then came August 1, 1943, and with "a bullet-injured right hand, the 22-year-old blonde sortied at daybreak." She and her companions encountered bombers and fighters. Lydia briefly disappeared in a cloud while tangling with two Me 109s. Minutes later, through a break in the clouds, one of her fellow Yak pilots caught a glimpse of Lydia's fighter smoking, with eight German fighters in pursuit.

No wreckage, no body, was ever found. If only the memorial statue at the town of Krasny Luch, close to where Lydia Litvak vanished that August morning, could speak, perhaps it would tell the exact details of her final fate.

From Truman R. Strobridge in *Military History* Magazine, December 1986

# ■ Churchill Narrowly Missed

In the midst of the 1943 Quebec Conference, staff officers attending a strategy session with Churchill, Lord Mountbatten, Hap Arnold and others were ushered out of the room while the really top brass argued in rarified secrecy over the British role in the war against Japan. Minutes later, the officers waiting outside the closed door were horrified to hear the sound of heavy blows inside, a scream of pain, and then two pistol shots.

This was moments after a Mountbatten staffer had wheeled in two large blocks of ice on a dumbwaiter.

As Churchill publicly revealed later, one block was the common, garden variety, but the other was a chunk of the highly experimental Pykrete, an odd "alloy" of ice and wood pulp that was being considered for use as a floating "island" or rudimentary aircraft carrier. The tough stuff resisted melting and presumably could bear the weight of aircraft and their support facilities.

Determined to demonstrate its toughness, Mountbatten, Chief of Combined Operations, challenged the strongest man in the room to assail the two chunks of ice, each about three feet high. American Air Forces Chief Hap Arnold gladly took the proffered chopper, rolled up his sleeves and split the true ice asunder in one chop. When he turned to the Pykrete, though, it was so resistant to his blow that he dropped the chopper "with a cry of pain, for the Pykrete had suffered little damage and his elbow had been badly jarred."

Mountbatten then took out a pistol and fired a shot into the ordinary ice. It shattered. Without realizing the possible consequences, he now aimed at the Pykrete and pulled the trigger. The bullet merely bounced off the amazingly tough material—but in ricochetting, it "narrowly" missed the onlooking Sir Charles Portal, Chief of the Air Staff. It, in fact, was a close thing for anyone in the room, Churchill included. The bullet could have bounced in any direction.

While the aircraft carrier of ice never was put into use, the incident provided a moment of gallows humor in the midst of war and carnage. "But who in war will not have his laugh amid the skulls?" wrote Churchill later. "And here was one."

From *Closing the Ring, The Second World War*,
by Winston Churchill (Houghton Mifflin Co.,
Boston, 1951)

# ■ *Hey, We're On Your Side*

Off the island of Ustica, 30 miles north of Palermo, one August night in 1943, the U.S. Navy subchaser SC 530 was in a bit of a quandary—if ships can be imagined to feel a quandary sort of situation. Earlier in the day—evening, really—SC 530 had finished escorting a slow-moving, freshwater barge to the dry, thirsting island from Sicily's port city of Palermo.

Moving along at all of four knots, the two vessels didn't arrive until the middle of the night. Soon after, radar showed two large blips roaring up on the minuscule subchaser and her ward. At half a mile, visual identification established the two intruders as cruisers.

SC 530's concern at this point was to make it clear that she, herself, wasn't the enemy. Allied ships, by mistake, had been known to fire at Allied ships. So 530 quite properly "challenged the lead cruiser by flashing light."

The reply was a salvo of cruiser shells—they flew overhead, happily enough.

Disconcerted but stubborn, SC 530 tried again, after double-checking the correct naval routine. Again a mean salvo from the lead ship.

Still game, SC 530 next tried turning on her coded recognition lights. Any Ally would get the point. This time, both advancing cruisers unleashed their fire.

The moment had come, really, to make sure the cruisers understood whose side SC 530 was on. SC 530 turned her 12-inch signal light on herself, then directed the light at the cruisers.

"That did it," writes retired U.S. Navy Commander Edward P. Stafford. "The two cruisers ceased firing, reversed course, and sped off into the night."

Naturally, there would be an epilogue. "The next morning, back in Palermo, the 530's skipper stormed into Operations and complained bitterly about being fired on by his own ships when he had been doing all the right things to establish his identity. But he became very calm and quiet when the duty officer informed him that the ships he had encountered were not friendly but Italian cruisers, probably bound for Palermo to shoot up the harbor. Apparently his illumination had spoiled their intended surprise and they had returned to base."

Indeed, as later established, they had been the *Raimondo Montecuccoli* and the *Eugenio di Savoia*, out of Sardinia and headed for Palermo, but thwarted on their way by the prim and proper SC 530.

From *Subchaser* by Edward P. Stafford
(Naval Institute Press, Annapolis, Md., 1988)

# ■ *Am I Smoking Too Much?*

At Salerno the second week of September 1943, the going for the American and British Allies was rough—so rough that overall commander Mark Clark came within an ace of withdrawing the entire landing force. The British Eighth Army had landed near the tip of the Italian boot earlier, but the Fifth Army show at Salerno, on Italy's west coast, was the big one, the main Allied thrust.

It had to succeed and almost didn't.

The Italians had just surrendered, but the German forces under Albert Kesselring wasted no time in establishing their own control of the country—and moving to block the two Allied armies invading Italy.

Going ashore at dawn on September 9, the American VI Corps (36th and 45th Infantry Divisions) and the British X Corps (56th and 46th Divisions) had won their narrow beachhead, it appeared. On September 12, however, Kesselring's forces struck back so furiously that the outcome of the Allied invasion was very much in doubt.

As many as 2,000 Allied air strikes and repeated bombardment by off-shore navy ships greatly aided the troops ashore in finally turning back the German counterattack. The Eighth Army, moving up from the south under Sir Bernard Montgomery, made its link-up with the newly-landed Fifth Army on September 16—the Allies were in Italy to stay, although they still faced a stubborn, vicious campaign that would not truly end until the war in Europe was over in the spring of 1945, a year and a half later.

Richard Plunkett, an American sailor aboard the U.S. light cruiser *Boise*, kept a diary during the Salerno campaign, highlighted by his argument, "The Fifth Army would have been pushed back into the ocean if it hadn't been for the Navy!"

126

His cruiser was elsewhere the very day of the invasion at Salerno, busy dropping off British Commandos at the Italian naval base of Taranto, since the Italians had just surrendered. The *Boise* then dashed to North Africa, where orders suddenly changed and *Boise* set out for Salerno at high speed.

The warship arrived in Salerno Bay September 12, the day of the major German counterattack, and soon was in the thick of a desperate fight to sustain the beachhead.

*Sept 12: Around 12:30 p.m., six Fw 190s attacked us. Dropped bombs. No damage.*

*Sept 13: Germans bombed one of our hospital ships. Another dive-bomb attack. Were Me 109s. Tried like hell to get us.*

There were more air attacks that same day, with a near miss on *Boise's* sister ship, the *Philadelphia*.

*Sept. 14: Fired 1,500 rounds of ammo. While firing, had air raid. Dive-bombers got one transport and one LST. They came at us again and dropped one radio-controlled bomb which exploded right off our fantail—missed us again (pretty lousy). One plane was shot down.*

*Sept. 15: We are still in the gun turret firing on the beach, while air raids are going on all day long. Dive-bombers got two more LSTs. Bomb after bomb were dropped all around us. What a hell of a place! Smoking too much.*

On the 16th, the *Boise* stopped firing at 5:10 a.m. with only 503 six-incher shells left. But 30 minutes later, "we fired all of that." As more *Luftwaffe* dive-bombers appeared, shrapnel flew all around.

*Sept. 16: We are very lucky, furious fighting on the beach.*

Now, the *Boise* headed back to North Africa for more ammunition, arriving about 11 a.m.

*Sept. 16: Loading 3,000 rounds of 6-inch; fuel up. Worked like hell.*

*Sept. 17: Arrived in Salerno, laid smoke screen to protect ship. USS Savanah hit with radio-controlled bomb on Turret No. 3. Badly damaged. 200 casualties.*

But later that same day, for the *Boise* anyway, it was all over.

*Sept. 17: Beach under control. Got underway for Palermo, Sicily. Very glad to get out of here, am very tired.*

From letter by Richard R. Plunkett, retired plumber,
former U. S. Navy sailor aboard the USS *Boise*

# ■ *Close Call For FDR*

The excitement aboard the brand new battleship *Iowa* was brief but palpable one mid-November day in 1943. On her way to Oran, Algeria, with a screen of destroyers, *Iowa* played "target" for a destroyer simulating a torpedo run on a battleship.

The *William D. Porter* wheeled into her "attack." So far, so good . . . nothing unusual.

But suddenly the destroyer's whistle shrieked in alarm, and the *Porter*'s Officer of the Deck came hard on the radio: "Lion, Lion, Lion: come right, come hard right!"

Inadvertently, the *Porter* had loosed a live one—the *Iowa*, commissioned only the previous February, really was at the wrong end of a torpedo track.

While a visitor on the big ship's bridge continued to watch the flotilla's tactical exercises, the *Iowa* surged into a hard turn. Seconds later, the errant "fish" hit the battleship's wake and exploded, just a half mile astern.

And now the voice radio did some exploding, as both the *Iowa* and the commander of the destroyer division gave vent to their respective reactions. The language, they say, was purple.

One concern, of course, was the brand new ship and her crew. Another was that man on the bridge; the one on the first leg of a journey to Teheran for a conference with Joe Stalin and Winston Churchill; the wartime Commander-in-Chief, Franklin Delano Roosevelt.

From John C. Reilly in *Pull Together*, newsletter of the
Naval Historical Foundation and the Naval
Historical Center, Vol. 27, No. 1,
Spring/Summer 1988

# ■ *Sure Am Sorry*

The mules brought them down from the Italian mountains to a place in the valley where there was a road, a low stone wall and a cowshed. The dead.

Casualties from the 36th Division.

Texans for the most part.

Ernie Pyle's dateline said January 10, 1944. *From the front lines in Italy.* In the moonlight, he was down there at the bottom of that long trail negotiated by mules with their awkward, stiff-legged burden.

"I don't know who that first one was," he wrote for the folks back home to read. "You feel small in the presence of dead men, and ashamed of being alive, and you don't ask silly questions."

He got one name though—Captain Henry T. Waskow of Belton, Texas, a company commander in the 36th. Mid-twenties, he was— had been.

Ernie Pyle "never crossed the trail of any man as beloved."

They laid them all down tenderly. By the stone wall, and in a shadow.

He came down and his body was unlashed with four others, and all were laid down there by the wall, end to end.

Something special about Captain Waskow, though.

"After my own father, he came next," a sergeant told Ernie Pyle.

"I've never knowed him to do anything unfair," said another GI.

"He always looked after us," said a third. "He'd go to bat for us every time."

His men didn't want to leave him.

"They stood around, and gradually one by one I could sense them moving close to Capt. Waskow's body. Not so much to look, I think, as to say something in finality to him, and to themselves."

One by one they went close and spoke their goodbye. Or *thought* it.

Out loud, one of them said, "God damn it," and a second one said, "God Damn it to hell anyway."

Another, possibly an officer himself, came close and said, "I'm sorry, Old Man."

A GI followed. "I sure am sorry, Sir."

The first man came back, squatted by his dead captain and took his hand. He held it for five minutes, looked into his captain's face and said no more, nothing at all.

"And finally he put the hand down, and then reached up and gently straightened the points of the captain's shirt collar, and then he sort of rearranged the tattered edges of his uniform around the wound. And then he got up and walked away down the road in the moonlight, all alone."

From *Brave Men*, by Ernie Pyle
(Grosset and Dunlap, New York, N.Y., 1943)

# ■ War Story

Ah, the stories they do tell! Like maybe the B-17 that made it back with holes in the fuselage big enough for a jeep to drive through! Like the time, on a bombing run against a German airfield near Rheims, France, on March 28, 1944, fighter-pilot Chester A. Hallberg (55th U.S. Fighter Squadron, 20th Fighter Group) saw the "Whodat" out of Ridgewell catch a direct flak hit that threw the Flying Fortress into a violent spin . . .

Flying escort for the bombers, Hallberg and his mates were above, at 8 o'clock high. "I watched for parachuters as the big friend spun down—from an altitude of about 24,000 feet, as I recall. There were none. But while I watched, the pilot pulled the plane out of the spin at about 12,000 feet."

Aboard the "Whodat," both waist gunners and the tail gunner had been killed by the hit. Pilot Daniel C. Henry had rung the bail-out bell. Seconds later, fighting to control the stricken craft, he rescinded the "jump" order.

While Henry and his co-pilot, Bob Crisler, fought the controls, their rudder cables severed and the elevators jammed at "up," Flight Engineer Sebastian Quarema spliced the cables together with loose wiring. But the result was that pulling back on the controls nosed the ship down, and pushing them forward pulled her up. Just the reverse of normal operation.

Outside, Hallberg took his flight of P-38 Lightnings down to the big bomber's assistance. Obviously, if "Whodat" somehow could stay in the air, she would need close escort all the way home. As Hallberg slowed and pulled in close to see the extent of the damage, however, he was "horrified."

The starboard side of the fuselage "had been blown away from the waist gun to the rear door." On the port side was another hole half as big. "It was a miracle that the crate held together."

But it did, and the "Whodat" staggered back to England, where it was decided that the crew should bail out rather than attempt even a crash-landing in their battered ship. Five of the seven flak survivors successfully jumped above their Ridgewell base, then pilots Henry and Crisler headed their Fort over the English Channel before safely bailing out themselves. The big Fort crashed harmlessly in the water.

For years, though, fighter-pilot Hallberg had no idea how the difficult flight home really ended. He and his wingman, Philip Pearson, had stayed with "Whodat" as far as the English coast, but then they had to fly for home themselves, their fuel gauges "flirting" on empty. "I never knew if they landed safely or if they lived through the war," he wrote in 1986. Hallberg found out, though, through an article appearing in the *Friends of the Eighth* [Air Force] *Newsletter*; he thus learned that all seven men still alive on "Whodat" after the flak hit *did* get home safely and that all seven *were* able to finish their combat hours in Europe unscathed.

Hallberg, like them, had never forgotten the "Whodat" and the crew's feat of getting her home again. "The fighter escort mission on March 28, 1944, was relatively uneventful—except for one unforgettable moment when I witnessed one of the most fantastic displays of skill and courage to be seen in my 74-mission tour of duty in the ETO."

From *King's Cliffe Remembered,*
20th Fighter Group Association,
Vol. 5, No. 1, January-May 1987

# ■ *Strife At High Levels*

Spring 1944, and in Burma the Japanese were driving upon the harried, weakened and considerably thinned British forces along the India-Burma border. As General William Slim, commander of the British 14th Army, once said of his adversary in that jungled theater, they were "ruthless and bold as ants while their designs went well."

Shortly after the Japanese launched their two-pronged Imphal-Kohima offensive, however, their designs were not going so well as they once hoped. Those hopes, actually, had been pretty much the inspiration of General Renya Mutaguchi—many of his fellow Japanese generals were skeptical of any victorious outcome for the offensive by his 15th Army. Mutaguchi nonetheless, committed 91,000 troops to his plan, with Japan's future fortunes in Burma at stake. The pressure was on Mutaguchi, already known for a bad temper.

He drove hard early in March against Slim's 14th Army, and in three weeks the Japanese had succeeded in isolating 60,000

British and Indian troops. But the under-supplied Allies grimly held somehow and still blocked his attempt to penetrate into India, with the British base at Imphal in Assam Province the first major Japanese objective.

If Mutaguchi were now frustrated, so was his own subordinate, Lt. Gen. Kotuku Sato, commander of the 15th Army's 31st Division. For Sato had been given the unenviable assignment of leading a full division for many difficult miles through jungle, across rivers, over mountain ranges, to tiny Kohima in a 4,000-foot mountain pass at the India-Burma border as a secondary but vital prong in Mutaguchi's strategy.

Mutaguchi already had encountered problems with the commander of his lead-off 33rd Division. When, as early as March 23, that commander's momentum ended, he was replaced. The commander of another attacking division then died of malaria.

After five weeks on the march, meanwhile, Sato and his division had taken heavy casualties from air attacks and run so low on supplies that his men were eating their own pack mules. He now suggested that his force should retire. The answer was no.

His problems only mounted when his division failed to crack the dwindling defensive "box" at Kohima early in April, then faced an influx of British reinforcements later in the month.

With fierce fighting encountered in the direction of Imphal also, Mutaguchi saw both his 15th Army and his plan for a grand "March to Delhi" beginning to come apart. But the stubborn general wouldn't back down.

"Continue in the task till all your ammunition is expended," he ordered his men. "If your hands are broken, fight with your feet. If your hands and feet are broken, use your teeth."

By now he had relieved two of his division commanders, and Sato was in a most mutinous mood.

"This is shameful," Sato told his own staff officers. "Mutaguchi should apologize for his own failure to the dead soldiers and the Japanese people. He should not try to put the blame on his subordinates."

After repeated denials of his requests to withdraw, Sato on May 3 radioed to Mutaguchi that he would withdraw his battered division anyway. Retorted Mutaguchi, "Retreat and I will court-martial you."

Sato, though, was adamant. "Do what you please," he replied. "I will bring you down with me."

Sato also informed the Japanese Army headquarters overseeing

132

the entire Burmese campaign that the tactical ability of Mutaguchi's staff "lies below that of cadets.'

At his own headquarters, Mutaguchi ranted, "He has lost the battle for me."

Since Sato had broken off radio contact, Mutaguchi now had to send his chief of staff into the jungle with personal orders for Sato to rejoin the battle. When they met, Sato shouted that Mutaguchi's 15th Army had failed to send him any supplies or ammunition from the very start of the offensive. "This failure releases me from any obligation to obey the order," he declared. "And in any case, it would be impossible to comply."

That much was certainly true. His own division was shattered. Fifteenth Army was in tatters. The Japanese had suffered the greatest defeat of their ground forces in history.

Fired in the end himself, disgraced, Mutaguchi later was to mourn, "I have killed thousands of my men—I should not go back across the Chindwin (River) alive." Fired also, Sato later was spared court-martial because of a mental condition.

Fair to say that, apart from bodily harm, generals suffer their own kind of wounds.

From *China-Burma-India* by Don Moser and the editors
of Time-Life Books (*World War II* series,
Alexandria, Va., 1971)

# ■ *Search For Big Stoop*

Someone, it was thoughtfully decided in the midst of World War II, should check out the potential invasion beaches northwest of Hong Kong, along China's Japanese-occupied coastline. "My job," recalled retired U.S. Navy Captain Phil Bucklew, "was to carry out the reconnaissance in reverse of what we had done before. This time we went overland."

Before, the charter member of the Navy Scouts and Raiders had been a waterborne advance man for the Allied invasions of Sicily, Salerno and Normandy. Six months prior to Normandy, in fact, he had been ashore at the future Omaha Beach to collect a bucket of sand for engineers involved in the planning of history's greatest invasion.

It was after Normandy that an invasion of the China coast briefly came under consideration. Before anyone thought better of the notion, Scout/Raider Bucklew was on his way. A combination of wings and wheels took him as far as the Chinese mountain village of Kienyang, but from there it would be a 200-mile trek to the coast—on foot and dressed as a Chinese coolie. "They had come up with a very sacklike coolie suit and a huge straw hat. I was also provided with two hand grenades and a .45 caliber revolver."

Accompanied by ten Chinese guerrillas, Bucklew did his best to fade into the local scenery as his guides took him along mountain trails, through tiny villages, past Japanese encampments with bonfires and sleeping soldiers. "Fading" was a bit difficult, since Bucklew stood six-feet two, weighed nearly 240 pounds and had played professional football in America before the war.

"We'd be walking along and pass another group of coolies, who would just look up at me in wonder," said Bucklew years later. "I was just so out of proportion in size to them and everyone else there. The sandals didn't do too well, either, but later on I got some tennis shoes."

The Japanese soon heard about the mysterious "coolie" tabbed "Big Stoop" and began looking for him. "They knew an American was in the area and they sent out a search patrol. I lost face with my Chinese guerrilla leader because I wouldn't give him one of my two grenades to wipe out this enemy patrol, but my recon mission would have been blown right away."

In one close call, Bucklew hid in the center of a haystack while members of a Japanese patrol ate their lunch nearby. "It was rather foolish, with all my guerrillas sitting completely encircling the haystack. Anyone would have known that something, or someone, was in there."

But they didn't and Bucklew soon moved on.

The reconnaissance trip took about three weeks in all. For the American Navyman in Japanese-occupied territory along the China coast, things were surprisingly humdrum. "When we arrived, there were so many fishermen and sampans minding their own business—with Japanese doing the same—that we were hardly noticed. We made our run down the coast and I got the data I needed on the coastline."

The risk, of course, still was great—shunted from one place to another by sampan, Bucklew had to count on the integrity of his Chinese contacts. But . . . they stood by him.

Not that the mission was completed without further incident. One day, Bucklew's guerrilla leader sold his camera. "He convinced me that he could go into the village and bring back pictures. Later, he told a whopping story that he had been captured by the Japanese, who had both taken the camera and made him work as a coolie for a day."

Another time, joining up with a fellow American sent on the China coast reconnaissance, Bucklew weathered a slight accident. "Rocky Ruggieri and I decided to ride downhill on bicycles that we'd gotten hold of. It was okay until we came upon a sharp, right-angle turn on a three-foot pathway and crashed, flying spread-eagled into a nearby rice-paddy—which wasn't filled with roses! As far as I know, there are still two bicycles at the edge of that path, because we didn't bother to go back. We found a river and cleaned off—I haven't ridden a bike since."

Later, safely returned, Bucklew presented his report in Calcutta, India. The China coast, he advised, offered poor beach conditions for amphibious landings. "From there it was evidently decided to forget about China and go on north to Japan instead."

Fortunately, the war ended before either invasion proposal could be set in motion.

From interview by Blaine Taylor,
*Military History* Magazine, October 1987

# ■ *One-Man Army*

Who finally got the troops moving off "Bloody Omaha"—Omaha Beach in the Normandy invasion?

If such a confused, potentially disastrous experience could be said to have been salvaged by the pure grit and leadership of any one man, even a few, nominations for that honor must start with a West Pointer, a single-star general in his 50s who was practically elderly in comparison to the men all around him.

That would be Brig. Gen. Norman ("Dutch") Cota, 51, assistant commander of the 29th Infantry Division, a veteran of the

Allies' North African campaign who spent most of his time with the troops in the field, rather than shuffle papers at headquarters. Both fierce and absolutely fearless in combat, he held to an easily understood credo.

"Now look," he once told a well-meaning officer who suggested that perhaps he should not take so many risks, "I was a poor country boy from the Pennsylvania Dutch country. I heard about West Point, and that it was free, and I went. I made a contract with the government; if they paid for my education, I would serve them. Part of my contract was to die for my country if necessary. I intend to stick to it. If I get killed, then so be it, but I don't expect to be."

After taking over the training of the National Guardsmen who made up the 29th, Cota was just about everywhere with his walking stick, while chomping upon an unlit cigar. That was back on the moors of England, beginning in the summer of 1943. There, Cota had done his best to indoctrinate his men in the sights and crashing sounds of battle. And the confusion.

"The air and naval bombardment and the artillery support are reassuring," he told his staff. "But you're going to find confusion. The landing craft aren't going in on schedule and people are going to be landed in the wrong place. Some won't be landed at all. The enemy will try, and will have some success, in preventing our gaining a lodgement. But we must improvise, carry on, not lose our heads. Nor must we add to the confusion."

His prophetic words described exactly the situation on Omaha Beach moments after the first waves of American troops—the 29th included—stepped ashore on continental Europe, June 6, 1944. Omaha was a nightmare—noise, confusion, whole units landed at the wrong places, others still far from shore, and just about everybody pinned down by murderous crossfire. And bodies . . . bodies everywhere, in the water, on the beach itself, draped over the beach obstacles. All of them American.

In the area assigned to the 29th, those GIs still living and able to move had scrambled and crawled to the base of a low seawall 150 yards beyond the water's edge. There, the invasion had stopped. No one dared move. A carpet of men hugged the sand, face down.

General Cota came in with the staff of the 29th's 116th Regiment, dropping into waist-deep water from their landing barge 50 yards from shore and wading in from there. Right next to Cota, Major John Sours was hit by machine-gun fire and killed on the spot.

Looking at the masses of men jumbled up, unmoving, behind the seawall, the German fire only increasing with each passing moment, Cota realized the paralyzed 29ers had to be galvanized into action. Accounts vary on what happened next, but Cota nonetheless was the catalyst.

According to Cornelius Ryan in his famous book *The Longest Day* and to Max Hastings, British author of *Overlord: D-Day and the Battle for Normandy*, Cota scooted to a halt in the sand by the seawall next to men of the 5th U.S. Rangers who were mixed in—by erroneous landing—with the 29th Division men. "If you're Rangers, get up and lead the way!" exploded Cota (says Hastings). Another version: "Lead the way, Rangers!" (Ryan).

A 5th U.S. Ranger who was there has got it still another way. According to Stan Askin, the Rangers and their CO, Colonel Max Schneider, had just arrived by the base of the seawall when suddenly they saw a figure running toward them, "followed by another man shouting, 'Keep down, General, keep down.' " The two were Cota and his aide. "Cota threw himself down beside Max Schneider. 'Morning Schneider,' he said. 'Morning, General,' replied Schneider. 'Well,' said Cota, 'it looks like the Rangers are going to have to get us off the beach.' " (Stan Askins in *World War II* Magazine, May 1987).

By all three accounts, specialists armed with bangalore torpedoes blew vital gaps in the thick barbed wire just beyond the seawall, and the others then began to follow—a trickle that in time would become a flood, as the German defenders ultimately were pushed back.

Says Askin: "The rest of us followed (the bangalore men) on the double, but found ourselves slowed to a crawl as we began the climb up the steep hillside." The troops pushed and pulled and made their way forward, anyway. And the credit for leadership would go to Ranger Colonel Schneider.

In his book *Beyond the Beachhead: The 29th Infantry Division in Normandy*, Joseph Balkoski has it another way entirely. The Rangers were there, huddled and pinned like the 29ers, only it was Cota himself who led the breakout at his section of the beach.

Here and there a few brave men up and down the long line were edging forward. Others sometimes followed, discordant but brave sallies forward. Cota "cajoled a motley collection of infantrymen to get up and move." He, himself, crawled beyond the seawall to a protective rise five yards ahead. He brought a BAR man to his side to provide fierce covering fire, and another 29er blew the wire just ahead with a bangalore.

But then, disaster. The first man running through the fresh gap was cut down by machine-gun fire. "Medic," he sobbed, and "Mama!"

With that piteous cry, Cota knew the men behind would be frozen in place. He had to show them it could be done. And so— "He leaped up, dashing across the road and through the gap."

He turned and shouted for others to follow. A few brave souls did, and when they weren't hurt, "their success convinced dozens more to try it."

Soon Cota had a "scraggly column" advancing through a field beyond the beach bluff, the road and the wire. They passed through mine fields, losing several men on the way; they topped the high ground beyond the beaches, encountered German resistance and forced it back. They reached the French village of Vierville . . . and took it. All the while, more and more men were streaming up from the beaches behind. One group met Cota on the town's main street, "twirling a pistol on his index finger like an Old West gunfighter." He looked at the newcomers: "Where the hell have you been, boys?"

Not through with his beach heroics yet, Cota then returned to the landing area to speed the flow of men and vehicular equipment such as tanks. The Vierville "draw," a natural depression leading from the beach, still was in German hands. Cota, with six men, took it—from the rear.

Back on the beach, he set about bringing further order to a still chaotic and dangerous scene. He reported the draw was now clear for troop and supply movement; he cajoled a group of GIs until one finally agreed to drive forward a bulldozer loaded with TNT needed up forward.

Thus, 50 years later, the accounts of Cota's exact role differ in detail, but they agree in the essential fact that he was a key figure in moving a demoralized mob of men from their pinned-down position at a key point of Omaha Beach.

Not that Cota ceased his aggressive activity with D-Day itself . . . not at all!

On June 7, adds the 29th Infantry story by Balkoski, "Cota was a one-man army again." After prodding and pushing his troops, now toward the village of St. Laurent, he found an infantry captain and some men stymied outside a house occupied by Germans. When asked why they were not trying to eliminate the enemy and take the house, the inexperienced captain said, "The Germans are in there, shooting at us."

Clearly that would never do for a man of Cota's mettle. "Well, I'll tell you what," he said to the young captain. "You and your men start shooting at them. I'll take a squad of men and you and your men watch carefully. I'll show you how to take a house with Germans in it."

The general had been unbuckling two grenades as he spoke, and now he led his men to a hedge, then they dashed toward the house, "screaming like wild men," and threw their grenades through the windows. "Cota and another man kicked in the front door, tossed a few more grenades inside, waited for the explosions, and then disappeared inside the house."

The Germans surviving the assault ran out the back doors and windows, and soon General Cota was able to report back to his stunned captain.

Does the captain now know how to take a house? "Yes Sir!"

"Well, I won't be around to do it for you again. I can't do it for everybody."

But Cota did what he could for almost "everybody," always in the thick of things as the Americans who landed in Normandy gradually fought their way out of the bocage country with its damnable hedgerows until the 29th helped to take St. Lo in mid-July.

Typically, he entered the battered French city "close behind the head of the column." Talking things over with a fellow 29er shortly afterwards, General Cota took a piece of shrapnel in the arm. His colleague noticed blood running from his sleeve, forming drops on his fingers. "He just stood there talking; it didn't bother him in the least."

Cota had a medic tend to the arm and spent the rest of the day with his arm in a sling. That night, he was evacuated for a week's stay in a rear-area hospital. But, typically, he was not down for long.

The end of the month found him in a proud new role—commander of his own infantry division, the 28th. And, on August 29, there was Cota, at the head of the 28th, marching down the Champs Elysees of Paris and taking the salutes of Charles de Gaulle, Dwight Eisenhower and Omar Bradley—a long way from that bloody, pinned-down stretch of beach called Omaha.

From sources cited in text

# ■ New Hope For 'Kitty'

"Bad weather," she wrote Monday evening. "Heavy bombardments against the French coast continue."

What could it mean? The next day, at 8 o'clock the very next morning, she knew. They all knew. The radio in their hiding place spoke.

"This is D-Day. This is *the* day."

They heard it in English, exactly that way.

Even the German news provided more of the terribly exciting news. English paratroops in France.

English landing craft off the coast, in battle with the German Navy, added the BBC.

"We discussed it over breakfast: Is this just a trial landing like Dieppe two years ago?"

She didn't say so quite yet, but their excitement—and hope—in their "Secret Annexe" had to be great.

By 10 a.m., June 6, 1944, the reports were even more thrilling. From the English and given in several languages: "The invasion has begun!" And that meant the "real" invasion.

The hour of 11 a.m. brought more—a speech by "the Supreme Commander, General Dwight Eisenhower."

And at 12 noon: "This is D-Day." In English. Followed by more from Eisenhower, to the French specifically. "Stiff fighting will come now, but after this, victory. The year 1944 is the year of complete victory; good luck."

At 1 o'clock, more English news, more detail—good, hard, encouraging detail. Eleven thousand Allied planes. Four thousand landing craft depositing their men and cargo between Cherbourg and Le Havre (Normandy, of course). English and American troops "already engaged in hard fighting." And more speeches. "Speeches by Gerbrandy, by the Prime Minister of Belgium, King Haakon of Norway, de Gaulle of France, the King of England, and last, but not least, Churchill."

By now their reaction has caught fire. "Great commotion in the Secret Annexe! The long-awaited liberation still seems *too* wonderful, *too* much like a fairy tale."

And could Eisenhower be right? "Could we be granted victory this year, 1944? We don't know yet, but hope is revived within us. The great thing now is to remain calm and steadfast. Now more than ever we must clench our teeth and not cry out."

Often clenching her teeth and not crying out in all those months since they went into hiding in July 1942, she addressed her diary as a friend called "Kitty." In hiding with her were her mother, father and sister; another couple with a teenaged boy and an elderly dentist. As Jews, they were hiding from what later became known as the Holocaust.

Their hiding place was a group of rooms in the upper rear of a combined warehouse-office structure on the Prinsengracht Canal in occupied Amsterdam, Holland.

"Kitty" had become teenaged Anne Frank's only friend in the absence of any social contact beyond the seven persons trapped with her. Obviously, the young Jewish girl longed for friends. "Oh, Kitty," she wrote the day of the Normandy invasion, "the best part of the invasion is the feeling that friends are approaching. We have been oppressed by the Germans for so long that the thought of friends and delivery fills us with confidence!"

She went on to say the issue at hand no longer was the fate of the Jews in hiding and fear. Rather, it concerned all Holland and all Occupied Europe. Maybe too, her sister Margot had said, maybe Anne could even go back to school that very fall!

Seven days later, she noted the passage of her 15th birthday.

And still, "excellent" news of the invasion. Churchill and Eisenhower visited newly liberated villages, she had heard.

On July 21, she noted the "super news" that an attempt had been made on Hitler's life the day before. Hitler escaped real harm, but, "It certainly shows that there are lots of (German) officers who are sick of the war and would like to see Hitler descend into a bottomless pit."

On August 4, with the Allies still fighting their way through France, the "Secret Annexe" was raided by the Gestapo. All its occupants were shipped off to the concentration camps. Anne's "friend" Kitty was left on the floor, tossed there by the intruders.

Confined to the Bergen-Belsen camp, Anne survived almost to the end of the war, but not quite. In March 1945 she died. The war in Europe (and the occupation of Holland) ended just a few weeks later.

Only her father survived the camps, among those who had hidden in the annex for more than two years. He returned, found the diary exactly where one of the intruders had thrown it in August 1944.

"If he had taken the diary with him," said Anne's father later, "no one would ever have heard of my daughter." As it was, a publishing sensation, her "Kitty" appeared around the world in 32 languages, fostered a successful stage play and generated a widely seen movie.

The annex in the building on Prinsengracht Canal became a sort of shrine visited by hundreds every day, especially young people like Anne. Others, including many young Germans, for many years visited the Belsen site, specifically to pray for the brave and sensitive young girl's soul.

From *Anne Frank: Diary of a Young Girl*,
(Doubleday & Company, New York, N.Y.,
renewed copyright 1980 by Otto H. Frank)

# ■ *Two In Single-Seat Fighter*

Not so remarkable for *where* they were going but rather *how* to get there were two intrepid American airmen winging their way north in June 1944 from one of those difficult air raids on the Ploesti oil works in Romania.

Headed for a Russian air base at Poltava as their nearest sanctuary, Lieutenants Richard T. Andrews and Richard E. Willsie sallied hastily along in their single-seat, twin-engine P-38 Lightning.

Normally, of course, the World War II fighter carried a "crew" of exactly one.

But this wasn't "normally." To begin with, American P-38s from the 15th Air Force had been sent to the hot Polesti complex in an all-fighters saturation strafing raid, rather than risk still another bomber strike.

Strafing trains, trucks and German air facilities in the oil-field area, Willsie related years later, "I could feel the bullets hitting the aircraft and they actually made my feet bounce on the rudder pedals." As he saw oil leaking from his left engine, it lost all pressure. "I feathered that prop at once."

Willsie pressed on with his one good engine at full power—but then he saw coolant streaming from the right engine. "Knowing that I had only a few minutes left, I reported that I was going down."

142

Enter, at this point, 19-year-old Dick Andrews of the same 82nd Fighter Group, a youngster with only 100 hours in the P-38 and guns already emptied. "Pick a good field," Andrews radioed tersely, "and I will come in after you."

Willsie was too busy to dwell on the startling message. With his remaining engine popping ominously and a fresh hit cracking his windshield and causing a bloody head injury, he made for a freshly plowed field just ahead. "As I slid over the last obstacle and touched down, with wheels up, I placed my head against the rubber shield on the gunsight for protection. But my nose still took a pounding as the plane skidded to a stop."

Willsie got out in a hurry, destroyed his plane with a small phosphorous bomb (as instructed for such circumstances), then ran for the cover of nearby trees.

Beyond the trees, truckloads of German troops were racing toward the field. Six Me 109s appeared in the sky above. But here came Andrews anyway, his landing gear down, in line with the field's furrows. "You just can't leave a man like that to walk back through enemy territory," Andrews later explained in a letter to his mother. "I was determined to get him out of there."

While fellow P-38 pilots tangled with the Me's in dogfights above, Andrews made his landing, and Willsie sprinted for the Lockheed Lightning that could be his salvation.

But would they both fit in the single-seat cockpit? As Andrews tossed out his parachute and other gear to make room, there wasn't time to think it through. "We both jumped into the cockpit with miraculous precision," said Willsie later.

Seconds later, with senior pilot Willsie taking the controls at Andrews' suggestion, they were rolling down the soft, furrowed ground, their canopy securely locked. Willsie was on the front edge of the bucketseat, and Andrews was scrunched behind, one cramped leg draped over Willsie's shoulder.

They barely cleared the trees at the end of the field, then they ran into "weather" and lost their fighter escort and had to fly instrument. They had no map of their route to Poltava, and they just might expect "friendly" Russian fire at their unfamiliar plane, but to make a long story short, they made it.

The next day Lockheed technician Richard "Stumpy" Hollinger asked the intrepid pair to pose in simulation of their contortions for what may have been the first rescue of a downed combat pilot by a modern single-seat fighter landing on enemy soil. But . . . they couldn't do it. "They could not both get in and close that canopy," said an admiring Hollinger later. "No matter how hard they tried, it was impossible to fit in tightly."

In fact, when word spread of their feat and others tried to emulate it, there were so many casualties that American pilots were forbidden to attempt such a rescue procedure. In the meantime, Andrews was awarded a Silver Star for his onetime effort.

From interview notes and supporting material supplied by<br>
Mary Lou Colbert Neale, Co-editor, Lightning<br>
Strikes, P-38 National Association

# ■ *A General And His Dog*

As the men of George S. Patton's Third Army could attest, rare is the bond to equal the unique relationship that seems to develop between a general on campaign and his pet dog.

And, in World War II, if Patton had his famous bull terrier Willie, General Charles Gerhardt, commander of the 29th Infantry Division, had his own handsome pup of black and white coloring, longish hair, hound-dog ears—and distinctly mixed (but French) parentage.

The pup had appeared in the division's headquarters area on June 12, 1944, just six days after the 29th landed on "Bloody Omaha" as a leading element of the Normandy invasion. For Gerhardt and the months-old dog, it was *bonding* at first sight.

Gerhardt, known to his men as "Uncle Charlie," named his new constant companion "D-Day." In no time at all, the division would see the general's jeep racing about the advancing front with only a driver, general's aide, general and D-Day aboard.

The French-born dog usually occupied the rear jump seat with the aide, Lieutenant Robert Wallis. D-Day soon realized his exalted status and took full advantage of it. "The pup rides around in the general's jeep and his behavior is such that he seems to sense that this vehicle sports a red sign with two stars and that he is something special," reported the alert division newspaper, *29 Let's Go.*

144

Gerhardt was an aggressive, no-nonsense general. One of his pet peeves, for instance, was the loose chin strap attached to one's helmet. If the general was in the area, the men of the division knew they had better buckle their chin straps, *pdq*.

His pet D-Day became a sort of early warning system. Given nearly total freedom to roam where he chose, he often appeared in the van of the visiting general. Thus, a front-lines spy would have seen large numbers of grown-up men buckling straps, smoothing down rumpled uniforms and otherwise primping as best they could when a mere dog hove into view. The general, of course, would not be far behind.

D-Day, clearly, was no *mere* dog. Soon quite used to artillery, he stuck to the general like glue. He slept on the general's cot. He had K-rations with the general and his staff at mealtimes. He dashed in and out of headquarters with no apparent restraint.

Their bond was such that the general one moment would fulfill his reputation by delivering a fierce tongue-lashing of momentarily wayward officers, and in the next, turn to D-Day with cooing "baby talk" that was most unsuited to the general's usual image.

D-Day had his faults, naturally, His greatest sin—with ample opportunity to indulge—was the impulse to chase jeeps and trucks. This particular flaw could ruin a perfectly good day for Gerhardt's driver, Sergeant Robert Cuff. At the sight of an enticing convoy, D-Day thought nothing of leaping from the cruising jeep and giving chase. At the alarmed general's quick order, Cuff was constrained to pursue and collar the wayward dog, hoping all the time that they would not be blown up together by unmarked mines.

The same character flaw was very nearly D-Day's undoing. One of the trucks he chased accidentally struck the dog and left the animal near death.

A distraught General Gerhardt allegedly told the truck driver: "If that dog dies, you're history!"

Happily for all concerned, a division surgeon managed to tend D-Day's wounds, and the dog recovered. He recovered in such exemplary fashion, in fact, that he was able to accompany General Gerhardt back to Stateside after the hostilities were all over. He then assumed a more normal dog's life for another 10 years.

One day, though, former Sergeant Cuff heard again from his wartime commander. "D-Day is dead," said the sad note. If the

general's onetime driver shed a tear, was it one of soulful sorrow—
or delayed syndrome relief?

From *Beyond the Beachhead: The 29th Infantry Division
In Normandy*, by Joseph Balkoski, (Stackpole
Books, Harrisburg, Pa., 1989)

# ■ *Faint Sound In The Distance*

Ambush. Somehow, the word smacks of ancient tribesmen lying in wait around the next bend for the interloper. In the more
modern world, it rings of jungle-fighters or insurgent guerrillas.
Whatever the case, at Normandy three days after D-Day, it clearly was not a thought uppermost in the minds of the weary men
making up the 2nd Battalion of the U.S. 29th Infantry Division's
115th Regiment.

In the past 20 hours, they had marched 15 miles, effected a
difficult river crossing, and then warily threaded their way along
the road leading to St. Lo. As they plunged more and more deeply into the bocage past the Aure River and its swamps, they saw
less and less of the enemy.

The troops, 600 of them, were tired, merely trudging along,
and they were hungry. They were ahead of most other American
units and behind them, unknown to either side at first, was a
retreating task force of the German 352nd Infantry Division.

Long after dark—at 2 a.m., actually—the exhausted infantrymen were guided off the road into the bivouac area their officers
had found for them, two pastures enclosed by the hedgerows and
embankments that criss-cross the Normandy landscape as a giant
maze. Just to the north stood several houses—the French hamlet
of Le Carrefour, meaning "crossroads."

The Americans didn't know the German task force was right
behind them. The Germans, however, had discovered the presence
of the American column ahead—and its bivouac area.

In the pastureland, the 2nd Battalion threw up its sentries, while
the main body of men simply spread out and found places to sleep.
No foxholes, for once, were dug. Men fell asleep in minutes
without even shedding their packs.

"From somewhere in the distance sentries could hear the faint sounds of vehicle engines—probably the jeeps of the 3rd Battalion, they figured. The 3rd was supposed to be somewhere east of the 2nd.''

In a stone farmhouse by the road, Lt. Col. William Warfield, commander of the 2nd Battalion, was still up, conferring with his staff. None of the Americans had any idea the Germans were so near . . . so near they had virtually surrounded the bivouac area, filtering behind the hedgerows, emplacing their machine guns and mortars, even bringing forward three motorized assault guns, *Sturmgeschutze*, that looked like tanks.

With flares suddenly lighting the two pastures, the Germans behind the hedgerows let go with all their ordnance at once—machine guns, mortars, and the three *Sturmgeschutze* with their long-barrelled cannon.

"The 29ers never stood a chance. With no time to set up a coherent defense, the frantic 29ers ran to and fro looking for a way to escape the death trap, but the Germans on top of the surrounding embankments could easily pick off the Yanks. Along one hedgerow, a platoon of dozing 29ers had only just risen when most of the men were cut down by a burst of machine-gun fire. As the GIs were hit, they tumbled back against the hedgerows in heaps.''

Those who tried to fight back couldn't see anything beyond the flare-lit fields. Still, they managed to silence two of the assault guns with bazookas. "It was terrible,'' said a survivor later. "We had crawled about 100 yards away from the field when we heard a lot of the guys screaming. I think the Germans may have been making a bayonet charge.''

The entire firefight consumed all of 20 minutes. Fifty battalion members were dead; another 100 were either wounded or captured, while the rest fled singly or in small groups, to slowly wend their way back to the American lines to the rear.

At the farmhouse quartering Warfield and his staff, the situation was no better. The Germans had shouted, in English, their demand that the officers surrender. The stunned Warfield shouted back, "Surrender, hell!'' He and his staff then attempted a dash to the bivouac area, but they, too, were cut down by machine-gun fire.

To the rear, Division Commander Charles Gerhardt had been concerned at the lack of reports from the 115th all during the day of June 9. A staff officer, Major Glover Johns, finally located the regiment's command post about dusk, but learned the personnel there "had no idea where any of the 115th's three infantry battalions were."

Apprised of this news, an angry General Gerhardt turned up at the command post at about 2 a.m., about the time of the ambush. There still was no news until, about 4 a.m., the first survivors of the ambush began to straggle in with their grim report. Gerhardt couldn't believe what he heard. "No security!" he shouted. "They just went into the field and went to bed!"

He and Johns set off by jeep at dawn to find the ambush site, with Gerhardt ignoring the possibility that the area ahead might now be under German control. On their way, they encountered two dozen more survivors, traveling together. As Gerhardt heard their accounts, he praised their decision to stay together and determined to award them all a Bronze Star.

A mile up the road, he and Major Johns came upon the ambush site itself. Two elderly French women were placing flowers on the bodies. They didn't know any details of the fight. Nearby was Warfield's body, his Colt .45 still in his hand. "If you have to die," said Gerhardt bitterly, "that's the way to do it."

The German task force that had struck during the night was long since gone. It had continued its retreat as ordered earlier—the 352nd was by now taking up defensive positions south of the Elle River.

All during the day of June 10, more and more 2nd Battalion survivors filtered back to their lines. With 100 replacements, a new CO and a battalion reorganization, it set out again later in the day on the same road to St. Lo. By the time the reconstituted 2nd Battalion again approached Le Carrefour, the bodies had been removed. All three battalions of the 115th moved forward that day without encountering any significant numbers of the enemy. One battle, an ambush, was over. Many battles still lay ahead for the Blue and Gray Division before it would end its wartime duty in the industrial Ruhr and the Klotze Forest in May 1945. But still, on the early morning of June 10, 1944, that was one terrible ambush.

From *Beyond the Beachhead: The 29th Infantry Division In Normandy*, by Joseph Balkoski, (Stackpole Books, Harrisburg, Pa., 1989)

# ■ Hitchhiker To The Rescue

Limping from a severe leg wound suffered a few weeks before, the hitchhiker on the battle-scarred road to St. Lo, France, was a U.S. Army captain determined to catch up with his company of the 2nd Battalion, 60th Infantry Regiment, 9th Infantry Division. With his men in tough battle again, Capt. Matt Urban, a native of Buffalo, N. Y., had checked out of the convalescent wards in England and made his way back to France on his own. They might need him.

*Arriving at the 2nd Battalion Command Post at 1130 hours, 25 July (1944), he found that his unit had jumped off at 1100 hours in the first attack of "Operation Cobra."*

Cobra, quickly following on the heels of St. Lo's capture, was the operation that finally carried U.S. forces beyond the hedgerows of Normandy's bocage country, where they had been stymied and held to small advances ever since D-Day, June 6.

Captain Urban had suffered his leg wound just about a week after the Normandy landings. At Renouf on June 14, he and his company ran into two German tanks and heavy small-arms fire. The tanks soon were "unmercifully raking his unit's positions and inflicting heavy casualties."

With his company's very survival at stake, Urban grabbed a bazooka, worked his way forward among the hedgerows despite the "barrage of fire" and drew near the tanks.

*He brazenly exposed himself to the enemy fire and, firing the bazooka, destroyed both tanks.*

With that, his men routed the German infantry ahead and moved forward. Later the same day, though, near Orglandes, Urban suffered his severe leg wound—"by direct fire from a 37mm tank gun."

Refusing medical evacuation, he saw that his men were settled into defensive positions for the night. At dawn the next day, he led them in still another attack—an hour later he suffered another wound. He was then evacuated to England.

During his convalescence, however, he heard about his unit's heavy casualties in the bitter fighting that continued in Normandy for several weeks. With the "big push" on for Operation Cobra in late July, he couldn't stand to sit still any longer and "hitchhiked his way back to his unit near St. Lo, France."

Now, still limping, he caught up with his men just as they were again held up by strong opposition. Two American tanks supporting them had been knocked out, while a third stood by, "intact but with no tank commander or gunner." It simply wasn't moving.

Urban found the young officer, a lieutenant, in charge of the tanks and with him worked out a plan of attack against the German strongpoint ahead. But when the lieutenant and a sergeant climbed aboard the immobile tank to get it rolling again, they came under fire and were killed on the spot.

That left the job to the infantry captain himself.

*Captain Urban, though physically hampered by his leg wound and knowing quick action had to be taken, dashed through the scathing fire and mounted the tank. With enemy bullets ricochetting from the tank, Captain Urban ordered the tank forward and, completely exposed to the enemy, manned the machine gun and placed devastating fire on the enemy.*

Inspired, indeed "galvanized" by the sight, the entire 2nd Battalion now sprang into action, attacked and eliminated the German position that had been holding up the Americans.

Urban, though, was not yet through with the war or his heroics. About 10 days later, he suffered a chest wound from shell fragments and again refused recommended evacuation. He took command of the entire battalion on August 6, and on August 15 was wounded a fourth time, but still insisted upon staying with his men.

As the Allies now mounted their relentless march across France toward the German homeland, they came upon the same Meuse River that the German panzers had crossed in May 1940 to bring about the collapse of France early in the war. Urban and his 2nd Battalion were ordered to effect a crossing of the river near Heer, Belgium, in early September.

*The enemy planned to stop the advance of the Allied Army by concentrating heavy forces at the Meuse.*

As the battalion attacked toward its assigned crossing-point, German artillery, mortars and small-arms fire stopped Urban's men in their tracks. Leaving his battalion command post to take the lead personally, Urban reorganized his forward elements, then led a charge against the German strongpoint ahead. The advance took him and his men across open, exposed ground, and he suffered still another wound, a serious neck injury.

*Although unable to talk above a whisper from the paralyzing neck wound, and in danger of losing his life, he refused to be evacuated until the enemy was routed and his battalion had secured the crossing-point of the Meuse River.*

150

It should be no surprise that Captain Matt Urban, 26, for his "personal leadership, limitless bravery and repeated extraordinary exposure to enemy fire (June 14 to September 3, 1944)," was awarded the nation's highest military decoration, the Medal of Honor.

From Lt. Col. Matt Urban's Medal of Honor citation

# ■ *Fear And Trembling*

If Hitler struck fear and trembling in his generals, this was especially true after the open attempt on his life on July 20, 1944, an event that was not isolated unto itself but came as the Allies were breaking out from their continental foothold at Normandy. Hitler's vengeful wrath was expectantly terrible, and among those who went to their deaths as a result was Erwin Rommel (as a forced suicide).

Lesser-known was General von Stulpnagel, military governor of occupied Paris. Upon hearing the *erroneous* news that Hitler was dead, he ordered the arrest of all Gestapo agents in Paris. When it turned out that Hitler was only injured in the bomb blast meant to kill him, Stulpnagel was ordered back to Berlin. He drove by way of Verdun, where he had fought in World War I, stopped at the battlefields there and shot himself in the head.

He only succeeded in blinding himself, however, and he later was hanged.

Also affected by the bomb plot, and in his case *not* a directly involved conspirator, was Field Marshal Günther Hans von Kluge, who had replaced Gerd von Rundstedt as commander of German forces in the western part of France shortly before July 20. According to his chief of staff, General Günther Blumentritt, Kluge knew there was a plot against Hitler, but had declined to take part in it. Nonetheless, his name turned up in the investigation that followed the abortive July 20 attempt.

Worse, cut off at the front by artillery fire during the Battle of Avranches, he was out of touch with his own headquarters for more than 12 hours one day. Hitler's suspicions were immediately excited; his orders to Kluge became "brusque and even insulting," recalled Blumentritt later.

Kluge, the commander charged with stopping the Allies, now carried a double burden. "All this had a very bad effect on any chance that remained of preventing the Allies from breaking out," added Blumentritt. "In the days of crisis Field-Marshal von Kluge gave only part of his attention to what was happening at the front. He was looking back over his shoulder anxiously—towards Hitler's headquarters."

So were many others. "He was not the only general who was in that state of worry for conspiracy in the plot against Hitler. Fear permeated and paralyzed the higher commands in the weeks and months that followed."

Shortly after July 20, the German front in the West collapsed, and, unannounced, Field Marshal Walther Model arrived to replace Kluge. "His arrival was the first news of the change that Field-Marshal von Kluge received—this sudden arrival of a successor had become the customary manner of dismissal at this time. . . ."

A crestfallen, fearful Kluge left for home the next day. In the evening of the day after, Blumentritt received a telephone call informing him that Kluge had suffered a fatal "heart attack." Two days later, the report was changed to "cerebral hemorrhage." Then, he was to receive a state funeral, with Rundstedt slated to deliver a resounding funeral oration.

But no, then there would be no state funeral. "I then heard that Field-Marshal von Kluge had taken poison—my opinion is that he committed suicide, not because of his dismissal, but because he believed he would be arrested by the Gestapo as soon as he arrived home."

Narrator Blumentritt had fears of his own, for that matter. He, too, had been privy to discussions about the plot against Hitler, who was in it, and who was not. And now came his own summons to Hitler's headquarters.

He visited with his family in Marburg on the way east ("in case of what might happen"). While at home, he quivered every time the telephone rang or he heard a car approaching the house. He pressed on to Hitler's headquarters in East Prussia, where he first was told that Hitler was too tired to receive him but to attend the daily conference at noon.

Arriving at the appointed place, he found a group of fellow generals informally gathered in front. Among them were Heinz Guderian, recently appointed Chief of the General Staff, and

William Keitel, headquarters lackey who later was hanged as a war criminal. The apprehensive Blumentritt noticed that Guderian made no attempt to shake hands, "while Keitel and others stood aloof." Even worse, Guderian in a loud voice said, "I wonder you dare to come here after what has happened in the West (the Normandy debacle)."

As it turned out, Hitler was very cordial to Blumentritt. When his fellow generals learned that the *Führer* had been so pleasant to him, *they* suddenly became very pleasant, too. Keitel even invited Blumentritt to tea. And the reason for his summons to headquarters, by one account, was Hitler's wish to award him the Knight's Cross of the Iron Cross in person. Replaced by a more experienced man as chief of staff in the West, Blumentritt was to return to that fighting front in command of his own army corps. As he left Germany's military command center, he felt, "I had a lucky escape."

From *The Other Side of the Hill* by B. H. Liddell Hart
(Cassell and Company Ltd. London, 1981)

# ■ *Destruction, Destruction Everywhere*

For a time during the German campaign against the great Black Sea naval base of Sevastopol in the winter of 1941-42, the defenders and residents of the city thought their ordeal had ended.

During December 1941, the advancing Germans had pushed to within six miles of the city. The German offensive was halted, however, by amphibious landings the Soviets mounted on the Kerch Peninsula to the German rear, an operation pressed forward despite the wintry weather.

In the respite, lasting for a few months, Sevastopol's citizens returned to their homes from caves and other shelters and began repairs to the damage wrought before the Kerch landings. The expectation was that the Soviet troops to the east soon would liberate the entire Crimea—the diluted German forces at the city's gates would be driven off.

Instead, the offensive to the northeast was a disaster, and soon the German 11th Army once again was drawn up before the city at nearly full force. The German shelling then resumed in earnest.

Both before and after, however, the defenders and citizens of Sevastopol responded in ways that inspired song, poetry and the stuff of legend. "The Five Sailors of Sevastopol" were five Black Sea navy men who threw themselves bodily under German tanks with hand grenades. In the city, underground factories turned out mines and hand grenades, clothing and footwear, while children learned their lessons in subterranean schools.

Pounded into submission, the Sevastopol of Crimean War fame at last fell. But then it would be the turn of the German occupiers to withstand a siege and vicious, constant shelling by *their* resurgent enemy at the gate. Once again, the population went underground . . . their city above given no such refuge.

Two years later, after the Soviets finally recaptured their Black Sea port, Russian-born British journalist Alexander Werth visited Sevastopol. The once-lively and beauteous Crimean city, he found, was dead. "Even in the suburbs . . . there was hardly a house standing. The railway station was a mountain of rubble and twisted metal; on the last day the Germans were at (Sevastopol) . . . they ran an enormous goods train off the line into a ravine, where it lay smashed, its wheels in the air. Destruction, destruction everywhere."

Werth came across an inscription scratched into an old navy monument by the sea. It was probably written during "the last days of agony of July 1942," he decided.

"You (Sevastopol) are not the same as before, when people smiled at your beauty," it said. "Now everyone curses this spot, because it has caused so much sorrow. Among your ruins, in your lanes and streets, thousands and thousands of people lie, and no one is there to cover their rotting bones."

The sidewalks of the newly liberated city were deserted, Werth found in 1944. The mayor explained that survivors living in the outskirts still looked upon the city proper as *verboten*. Werth walked the empty, shattered streets recalling the Crimean War of the 1850s and a fort, still visible across the bay, where a young Leo Tolstoy had been stationed.

Now, in 1944, proceeding to the Khersones Promontory, where some 750 German SS men had fought to the last, Werth found the ground had been "ploughed up by shells and scorched by the fire of the katyusha rockets." The ground was littered with

154

German equipage and "thousands of pieces of paper—photographs, snapshots, passports, maps, private letters." Floating in the surrounding bay waters were rafts and the bodies of men who had tried to escape but did not.

From *Russia At War: 1941-1945* by Alexander Werth
(Dutton, New York, N.Y.,1964)

# ■ *Million And One Heroes*

At Cap Cavalaire on the French Riviera the morning of August 15, 1944, Sergeant James P. Connor's infantry platoon stumbled into a German minefield just beyond the invasion beaches. He tried to shout a warning, but too late. His platoon leader, Lieutenant John J. Criegh, tripped the wire of a hanging mine. In the explosion that followed, the young officer was torn to bits and Connor was blown 10 feet away.

Stunned, bleeding from fragmentation wounds in the neck, Connor got to his feet and helped regroup remaining members of the platoon for the dash to the "safety" of the nearby coastal road. The road, though, was nothing but a bowling alley for depressed 20mm German flak guns.

Vastly superior in numbers, the Germans were entrenched on a peninsula affording them a commanding view of the road and the beaches where men and equipment of Connor's U.S. 3rd Infantry Division were still landing as part of the Allied invasion of Southern France. It was the platoon's job to penetrate several thousand yards of terrain that was alive with the shot and shell of the flak guns, of mortars, machine guns and sniper-held weapons. They were to destroy the fortified enemy position—and all with utmost speed.

As Connor's patrol pushed forward to a road bridge just outside the village Cavalaire-sur-Mer, he shot and killed one enemy rifleman who jumped into view not ten feet away. Seventy-five yards beyond the bridge, he killed a second sniper, but still another had killed the acting platoon leader. Connor, a native of Wilmington, Delaware, was left in charge of the 36-man platoon.

The number of men still available to him had been reduced to 20, however, and now they were anxious to take cover from the heavy mortar fire dropping all about them. But no—get the hell out of here, he ordered them. The only way to escape the mortar fire was to advance and attack its origin, the enemy strongpoint on Cap Cavalaire.

They started forward again. A nearby machine gun opened up and caught Sergeant Connor in the left shoulder. As one of his men knocked out the machine gun with a BAR, he refused medical attention and directed his platoon members in a flanking movement against nearby snipers. The platoon continued its assigned course, through groups of buildings and light woods; it began the ascent on the Cavalaire side of the enemy-held point above the invasion beaches.

Rising from a hole in the ground ahead, a German shot Connor in the leg, his third wound of the day. He fell. He tried to stand, but couldn't. "Nevertheless," says his official citation, "from his prone position, he gave the orders and directed his men in assaulting the enemy. Infused with . . . (his) dogged determination, the platoon, though reduced to less than one-third of its original 36 men, outflanked and rushed the enemy with such furiousness that they killed seven, captured 40, seized three machine guns . . . and took all their assigned objectives."

With more than 10 million Americans in uniform for World War II, Connor was one of 434 who received the Congressional Medal of Honor. In the eyes of his own nation, the 434 are a special number, members of an exalted order, but there were millions of other heroes, too. They were the American GI sent to Continental Europe like Connor (nearly four million, excluding those in the rough Italian campaign); they were sailors, Marines, Coast Guardsmen, spies, airmen, generals and admirals, too.

Not all were Americans, nor even combatants. They were, too, the soldiery of the Allies; they were the Resistance, and they were the civilians pushed, pummeled and pilloried by war.

Compared to both allies and enemies in World War II, America entered the fray a most unwarlike nation, its experience in war, or taste for it, limited. But its 10 million quickly adapted. "What was really amazing," said German Field Marshal Erwin Rommel at one point, "was the speed with which the Americans adapted themselves to modern warfare." They succeeded in an unprecented way. "Starting from scratch, an army has been created in the very minimum of time, which, in equipment, armament and organization of all arms, surpasses anything the world has yet seen.''

From *World War II* Magazine, May 1986

# ■ *Marooned In Modern France*

Tom Maloney, 20, might as well have been shipwrecked, marooned on a remote island in the Pacific. Within easy view was a "tower type" structure. Normally, it would take him only minutes to walk over to it.

In August of 1944, it took Tom Maloney five lonely days to reach the tower.

In the middle of the European War, in the days immediately after a massive invasion of Southern France pitting hundreds of thousands of fighting men against each other, Tom Maloney had found himself marooned in a world of pain and desolation on the coast of the same modern but war-racked country, with all those thousands of soldiers, and their civilian onlookers, quite close by.

On August 15, 1944, Maloney was healthy, young . . . a hot-shot P-38 pilot with the 15th Air Force's 27th Fighter Squadron, 1st Fighter Group. On that day, on his 60th mission, the 20-year-old ace shot down two German Me 109s over St. Tropez, France, to give him a total of eight victories for the war thus far. The 15th would stand out in his memory also as the day the Allies mounted their second invasion of France, a near-perfect amphibious exercise that landed thousands of Americans, French and British troops along the French Riviera.

For the fighter pilots based at Foggia, Italy, the invasion meant a flurry of combat missions over the next few days. Thus, Maloney flew his 63rd and 64th missions in one day, August 19—with No. 64 destined to be his last.

Dive-bombing a German truck convoy near Avignon, France, Maloney hit one truck so squarely that he saw "the back half of the truck, with the wheels still attached, going end over end by his airplane, plus a heavy concentration of debris." In no time at all, his twin-engine Lightning lost oil in the left engine, which he quickly shut down. He turned for the coast, 30 miles distant, while his right-hand power plant was still going.

He reached the Allied-controlled Mediterranean, but with his right engine also failing due to low oil pressure. He made the fateful decision to ditch his ''Maloney's Pony'' five to six miles offshore between the Gulf of Lions and the Cote d'Azur, and so far, so good, considering. The plane nosed quickly into the water, like ''a submarine,'' but he managed to wriggle out, inflate a dinghy and head for shore.

In the hours ahead, two sea rescue boats cruised by without spotting him in the tiny dinghy. They turned and passed him again.

He put to shore, finally, near the mouth of the Rhone River. By now, it was after dark.

He walked inland a short ways, just 40 to 50 feet, when ''he heard a click, as though someone was cocking a hand gun.'' He froze on the spot, rooted.

It hadn't been a hand gun, of course. It was a mine, and he was practically standing on it. The explosion drove steel shards through his feet, severely lacerated his left hip area and caused numerous other shrapnel injuries.

With such injuries, Maloney was left immobilized. Semiconscious for a while, he rallied and somehow managed to pull some of the steel shafts out of his feet, the larger ones. He lay back . . . and three days later awoke, still in the same spot, still alone, still grievously injured. He awoke with a terrible thirst. Forty to fifty feet away there were some green bushes—perhaps there would be water nearby.

Half a day later, he reached the bushes. He could move, barely, by sitting, pushing himself backwards with knees bent, then arms taking up the slack, a bit like rowing.

At the end of the 50 feet, there indeed was a puddle of water! ''Tom says he will never forget the moment!''

Now he could see the tower structure, and in five days, he reached that goal, too.

Nothing there. But a short distance away was ''a lodge-type building.'' He back-pedaled to it, pushed the door open, and on the floor found some rotten carrots. He couldn't stomach them and couldn't break down a hard chunk of old black bread. Obviously, he would have to move on.

''The area was quite marshy, so Tom was able to fashion a raft of sorts. With this new mode of transportation, he slowly made his way toward what appeared to be a small settlement of the

French. He finally reached the settlement and got the attention of six men who were standing around an old truck.''

From there, Maloney was carried to a French hospital three miles away, and from it he was taken to an American field hospital and then to a U.S. Army hospital at Naples, Italy. There, the doctors wanted to amputate both legs, but held off at his insistence and that of his group commander, Colonel Robert Richards.

He recovered eventually, at last leaving his many hospital beds in September 1945, more than a year after he suffered his injuries. He married his childhood sweetheart back in the States, Patricia Jean Driggs. In future years, he would undergo further operations and medical treatment, graduate from Oklahoma State University, run his own oil drilling business, and serve his community as a school board clerk, city planning commission chairman and chairman of his church finance committee. Nor would he be any slouch on the golf course, either.

From Irv Styer in the *1st Fighter Group Association News,* Fall-Winter, 1986

# ■ *Resistance At Auschwitz*

The man repairing the roof, armed with a smuggled camera, was a spy. Earlier, saboteurs within the tightly guarded complex had damaged the roof with planned deliberation. That was the excuse for insertion of the ''roofer'' now watching, waiting, with his hidden camera.

The camera had to ''go in'' ahead of him, since he naturally would be searched upon his arrival.

That problem was solved by building a false bottom in a large soup kettle. Protected by a watertight cover, the camera was hidden beneath soup carried into the compound every day from kitchens located outside.

The workers inside had places to hide the camera until the day the ''roofer'' arrived.

He did, and he reported to the *Obersharfuhrer* in charge, a one-eyed man named Moll.

As usual, this widely dreaded sadist minced no words. "I want you to stay at your job like a dog chained to his post. If you move away from there for one minute you will not come out of here alive. You hear me, you *Schweinhund*?"

David Szmulewski meekly agreed, but when Moll left the compound to meet one of the frequently arriving "transports," the roofer took the camera from a waiting co-conspirator and secreted it under his flimsy jacket. He squeezed the lens through an enlarged buttonhole and while working upon the roof was able to snap three key photographs of the secret activity below.

He wrapped the film in a rag and hid it in his roofing tar, while others hastily buried the incriminating camera on the grounds of the compound. Szmulewski finished his repairs and left the compound uneventfully, the film safely hidden in the roofing tar.

He, himself, wouldn't go far, since he had merely stepped from one prison compound into the far larger boundaries of another one—Auschwitz. The film, though, would be smuggled out; it would show a group of naked women on their way into the gas chamber. Two other shots would reveal bodies being burned in open pits. The place where the "spy" had done his work was the crematorium compound at Auschwitz II, or the Birkenau camp built next to the original death camp, and both on marshy, pestilent ground 160 miles southwest of Warsaw.

Himself an Auschwitz inmate, Szmulewski had arrived in March 1942, while the camp was still being built. Volunteering as a "roofer," though he really wasn't, he had avoided the usual fate of the Auschwitz inmates by being classified "as a prisoner with special skills needed by the administration."

He eventually earned a *Passierschein*, or permit, allowing him "to move about the camp unguarded, including Auschwitz II (Birkenau), where the gas chambers and crematoriums were located." Thus, he was a vital liaison man for the Resistance cells scattered throughout the huge death camp—and the perfect prospect to obtain photographic evidence of what was going on in the new crematorium compound, "whose smoke-belching chimneys were visible to thousands of prisoners in the Birkenau barracks."

The camera itself had been no problem—the Nazis had whole warehouses full of personal belongings left behind by the condemned, some of whom innocently brought cameras with them to Auschwitz.

The camp Resistance was so well organized that the film now was smuggled out and sent to the Polish Underground at Crakow, together with a report from Jozef Cyrankiewicz, a leader in the camp underground who years later would be Premier of Poland. The report from Cyrankiewicz was a warning that the Nazis had begun a hideous massacre of Hungarian Jews "transported" to Auschwitz. (Indeed, 400,000 Hungarian victims killed at Auschwitz would outnumber those from any other nation under Nazi Germany's rule, including Germans.)

The photos that Szmulewski took "provided the outside world with the first photographs of Nazi atrocities inside Auschwitz, giving visual support to the word-picture painted by Cyrankiewicz in his secret report to the P.P.S. (Polish Socialist Party) . . ."

The camp Resistance, however, was not yet through with the crematorium compound. In this dread place, the workers were always several hundred Jews sequestered from the rest of Auschwitz and forced to operate the incineration system. Called the Sonderkommando, they, themselves were gassed and burned to ashes every two or three months, only to be replaced by a new group performing the same terrible task.

"But the brotherly hand of the underground extended even into the ranks of the Sonderkommando. Though cut off from the rest of the prisoners and condemned by the Nazis to spend the last months of their agonized lives burning the bodies of fellow Jews, the underground kept alive within them the spirit of revenge and revolt."

Thus, they had been happy to help David Szmulewski in his photography assignment. Thus, too, in the weeks before October 7, 1944, a young Polish woman by the name of Rosa Robota was a chief organizer in an underground chain that had been smuggling tiny bits of dynamite and other explosives into the crematorium compound.

The source of these forbidden materials was a munitions factory at Auschwitz employing prisoners as slave-laborers. Rosa had seen her own family and other Jews from her hometown of Ciechanow marched off to the gas chambers on her arrival in late 1942, and she was more than willing to help the Resistance when a contact told her what was needed.

She organized 20 factory "girls" in a smuggling operation that carried out the explosives in the form of tiny "wheels" that looked like buttons. The women stashed them in matchboxes tucked into their clothing. The "buttons" then went, through many hands, to a Russian named Borodin who was a demolitions expert. He created "bombs" with empty sardine cans as the casings. Rosa, herself, was again involved in smuggling explosives into the crematorium enclosure. "The explosives she received were hidden in the handcarts on which corpses of those who had died overnight in the barracks were taken to the crematorium."

Other bombs or their ingredients filtered throughout Auschwitz, since the inmates planned a general uprising, but inside the crematorium enclosure, the Sonderkommando learned their turn for liquidation had come. With no time to waste, they blew up Crematorium III (one of the four in use) on October 7, 1944, threw one of their four German overseers into the oven, killed four SS guards, injured many others, then cut through the barbed-wire fence and fled en masse.

They were about 600, and they still were within the larger Auschwitz bounds. A "large contingent of SS" men hunted them down and shot them. The subsequent investigation led the SS eventually to Rosa Robota. After interrogation and torture, she was hanged with three other young women conspirators, but not before she was able to scribble a farewell message to her fellow Jews, the Hebrew greeting of Hashomer Hatzair, *"Khazak V' Hamatz"*—"Be strong and brave." She and many others had been.

From Yuri Suhl in *They Fought Back: The Story of Jewish Resistance in Nazi Europe* edited by Yuri Suhl (Schocken Books, New York, N.Y. paperback edition, 1975)

# ■ *Apology Between Enemies*

Unlike the always ugly Pacific War, the American GI sent to Europe often was able to maintain an odd relationship of sorts with the German enemy. They shot and killed each other, true . . . but when the firing died down (and excluding the SS fanatics) there was this personal, sometimes almost intimate bond present. They could speak, interact, soldier to soldier. Or . . . young-boy-sent-to-war with young-boy-sent-to-war.

While not universally true, many an American veteran can recall the stories of unexpected battlefield *camaraderie*.

Elliott Johnson, for instance. An artillery lieutenant with the 4th Infantry Division, he landed at Normandy, made the crossing of France and wound up at the end of 1944 in the terrifying tangles of the Huertgen Forest.

His experience was not only with visible German troops taken prisoner, but with the enemy's invisible artillery, directed in many cases by a forward observer like himself. Sometimes it became a personal thing, a duel of sorts.

One day in Normandy, he was approaching a "huge old chateau" protected by a slimy moat. He heard the sound of a deadly German 88. "You could tell from the sound when it was pointed at you. I heard this *chok*! and knew it was mine."

Johnson leaped from his position in the middle of a road over the nearest hedgerow and landed in the moat, "all covered with green slime." The round missed.

Now he had to go back. He dashed across the road and behind a hedgerow on the far side. But—"Not before he took another shot at me. He was up in that church steeple, and he had a telephone going straight down to that guy. When he'd say fire, the guy'd pull that lanyard. I was the target."

The German artillerists were fast and accurate, Johnson realized. He had one more road to cross. They were waiting.

He took a running start and made the dash. The 88 fired again. It was a shade too low, and all that Johnson got was a piece of shrapnel in the thigh. Nothing serious.

A few days later, his friend Fitzpatrick ("a wonderful young man") was hit direct by an 88 shell. Nothing left.

So it went for Johnson, in combat across Europe from June of 1944 until May of 1945, end of the war in Europe. Killing or be killed, advancing, taking prisoners, friends lost or permanently maimed.

And yet—"I avoid using words like 'kill a man' because I like to divorce myself from that. We recognized that we were in a war, but we recognized that they came from families like we came from families and that they had loved ones and they were good guys and they were bad guys. We were called on by our government, that our country was in jeopardy. Therefore, we had to fight for it. Personally, I had no malice at any time toward the Germans."

The SS was a bit different—brainwashed and difficult to deal with. "Those people made me angry." The regular German, though, the ordinary boys they took prisoner, were just "glad to be out of it." The Americans would take off their shoes and send them down the road to the rear to be processed as POWs. "The last thing they'd do is come back and either shake hands with us or embrace us."

One day in December, near or at the Huertgen, Johnson as artillery observer looked down a steep bank into a small, tight valley and saw "enormous numbers" of German tanks and other vehicles move into a bloc of forest. He called in his artillery, a massive barrage of burning white phosphorous and one-half posit fuses that would explode just above the ground. "The devastation on that little piece of land, the accuracy of those boys in firing, was incredible. It's one of my bad memories, the suffering."

In the Huertgen Forest itself one time he was locked in an almost friendly artillery duel with a German counterpart, a fellow artillery observer. With his crew of three, Lieutenant Johnson had gone forward with their radio equipment to a forester's tower. At the base, they propped up some logs as their shelter from all the artillery tearing up gouges in the deep forest. They did their work, spotting, from the tower above.

On the second day at the outpost, Johnson saw another forester's tower. "There was a German lieutenant looking right at me. We waved at each other. I marked him on the map. I got my guns zeroed in on him, and I know in my heart he did the same thing to me."

Johnson had a view of a road that was a pathway for German tanks. They were Johnson's target. "He would watch my shooting. He was interested in my effectiveness."

And so Johnson brought in the artillery whenever a target presented itself. One day, however, three German ambulances held down the middle of a vehicular convoy—"hands off." Johnson was letting them go by, unmolested . . . but suddenly the American artillery came in anyway, ambulances or no ambulances.

Frantically, Johnson looked at his lieutenant counterpart and shook his head, "hard as I could." But the German thought Johnson had called down the fire. Johnson saw him pick up his telephone, and that was enough to "hit the ladder" and get down from the tower and into the little log shelter at the bottom.

Seconds later, the German artillery rolled in. The tower almost came tumbling down, but not quite. It was "his (the German spotter's) precision shooting," nonetheless.

As soon as the firing stopped, Johnson scrambled up his ladder to the tower cubicle. "I had my hands up and I was waving and shaking my head: not me."

The German looked at Johnson . . . studying. After a moment, the German carefully and symbolically took off his helmet.

"That was his apology to me."

From *"The Good War," An Oral History of World War II*, Studs Terkel (Pantheon Books, a division of Random House, Inc., New York, 1984)

# ■ *Prepare To Attack Japanese Fleet*

When the Japanese sent a powerful column of cruisers and battleships as battering rams against the back door of Leyte Gulf in the fall of 1944, few would have drawn the slightest equation to the flat lands of Oklahoma in distant America. Even more remote would have been any thoughts of the native Americans who roamed the virgin continent before the technologically advanced Europeans learned to bridge entire oceans in their great ships.

Indeed, what could have been less relevant in 1944, as the world's modern fleets gathered for the greatest naval battle in history? Relevant . . . except that it *was* an American Indian, a Cherokee from landlocked Oklahoma, who led the counterattack against the seemingly overpowering Japanese column at the critical moment of battle.

Among the 216 American ships engaged in the Battle of Leyte Gulf against 64 Japanese vessels . . . among the 143,000 American personnel (and 42,800 Japanese), few ships or sailors will be remembered so well as the U.S. destroyer *Johnston* and her fighting skipper, Commander Ernest E. Evans, an Annapolis graduate from Pawnee, Oklahoma.

As the situation unfolded October 24, 1944, on a gigantic chessboard of 500,000 square miles, Admiral Takeo Kurita's Center Force, approaching the island of Leyte from the rear, had been badly battered and turned away from the San Bernardino Strait. Or so it seemed.

During the night, 24-25 October, the Japanese Southern Force had been caught negotiating the narrow Surigao Strait and mauled so badly that the lower arm of a giant Japanese pincer appeared cut off. Meanwhile, the American invasion of Leyte—MacArthur's return to the Philippines—continued apace, apparently not to be overly disturbed by the last great sortie of the Japanese Imperial Navy.

But Kurita, last seen hightailing in the opposite direction after losing *Musashi*, one of Japan's two "super" battleships, on the 24th, was not to be so easily denied. Unknown to any on the American side, he had turned his Center Force about during the night and now was barreling down the San Bernardino alleyway after all.

And no one was watching its handy exit above Samar Island.

"One might have been in the age of Drake," wrote naval historian Samuel Eliot Morison later. "Lord Nelson would have left a frigate to watch . . . and give him advance notice of the approach of an enemy fleet. How could such a thing happen in broad daylight, in the age of air power and electricity? And to top it all, as if the god of battles wished to test the Americans, he shielded Kurita's fleet from the probing invisible fingers of radar almost until the lookouts sighted it with their own eyes."

Including Japan's second "supership," the *Yamato*, Kurita's juggernaut burst upon "Taffy 3," a weak flotilla of six slow-moving escort carriers and their seven "small boy" escorts. It was sharks against ducks in a mill pond.

Blowing smoke and spitting torpedoes, though, the incredibly brave *Johnston* turned to the attack despite the hopeless odds. As other destroyers joined in, even destroyer escorts, the hits they made, the confusion they sowed, the time they gave most of the unprotected carriers to escape, all combined to throw Kurita off stride. Also beset by a swarm of attacking aircraft, his powerful *Yamato* soon sent scurrying to avoid torpedo tracks, Kurita in the end did not plunge on into the vulnerable Leyte landing zone.

Why he didn't brush aside his waspish attackers has been a matter of debate ever since, but one major reason was the unex-pected ferocity of the "small boy" attacks, with "General Quarters Johnny," the *Johnston*, showing the way.

Fondly called "Chief" by his men, Evans never faltered in pressing his attack or interdiction tactics, even when the torpedoes were gone, when his upper clothing had been sucked right off him by the blast of arriving Japanese shells . . . when he had lost two fingers of his left hand. Or when, at the end, with all guns but one five-incher out of action, his *Johnston* was surrounded by a ring of enemy ships.

As she went down, a Japanese skipper was seen to salute the gallant *Johnston* from his own destroyer's bridge.

Later, a grateful nation bestowed upon its American Indian son the Medal of Honor. Sadly, it would be posthumous, since Commander Evans was one of the 186 *Johnston* crewmen lost in the memorable battle. But he undoubtedly knew those odds before taking his *Johnston* on what naval historian Morison later called "her mad, brave course" into the teeth of the oncoming Japanese column.

*Prepare*, Evans had told his crew at the very outset of battle, *Prepare to attack major portion of Japanese Fleet.* And no exaggeration—they did.

From various sources

# ■ *Unlucky Agent's Unexpected Role*

Laconic and taciturn, Jack Taylor was not entirely your mild-mannered orthodontist solely interested in retainers and braces. That was the California resident's civilian occupation before the war, true. But he also was a ham radio operator, a licensed pilot, a yachtsman (races in the Hawaiian islands and to Bermuda under his belt), and he once spent two days trapped inside a collapsed gold mine in the Yukon.

When he signed up for the Navy as a lieutenant, he spurned the relative safety of the medical corps to become a line officer aboard a subchaser.

The American OSS was taken with his extracurricular profile and soon had him instructing trainees in boat-handling, underwater demolition, navigation and related specialties. In short order, he, himself, was in the field as a behind-the-lines agent. Based in the Balkans, he survived 15 such missions in Corfu, Yugoslavia, and Albania. Taylor was tall at 33, a handsome man with short-cropped brown hair.

He did not, for all his various attributes that appealed to the OSS, always enjoy the luck of the draw. On one mission, he had endured 45 days of isolation upon an enemy-occupied island off

Albania. His survival was a testament to his inner resources, but the parallel fact was that he had been stranded there helplessly, and his sub-rosa colleagues had been forced to rescue him.

Then, on his very next mission, a parachute drop into Austria at the head of a four-man team, he was captured. As of late 1944, it appeared that his luck finally had run out; that even if he were fortunate enough to survive the horrors ahead, the war was over for him.

But fate had not counted upon the resilience and remarkable courage of the orthodontist from California.

Taylor was beaten into unconsciousness at the moment of his arrest, and from the first his interrogation at the Gestapo headquarters in Vienna's Metropol Hotel was accompanied by slaps and kicks. To his amazement, Taylor learned he "knew" one of interrogators—a fellow ham radio fan who had "talked" with him before the war.

The peacetime contact did Taylor little good, though. Held for months in solitary confinement at the Metropol facility, he survived bouts with dysentery and pneumonia. He was under threat of death for espionage, but he argued he was a visible combatant, a soldier in the war, since he had operated in Austria dressed in a brown Navy officer's ground-combat uniform.

In early March 1945, American bombs heavily damaged the Metropol —along with other Gestapo prisoners, Taylor was moved to a commandeered villa, also in Vienna. He regained some of his strength working outdoors—pruning trees, splitting wood. But then came a final ruling from Berlin. Uniform or no, he was considered a spy. The sentence would be execution, to be carried out at the widely dreaded Mauthausen concentration camp near Linz, Austria.

Taylor had no way of knowing then, but the move to Mauthausen would take him to the most deadly of all German concentration camps (not to be confused with "officially designated" *extermination* camps like Auschwitz). By war's end, Mauthausen would lead all concentration camps by sending 36,000 inmates to their deaths.

But Taylor needed no briefing to appreciate Mauthausen for what it truly was—a torture chamber and center of extermination, whatever its official designation. He was put to work with labor gangs building a crematorium that would double the camp's number of executions.

Typically, Taylor's greeting upon his arrival on Easter morning, April 1, 1945, was a three-hour beating by SS men and the shooting of a prisoner who allegedly had attempted to escape some time before. In all other respects, Mauthausen was a worst-case scenario of concentration camp horror—sadistic guards, starvation diet, unremitting labor, overcrowded, unsanitary living quarters. A chilling specialty at Mauthausen, though, was its gigantic rock quarry by the banks of the romantically storied Danube.

Not only was the primitive quarry work hard and dangerous for the emaciated inmates, but the guards had a game called "parachutist." That involved dropping a prisoner from the quarry's lip to the rocky floor 150 feet below. If the victim somehow survived, he was carried up the 186 "Steps of Death" to be dropped a second time.

"Official" executions were carried out by gas, hanging or shooting (in the back of the head), usually in a building known as the "Death House."

Although still under a death sentence himself, Lieutenant John Hedrick Taylor, USN, now found the wartime role that fate had designed for him.

Clearly, he was a rarity among German concentration camp prisoners. As an American officer, his fellows realized, he could be a compelling post-war witness to the brutalities they were suffering at Mauthausen—if any of them survived, Taylor included. The European nationals with him, many of them professionals with strong anti-Nazi credentials, conceivably could be considered too "political," too anti-Nazi and vengeful to be taken literally in their horror claims.

The American among them would be a far more believable witness. "Thus, they unburdened their most painful memories on him, a litany of men torn to pieces by trained dogs, injected with magnesium chlorate in the heart, tossed into cement mixers, and given hot showers followed by naked exposure in sub-zero temperatures while having hoses turned on them. For each story, Taylor insisted upon two eyewitnesses. Then, he committed the accounts to memory."

On May 5, 1945, forward elements of George S. Patton's Third Army liberated the camp. Weighing a mere 112 pounds and still suffering from dysentery and fever, Taylor was sent to a U.S. Army hospital at Regensburg.

Three weeks later, though, he was back at Mauthausen, to help gather evidence against its surviving wardens and their collaborators. He found 18 "death books," a meticulous record of the executions carried out at the camp—and prime evidence against its captured, war-criminal personnel. He also discovered that his own execution had been scheduled for April 28, but that a fellow inmate, a trusty, had burned the order.

A year later, temporarily recalled to active duty again, Lieutenant Commander Jack Taylor was at Dachau for the war crimes trial of the Mauthausen personnel. He was the lead-off witness for the prosecution. His testimony was a major factor in the guilty verdicts that resulted—"the major surviving officials of Mauthausen were convicted and executed."

A year after VE Day, Jack Taylor then went back to his orthodontist's practice in California, his unexpected part of the war finally done.

> From *Piercing the Reich: The Penetration of Nazi Germany by American Secret Agents During World War II* by Joseph E. Persico (The Viking Press; Ballantine Books, New York, N.Y. 1979)

# ■ *Presidential Unit Citation*

For American blacks, too, the war began with Pearl Harbor. One was Dorie Miller, Mess Attendant Second Class—at the time, weren't all blacks relegated to such jobs? Mess Attendant on the battleship *West Virginia*, a big man who also was the ship's heavyweight boxer.

As the Japanese planes bore in on the Sunday morning tableau at Pearl, Miller was serving the nearly empty junior officers' wardroom. Suddenly, for all, frenzied activity aboard ship. Up on the bridge, flying shrapnel from the *Tennessee* alongside struck down the *West Virginia's* skipper, Captain Mervyn Bennion, a fatal wound that nonetheless left him conscious for some time.

Another officer, racing for the command center that was the bridge, encountered Dorie Miller and brought him along. As a result, notes Dorie Miller's Silver Star citation, the share-cropper's son from Waco, Texas, "assisted in moving his Captain, who had been mortally wounded, to a place of greater safety." *Assisted while under "serious fire."*

Minutes later, Dorie Miller was busy with a nearby machine gun—by some accounts he shot down two of the attacking aircraft before he was finished for the day, before his ship sank. In the interim, he had earned the first Navy Cross to be awarded to a black . . . yet he died later in the war aboard the torpedoed aircraft carrier *Liscombe Bay* (Nov. 24, 1943) still as a mess attendant.

And so it was for most blacks, for most of the war—menial jobs in manual labor and housekeeping chores for the most part. Exceptions were the few all-black combat outfits, such as the intrepid airmen known as the Black Eagles (99th Fighter Squadron, later grown to the 332rd Fighter Group).

The flyers tended to get the publicity, but on the ground there were a handful of other all-black outfits (often led by white officers)—infantry, artillery, antiaircraft, tank destroyer and tank units. One was the belatedly recognized 761st Tank Battalion, which, while nominally assigned to the 26th Infantry Division, was in actuality on "roving" assignment that broke ground for several divisions in the long march across France and through Germany.

*Broke ground*? "The average life of a separate tank battalion was from ten to twelve days. Then they'd just redline it out and the few men who were left were attached to somebody else. So when there was a bad spot, they'd send the separate tank battalion in the area and the division would just bypass it. You were just gun fodder really. We went 183 days without relief and damn few replacements."

In the 183 days, also recalled former battalion commander Charles A. Gates, himself black, the battalion began with 750 men and ended with 35 killed in action. "We had 293 who received Purple Hearts. We had 60 who received Bronze Stars. We had 11 who received Silver Stars. Remember, these awards were granted through the divisions with whom we'd been attached. A division naturally is gonna take care of its own first. So for us to have received that many awards meant to me that any man who received a Bronze Star should have received a Silver Star and any man who received a Silver Star should have received a Congressional Medal of Honor. Because we got only the crumbs. So we must have done a very creditable job."

He recalls the day he and his men were having difficulty clearing a wooded area of German troops. For a time, the tanks had been firing low into the trees. Finally, Gates ordered, "Gentlemen, raise your fire so it will explode up in the trees."

That sent shrapnel and chunks of trees flying around—shortly, the Germans came pouring out under white flags. When they saw the American tankers were American blacks, however, they turned and started running for the woods again. A bit more fire halted them in their tracks. "Finally, they figured they'd better go along with these black soldiers."

Later, back home, hostilities over, the tankers of the 761st Battalion discovered at least 12 of the units they had served on temporary status had been awarded Presidential Unit Citations. Why not the 761st Battalion, apparently the first black tanker unit to be used in combat—and for 183 days *immersed* in combat?

"We had tried at the close of World War Two to get someone interested in reading our record and hadn't been successful. In '66 it was introduced in the House and it died as usual; '67, it was introduced and died. After President (Jimmy) Carter'd got into office, he said, 'Write the White House if you have a problem.' I wrote him a letter. On January 24, 1978, he signed our award for a Presidential Unit Citation."

From various sources: "*The Good War*" by Studs Terkel (Pantheon Books, New York, 1984); *Strength for the Fight: A History of Black Americans in the Military*, by Bernard C. Nalty (The Free Press, New York, 1986); "*0755*": *The Heroes of Pearl Harbor* by Donald and Helen Ross (Rokalu Press, Port Orchard, Wash., 1988); *Day of Infamy* by Walter Lord (Henry Holt and Company, New York, 1957)

# ■ *Escape From Auschwitz*

At Auschwitz, Rudolf Vrba's job was to greet the incoming transports and get the dead, dying and sick out of the boxcars and into a truck that would go straightaway to the crematorium. He and many others, of course—under extremely tight security. "The whole murder machinery could work on one principle: that the people came to Auschwitz and didn't know where they were going and for what purpose. The new arrivals were supposed to be kept orderly and without panic marching into the gas chambers. Especially the panic was dangerous from women with small children. So it was important for the Nazis that none of us give some sort of message which could cause a panic, even in the last moment. And anybody who tried to get in touch with the newcomers was either clubbed to death or taken behind the wagon and shot, because if a panic would have broken out, a massacre would have taken place on the spot, on the ramp. It would already be a hitch in the machinery. You can't bring in the next transport with dead bodies and blood around, because this would only increase the panic. The Nazis were concentrating on one thing: it should go in an orderly fashion so that it goes unimpeded. One doesn't lose time."

The man speaking, born Walter Rosenberg rather than Rudolf Vrba, had arrived at Auschwitz on June 30, 1942; two years later, he was a clerk in the huge extermination facility's "quarantine camp," a post allowing him relative freedom of movement and access to information on the "deportations, selections, and extermination of prisoners in Auschwitz." His friend Alfred Wetzler, also a clerk, was in similar position.

Both were active in the Auschwitz Resistance, but by April 1944, Vrba had concluded there was no chance of fomenting a general uprising. He saw that the Resistance "is not geared for an uprising but for survival of the members of the Resistance." He and Wetzler decided to escape and "inform the world" of what was going on at Auschwitz. "And I thought that if this would be made known by any means within Europe, and especially within Hungary, from where a million Jews were to be transported to Auschwitz immediately, in May—and I knew about that—that this might stir up the Resistance outside and bring help from outside directly to Auschwitz. And thus the escape plans are finally formulated and the escape took place on April 7."

What "took place" when the two Slovakian Jews vanished from sight that day was not what the searching guards assumed. Vrba and his companion had not yet really escaped; they had not yet really gone anywhere; they were still in Auschwitz itself. They merely had gone underground—into an excavated pit hidden by boards and pieces of wood filched from the camp barracks. "They protected themselves against police dogs by scattering gasoline-soaked tobacco around the bunker."

They stayed in their "bunker" for three days and nights, not 500 yards from a block commander's office. Only when the initial hue and cry over their escape had eased up did they move. With the perimeter guard deployment back to normal by the evening of April 10, they crawled their way out in the darkness and took to the countryside. "After a 10-day-long flight that was full of dramatic experiences, Wetzler and Rosenberg (Vrba) crossed the German-Slovakian border. They rested for three days and nursed their injured feet in the house of a farmer named Cansky in the Slovak community of Skalite." They then reached Zilina, where they made contact with Jewish leaders and imparted their account of the genocide being conducted at Auschwitz.

As their eye-witness details were being filtered through various organizations to a not-always-listening world, still another escape plan was developing back in Auschwitz, where in May the camp "conveyor belt" reached a record extermination figure of nearly 20,000 men, women and children reduced to ashes in one 24-hour period.

In Camp BB-II-d, where escapee Wetzler had served as a clerk, Jewish leader Arnost Rosin was suspected of complicity in Wetzler's escape with Vrba. "Rosin was called in for questioning and torture." As punishment, he was assigned to hard labor in a gravel pit. But there he met another determined Jewish prisoner, Czezlaw Mordowicz, a Pole. And they discovered in the wall of the pit "a short, narrow passageway—a bunker—that had been filled in with broken stones after the escape of other prisoners."

After surreptitiously preparing the hideaway while at their gravel-pit labors, they "vanished" the night of May 27. Like Vrba and Wetzler, they stayed hidden for three days, and when the initial alarm was lifted, with a lightening of the perimeter guard force, they, too, crawled free, swimming the Sola River and making their way toward Crakow. To avoid a round-up of forced-laborers, however, they had to change their plan. Riding on the roof of an overcrowded passenger train, they headed instead for Rosin's native Slovakia, which they reached after a trek through forestland. They also made the right contacts and reported on the events in Auschwitz, and still the outside world did little in response.

All told, there were 230 escape attempts by the thousands of prisoners sent to Auschwitz during the war years. Only about 80 inmates were successful. Eighty was a handful, relatively, but what a remarkable handful!

> From Erich Kulka's "Five Escapes from Auschwitz" in *They Fought Back*, edited by Yuri Suhl (Erich Kulka, with his 12-year-old son, escaped from Auschwitz during its evacuation by the Germans in January 1945 prior to its dismantling.); and from *Shoah: An Oral History of the Holocaust*, text of the film by Claude Lanzmann (Pantheon Books, New York, 1985)

# ■ *Remarkable Delaying Action*

A smalltown boy like Alvin York, he came from Right, Tennessee. He joined the New Deal's CCC—Civilian Conservation Corps—at age 17, and he joined the U.S. Army on December 1, 1942, his 21st birthday.

Two years later, of another December day, Tech Sergeant Vernon McGarity was a squad leader in Company L, 393rd Infantry Regiment, 99th Infantry Division, on the line near a place in Belgium called Krinkelt. That morning, December 16, 1944, the great German counteroffensive to be known as the Battle of the Bulge opened with an intensive artillery barrage. McGarity suffered a painful wound right then, but he was not yet ready to bow out.

*He made his way to an aid station, received treatment, and then refused to be evacuated, choosing to return to his hard-pressed men instead.*

With tanks and infantry swarming from out the snow-clad Ardennes, they needed him.

*The fury of the enemy's great Western Front offensive swirled about the position held by T/Sgt. McGarity's small force, but so tenaciously did these men fight on orders to stand firm at all costs that they could not be dislodged despite murderous enemy fire and the breakdown of their communications.*

Squad leader McGarity braved the same fire at one point to go forward and rescue a wounded comrade. During the night that

175

followed, he continued to exhort his men to fend off the swarming Germans.

*When morning came and the Germans attacked with tanks and infantry, he braved heavy fire to run to an advantageous position where he immobilized the enemy's lead tank with a round from a rocket launcher.*

That done, his squad laid down murderous fire of its own that again drove off the German infantry, plus three supporting tanks. McGarity in the meantime rescued another wounded American, then directed "devastating fire" on a light cannon the Germans had brought forward.

But now the squad's ammunition was running short—McGarity knew there was more ammunition stashed in a hole about 100 yards ahead of his squad's defensive line, in the direction of the enemy. He went and retrieved the ammo, despite "a concentration of heavy fire."

The Germans, meanwhile, circled the squad's position and managed to set up a machine-gun emplacement to its rear—along the squad's only prospective route of withdrawal.

*Unhesitatingly, the gallant soldier took it upon himself to destroy this menace singlehandedly. He left cover and while under steady fire from the enemy, killed or wounded all the hostile gunners with deadly accurate rifle fire and prevented all attempts to re-man the gun.*

But a squad is only a squad, and eventually McGarity and his men fired their last round. They would be POWs for the rest of the war, but they had done their bit—especially squad leader Vernon McGarity.

*The extraordinary bravery and extreme devotion to duty of T/Sgt. McGarity supported a remarkable delaying action which provided the time necessary for assembling reserves and forming a line against which the German striking power was shattered.*

Like his fellow Tennessean and Army Sergeant Alvin York, Vernon McGarity returned home after war's end to a Medal of Honor and various other military decorations—in McGarity's case including the Purple Heart and the POW Medal.

From *The Checkerboard*, 99th Infantry Division Association, June 1989, and Medal of Honor Citation: McGarity, Vernon

176

# ■ 'Miracles Do Happen'

From his B-24 Liberator above, navigator Jackson W. Granholm was sickened to see pilot Charles Giesen's B-24 nosing down, out of their formation over the snow-capped terrain upon which other men were fighting the Battle of the Bulge.

It was Christmas Eve, 1944, and the flak that day was incredibly heavy. Those people could really shoot, had been Granholm's unhappy thought. And now . . . now, he saw the flak burst right underneath Giesen's big ship, and it nosed down. "There was no external sign of damage to his airplane . . . no fire, no feathering engines."

Yet, "Suddenly, the whole tail section of Charlie's airplane fell off, taking the tail gunner down."

Mesmerized and horrified, Granholm had to keep on watching. "I looked anxiously for hatches to open, for crewmen to leap out, for the bomb bay to spill forth escaping people. There was nothing, no sign of anyone bailing out."

As Granholm's own Liberator churned onward, Giesen's stricken ship hit the ground with impact creating a "vast ball of fire." It appeared the entire crew rode the ship into the ground.

From another angle, another U.S. 8th Air Force crewman saw a slightly different, albeit still grim, scenario. He saw the ship break into three distinct parts—front complete with wings, tail end alone and mid-section of the fuselage.

Still, with such a mid-air "hit," how could anyone have survived?

Al Wolak of Foley, Minnesota, did. He was the left waist gunner that day, and he agrees with Granholm that the flak they ran into "was to be the most accurate and intense of any mission we'd ever been on." (For Giesen and crew, this was, in fact, Mission 23.)

Wolak recalls two hits, and then he blacked out. He came to in his waist section of the Liberator, apparently alone. He was unsure how long he had been "out." The waist section was "floating down like a falling leaf,"

Wolak tried to gather his wits, figure out what was next. "I got to my knees and wiped the blood from my eyes and face, saw my chest pack lying beside me and snapped it on. My steel helmet was lying there, too, with the front part smashed in, and that is how I got knocked out, I believe."

Oddly, Wolak felt in no great rush to depart his gently falling waist section. His unreasoning impulse was to stay with this light, balanced "leaf" floating in space. Fortunately, he knew better, and he leaped free, to truly float down to earth beneath a parachute.

On the ground, the Germans were waiting—Wolak would be retired from the war as a POW. No surprise in that, considering the circumstances, but just ahead would be a joyous and unexpected discovery after all. "I met the tail gunner and our co-pilot in a German prison camp!"

Their stories? The tail gunner, after his lone and severed section careened downward on its own, had bailed out at 2,000 feet. The co-pilot very nearly went all the way down with the Liberator's front section. Shaken by one flak hit, he was looking about the damaged cockpit "and then there was another explosion, and when he came to he was hanging in his parachute just above the ground."

Chancing many years later upon Granholm's eyewitness account of that day, Al Wolak in Foley, Minnesota, not only leaped from his chair, but also hastened to write: "As terrible as it looked to you, Mr. Granholm, and to the other boys up there that day, believe now, as I do, that miracles do happen."

From Jackson W. Granholm and Al Wolak in World War II Magazine, May and September 1988.

# ■ *Platoon's Heroics At The Bulge*

Bastogne, St. Vith . . . such are the place-names that usually symbolize American heroics and stubbornness in the Battle of the Bulge. But there also was a small town named Lanzerath, just south of the Losheimergraben crossroads on the northern shoulder of the long battle line that became known as the Bulge.

Lanzerath, you might say, was at the western end of a *funnel* through the Ardennes—at the opposite end was the German village of Losheim. In between, the corridor was the Losheim Gap. Germany had used the corridor to pour her troops into Belgium in World War I, and again at the start of the campaign against France and the Low Countries in May 1940, Rommel himself came right through the same Losheim Gap.

As the Battle of the Bulge began, 18 young Americans would be posted on the northern lip of that same funnel into Belgium, on a hillside overlooking the town of Lanzerath. And as the great German counteroffensive of the war began that morning, December 16, 1944, the main thrust was assigned to the Sixth SS Panzer Army in the same sector of the Ardennes front. A swarm of infantry, closely followed by tanks, would lead the desperate attack.

Aligned opposite the Germans here was the U.S. First Army, stretched out along a lengthy front reaching from Aachen to lower Luxembourg. After rolling eastward to the Siegfried Line in the weeks since the Normandy invasion in early June, the Allied armies liberating Europe had outrun their supply lines and had to stop and consolidate before mounting the final plunge into Germany itself.

In the center of the thin Allied line was the American V Corps, and of its three infantry divisions, the newly arrived 99th held the center front's southern sector, from Monschau down to Lanzerath and the Losheim Gap, a 21-mile stretch called the "ghost front" because of difficult terrain and forests expected to impede any German attack. As fate would have it, the division's 394th Infantry Regiment held the V Corps' southern flank and was positioned directly athwart the Sixth SS Panzer's proposed thrust.

For the Germans attacking all across the Ardennes front, north, center and south, speed in reaching key objectives was the name of the game. They had to shock their enemy, overwhelm his thin lines, disrupt his communications and penetrate quickly as possible. The offensive could not otherwise be sustained.

And they did shock and stun, they did disrupt communications, they did penetrate in many sectors . . . but they soon began to fall behind the all-important timetable. On the northern shoulder, one major reason was the 394th Infantry stationed all around Losheimergraben.

In the confusion of battle and deliberate disruption of communications, it was a series of small unit, sometimes even individual actions that held up Sixth Panzer Commander Sepp Dietrich's powerful thrust westward.

The artillery barrage announcing the Battle of the Bulge began at 5:30 a.m. It lasted for two hours.

The 394th's Intelligence and Reconnaissance Platoon was posted that morning at the town of Lanzerath to help fill a gap of more than seven miles between the V Corps' southern flank and the next American corps to the south, the VIII. The platoon thus was the southernmost unit of the V Corps.

Holding the south flank of his regiment, division and entire corps was platoon leader Lyle Bouck, a first lieutenant about to turn 21 the next day. He had established his men in log-covered foxholes on a small hill northwest of, and looking down upon, Lanzerath. Situated in the town itself were elements of a tank destroyer outfit that represented the VIII Corps' northernmost unit.

Bouck was counting upon the Americans in the town to provide warning of any German attack, since they had a better view of the approach from the German end of the Losheim Gap, the only natural funnel of appreciable size on the Ardennes Front.

The opening artillery barrage December 16 only briefly struck in Bouck's vicinity and soon lifted for more distant targets to the west, behind. But Bouck then was dismayed to see the men of the tank destroyer outfit hurriedly pull out—the village of Lanzerath suddenly was left empty.

Hustling down into the village with a few of his men, Bouck found a vantage point in the top floor of a building, looked down the road beyond the small town and saw a German column headed his way. He left two men in the town as an outpost and radioed the information to his headquarters staff. He was not entirely believed (the scope of the Ardennes offensive took hours to become fully appreciated at many points up and down the American front).

Soon, lead elements of the crack German 9th *Fallschirmjager* (Parachute) Regiment, 3rd Parachute Division, reached the village streets while Bouck watched from his hillside position. He would have waited for more of the Germans to come into range, but a blond-haired girl ran into the street and apparently alerted them. Bouck's platoon, 17 men, immediately opened fire, catching many of the enemy before they could take cover.

At least a full battalion now was alerted to the American platoon's presence. And it responded to the seemingly minor impediment with predictable fury.

For reasons unknown, however, the Germans foolishly, time and again, attacked across more than 100 yards of open ground before the hill, with no artillery support. They were cut down time and again. Bouck, himself, called for artillery fire from his distant rear but received little. Below him, as the minutes, then hours, passed, the dead Germans piled up. His men didn't like shooting such easy targets.

Radioing headquarters for instructions for his vastly outnumbered platoon, Bouck was told, ''Hold at all costs.''

The day, the untenable situation, stretched on, a mere platoon holding off the lead battalion of an entire German regiment. By afternoon, though, the platoon's ammunition was practically gone. Bouck told his radio operator that they had done all they could do, and anybody who wanted to leave, withdraw, could do so.

His radioman, Private William J. Tsakanikas, said he would go only if Bouck left, too. But Bouck said: "No, I have orders to hold at all costs. I'm staying."

In the end, no platoon member left the isolated position, except for two messengers Bouck used as runners to regimental head-quarters. The Germans, in their overwhelming numbers, finally eliminated the stubborn obstacle in their path with an assault from one flank. They systematically "cleared" the line of foxholes with MP40 submachine guns until every American was killed or taken prisoner. Bouck was among the latter. So was his radioman Tsakanikas, horribly wounded.

By then it was late afternoon; it had taken the German paratroopers eight precious hours to eliminate the few stubborn Americans holding them up at Lanzerath.

Likewise, all up and down the V Corps' southern flank, various elements of the 394th had held up the German advance at various points during the same day. One of those actions was at the Losheimergraben crossroads itself. By late afternoon, December 16, the advancing Germans had cleared most of the crossroads area, but a small group of Americans in houses at the intersection still blocked the way for the German 48th Grenadier Regiment. Finally, the Grenadiers' commander, Wilhelm Osterhold, shouted from behind a nearby building in English that there was no way the handful of GIs could hold out any longer. He threatened them with obvious mayhem from an American anti-tank mine thrown through the window of their building if they didn't surrender. They did, and Osterhold personally led them out of the building, and soon they shuffled down a road into Germany as POWs.

They could hold their heads high, though—they and their fallen compatriots at the crossroads had held up Osterhold's entire regiment for a full day.

Individual initiative at small-unit level is what the military calls it . . . and that's what the scattered pockets of the 394th practiced that grim day in the face of overwhelming assault by a long pent-up torrent of enemy forces.

The delays thus inflicted would be fatal to the German time-table on the key northern shoulder of the Bulge.

It often was the same story all up and down the American line. Neither the 394th nor the entire American force along the Ardennes was able, on that first day, to turn back Hitler's great counteroffensive, but small, brave actions here and there contributed to eventual victory by the delays they cost the enemy. Every delay like Lanzerath placed the Sixth SS Panzer Army further behind its crucial schedule.

Massive and overwhelming attack up and down the line at dawn the next day, the 17th, forced the 394th's withdrawal to Hunningen and, later, to the Elsenborn Ridge. Thanks to the small-unit actions at places such as Lanzerath or the Losheimergraben crossroads, however, Sepp Dietrich's Sixth Panzer Army was off to a fatally slowed start.

From "394th Infantry, Battle of the Bulge," by Captain Stephen Rusiecki in *The Checkerboard*, 99th Infantry Division Association, February 1989; and *A Time For Trumpets: The Untold Story of the Battle of the Bulge* by Charles B. MacDonald (William Morrow and Company, Inc., New York, N.Y., 1985)

# ■ *Practice Makes Perfect*

Late December 1944, and 1st Lieut. Harley L. Brown of the 55th Fighter Squadron, 20th Fighter Group, was at 25,000 feet over friendly territory test-firing the guns on his P-51 Mustang. He began a "big slow roll" to see how his speedy mount would react while he fired the guns on his back—upsidedown.

The Mustang didn't react well at all. "When I pulled the trigger, my Mustang stalled and I fell into an inverted spin."

After dropping several thousand feet, the startled young pilot recovered, but his ship then fell into a normal spin. And still dropping.

This went on for quite a while. First one spin, then recover, only to revert into the other spin. Ground coming up pretty fast by now. "I lost 15,000 feet fighting those damn spins."

Finally recovering at 10,000 feet, Brown realized what his mistake was, took his ship back up to 25,000 and threw her into another spin, intentionally this time. He recovered in 3,000 feet and in short time flew on home to base in England.

Three weeks later, those spins—and his mastery of them—probably saved his life.

This time he and his faithful Mustang were above German territory, near Magdeburg. Two to three thousand feet below, he spotted a German Me 109. Brown nosed down into a dive to close up and take on a dogfight that either would establish him as an ace with five kills . . . or possibly end the other way. One never knew.

He closed, and the German headed straight up, into a vertical climb. The American P-51D followed right behind. "I kept giving him short bursts and pieces of debris kept falling all around me." The moment finally came when Brown and his Mustang were within 20 yards of the 109, just under him . . . but neither plane was destined to reach the crest of their hill. Both now faltered and at nearly the same moment stalled out.

That meant, naturally, that each would collapse into a spin. And they did. "We fell several thousand feet spinning almost in formation. That black cross on his fuselage looked big as a barn!"

But here is where Brown's earlier practice session came into play—vital play for him. "I recovered from the spin and got on him just as he recovered."

Brown now had the advantage, but even then, it wasn't easy. This was his "toughest" dog fight, and the German pilot the smartest he ever had encountered in the air.

"The next three or four minutes he used the most evasive tactics I ever experienced, turning left and right, climbing and diving and slowing down." At one point, Brown had to drop his flaps, lower his landing gear and fire his six 50-calibers to keep from plowing right into the suddenly slowing 109—or streaking on past to become the hunted instead of hunter.

In the end, though, his guns found the mark. The 109 in front abruptly blew up, with just the wing tips and tail left "fluttering to the ground."

Brown "in a way . . . was sorry to see him go." But he also knew the practice spins three weeks before had saved him, since otherwise "Jerry would have recovered first and probably got me!" Instead, 1st Lt. Harley L. Brown reached ace status with his fifth air victory.

From *King's Cliffe Remembered*, 20th Fighter Group Association, Vol. 6, No. 2, Summer 1988

# ■ Fateful Tea Party

The tea party was held at the home of Elizabeth von Thadden, former headmistress and founder of a boarding school in Germany. Present were several associates in the German Resistance movement—among them, the Widow Solf and her daughter and Helmuth James Graf von Moltke, legal adviser to the German High Command and great-grandnephew of the famous Field Marshal Helmuth von Moltke.

Forced by the Nazi regime to leave her beloved school, hostess von Thadden had joined the Red Cross and the sputtering German Resistance. She and Frau Solf, widow of a former Colonial Minister for pre-war Germany, were the leaders of the Solf *Kreis* (Circle) near Heidelberg. Frau Solf and daughter Grafin Ballestrem had been active in quiet opposition to Hitler and in helping Jews to escape Nazi persecution.

Von Moltke, a distinguished young lawyer, had used his position as an adviser in the foreign office of the High Command to help hostages, prisoners of war and forced laborers, but would be best known for his *Kreisau* Circle, composed of bright young Germans who hoped to replace the Hitler regime with a morally based government.

The "Solf Tea Party" was fateful because of the presence of a newcomer to the group, a young doctor named Reckzeh who claimed to be a Swiss national. He persuaded Frau Solf to entrust him with a letter she wanted smuggled to contacts in neutral Switzerland.

Four months later, in January 1944, all who had attended the tea party, the hostess included, were arrested—"Dr. Reckzeh" had been a spy for the Gestapo. As a result, both the Solf and Kreisau Circles were broken up.

As time passed, all were executed, one by one—Elizabeth von Thadden on September 8, 1944; von Moltke on January 23, 1945.

All, that is, except for Frau Solf and her daughter. Their turn was coming, though. They would go on trial early in February 1945 before the widely dreaded People's Court Judge Roland Freisler, who had sent von Moltke and many others to their deaths for plots or imagined plots against Hitler and the Nazi regime.

Totally without mercy, Freisler was noted for the abuse he directed at the helpless prisoners brought before his bench. He had sent von Moltke, a conscientious Christian, to his death with the comment: "The mask is off. Only in one respect are we and Christianity alike: we demand the whole man."

Certain death also awaited Frau Solf and her daughter as their turn came for an appearance before Freisler's court in the plenary chamber of the Berlin Law Courts. But that very morning, February 3, 1945, a bomb from an American daylight air raid on Berlin ripped into the building and Freisler was killed right in his courtroom. Destroyed with him was the dossier on the Solf case.

A few weeks later, on April 23, the miraculously spared widow and her daughter were released from the Moabit Prison—by mistake. The war in Europe ended two weeks later. They were the only surviving conspirators from the tea party held on September 10, 1943, at the home of Elizabeth von Thadden.

From *Encyclopedia of the Third Reich* by Louis L. Snyder (Paragon House, New York, N.Y., 1976)

# ■ A Southpaw's Cruel Fate

Even in the midst of hot combat there can be the most accidental, totally chance tragedy, startling and dismaying to even the most battle-hardened onlookers. During the liberation of Manila, for instance, sheer accident called upon U.S. Army 2nd Lt. Robert M. Viale, a native of Bayside, California, to make the supreme sacrifice.

It was February 5, 1945, and Viale was leading his 1st Platoon, 148th Infantry Regiment, 37th Infantry Division, toward a small bridge. Held up by fire from three Japanese pillboxes nearby, he and two companions dashed across the bridge behind a grenade-laid smoke screen. He knocked out one of the pillboxes; the other two were taken out by various of his platoon members.

Fatefully, Viale had suffered "a painful" wound in his right arm. He and his platoon couldn't stay where they were, either —their planned pathway into the city had been blocked minutes before by enemy demolitions. Now, after crossing the small bridge, they pushed ahead "through mortar fire and encircling flames." Ahead, though, their only escape route was blocked by a machine gun placed at a street corner.

Searching for ways to overcome the latest impediment, Viale led his men into a nearby building. In one room were civilians "huddled together." In another, close enough to the machine gun, was a high, small window with a ladder leading up to it.

One of his men, a right-hander, tried to toss a grenade from the window, but the angle was wrong. Being, himself, left-handed, Viale decided he could get the angle with a southpaw throw.

Taking an armed grenade, he started up the ladder. But his wounded right arm failed him—as he tried to steady himself, the armed grenade fell to the floor of the room.

*In the five seconds before the grenade would explode, he dropped down, recovered the grenade and looked for a place to dispose of it safely. Finding no way to get rid of the grenade without exposing his own men or the civilians to injury or death, he turned to the wall, held it close to his body and bent over it as it exploded. Second Lt. Viale died in a few minutes, but his heroic act saved the lives of others.*

From Medal of Honor Citation: Viale, Robert M.

## ■ Maybe They're Still There

Navy Doctor Richard Hamilton had never seen anything quite like it in his young life. Offshore from a small volcanic island in the far Pacific, he was aboard the transport attack ship USS *Mellette* as for three days the big U.S. Navy ships around him simply pounded the island. From the battleships behind, the shells whistled overhead, and on the hapless island looming in front, leaping bursts of black, volcanic dust.

And then came the aircraft, what appeared to be *hundreds* of carrier-based dive-bombers. Surely their added ordnance would "sink the island." And surely, nobody on that island could survive so awesome a pasting!

But an officer with the grimly awaiting men of the 4th Marine Division thought otherwise. "Don't let this fool you," he told Hamilton, a recent graduate of medical school at Kentucky's University of Louisville. "They are still there."

In 1,500 fortified caves, in a network of interlocking tunnels, pillboxes, blockhouses, tunnels and plain old trenches, *they*, 21,000 Japanese defenders, *were* still there. For the pasting of their island, a mere 700 miles south of Japan, they merely ducked under. They didn't fire back. Figuratively, they didn't move. They merely waited.

Even before the Marines climbed down to their landing craft the morning of February 19, 1945, the young medical officer felt the somber mood that had taken over the transport ship. "There were no more jokes, no laughing, only silence. It was obvious that some were praying. He saw fear in their eyes. Some were trembling with fear. It was very serious now."

Hamilton, left behind on his ship, idle for the moment, could only watch as the first landing wave went in, the beaches black with their volcanic sand. And . . . nothing! With his binoculars: "He could even follow his navy medical team as they landed and set up their aid station without a shot being fired." And still, "It was like watching something going on across the street." He watched the Marines move in from the beach. So far he on his ship and his medical team on shore had nothing to do —no business.

One second they didn't, the next they did. As in concert, the waiting defenders and their instruments of death filled the air with noise, with shot and shell for all those distant tiny men on the beach shelf, and for the landing barges still nosing in. So intense was it, as well as so sudden, that Hamilton now was sure the Marines couldn't possibly cling on. Either they'd "be killed or be pushed back into the ocean."

In minutes, too, the 13·doctors and 40 medics aboard his ship were overwhelmed with the wounded hurriedly carried back from shore. And nothing in his training was preparation for the sights that now greeted him—a leg gone, a face shattered, or even worse. "But the most difficult thing for him were the combat fatigue cases. On a given day, the stress of battle with noises, sights, orders and constant threat to life and limbs was too much for some men."

They were, he recalls, "scared to death!" Many of them, trembling uncontrollably, could not calm down. "He learned that no medicine would relax them like two 2-ounce bottles of brandy."

Some he could send back to battle, others not.

For the Navy doctor, the battle of Iwo Jima lasted for 10 nightmarish days before his ship moved on to Saipan; for the Marines on Iwo, those surviving it all, the battle would last until March 26.

Off Okinawa not long after (April 1-July 2, 1945), Hamilton more personally came to know the fear of imminent death, just as his patients ashore did, since at Okinawa the supporting fleet endured weeks of *kamikaze* air attacks by suicidal Japanese pilots (who sank 26 ships in the process). Later still, the war by now stopped, the young American doctor was near Nagasaki. He saw a group of Japanese children who responded to the presence of Americans in sheer panic. "They ran into each other, and into things as they tried to get away. It was like a wild animal trying to outrun a bigger and faster predator."

Still, he wouldn't change the way the war ended—with The Bomb. "Without it, we never would have whipped them."

From Col. Arthur L. Kelly, USA (Ret.), in the
*Springfield* (Ky.) *Sun.*, May 25, June 1,
June 8, 1988

# ■ *Aboard An 'Apartment Ship'*

Smalltowner William Rowe decided on the Navy for its "better life" than the other branches of wartime service. "You had a decent place to sleep, no C-ration, no foxholes. As long as the ship was not shot out from under you, I figured it would be okay."

*As long as . . .*

After his initial training at Great Lakes Training Center near Chicago, he received his orders. Troop train to the West Coast. Then another train up the coast to Bremerton Navy Yard on Puget Sound, near Seattle, Washington. He then saw his "decent place to sleep" for the first time—the newly built U.S. aircraft carrier *Bunker Hill*.

She struck him as quite a sight. "When I first saw it, I thought to myself, 'I'm going on there?' I thought I was looking at an apartment building. It was a little city, with its own library, canteen and chapels."

Perhaps more impressive yet, her "crew of 3,200 men totaled almost as many people as I had left back in Painesdale (his hometown in Michigan)."

188

The *Bunker Hill* set sail for the Pacific, and she soon was on station to support the American landings at Iwo Jima. "I had experienced a large volume of noise from the drilling in Michigan copper mines, but Iwo Jima was something else. I'll tell you, the noise was really deafening, with both ships and planes hitting the island."

Seaman 2nd Class Rowe, a loader for a 20mm gun mount, began to see—and experience—things that would *not* have been commonplace for the infantry or the air corps. Like when, in that famous 1945 typhoon off Okinawa, the ship swayed so much her flight deck dipped into the water on one side. Or: "Sometimes the screws lifted out of the water, and when they did, the whole ship vibrated. That was scary."

One time, too, Seaman Rowe was on overhead lookout, a four-hour watch that he undertook by lying on the deck and staring straight up—"I was to focus my attention on the airspace immediately above the carrier."

He did, but still he was pretty startled when suddenly, "a Jap bomber broke through, coming right at us." Rowe was supposed to holler a warning to the other guys in his gun crew, "but I was so scared that nothing came out."

The enemy craft then released a bomb—"and it looked like the bomb was coming right at me, but it fell 50 feet short of our carrier."

When his crewmates upbraided him for failing to yell a warning, Rowe explained he simply had frozen. "So they said, 'Next time, Rowe, say anything at all—like son of a bitch, or something.'"

*Next time*, though, would be a lot more serious. During the campaign against Okinawa that April, the Japanese responded with their most intense *kamikaze* effort yet—suicide planes willfully crashing into American ships. The sailors aboard all ships felt the danger, but especially those on the carriers, prime targets in anybody's navy.

"We were living 24 hours a day on a floating target. This thought was always present, but especially so at Okinawa where Japan used the *kamikaze*. We constantly thought of being an open target. . . . It was like living on a large bull's eye."

And then came May 11, 1945. The men of the *Bunker Hill* were at "Condition Easy" at 10:45 that morning—manning battle stations, but with the leisure to read or write letters while others kept watch. Quite suddenly, not one, but two, *kamikazes* broke through the nearby clouds. How they eluded the fire of surrounding, lesser ships was a question no one had time to ponder. They were there, upon the *Bunker Hill,* before anyone could react.

The first one, a Zero, dropped a bomb that penetrated the wooden flight deck, went through a section of hull and exploded over the water. The Zero itself, however, turned for the 30 American planes bunched up on the after flight deck, all fully armed and loaded with aviation fuel—12,000 gallons of it. The Zero hit the aircraft parking lot directly, then bounced on into the ocean, an inferno springing up behind.

Just 30 seconds later, the second *kamikaze* came in—a dive-bomber coming down in "an almost vertical dive" until it struck. "The plane hit midships, about 40 feet away from me, flipped over, hit the superstructure (the carrier's 'island') and shook the whole ship." The dive-bomber's heavy engine careened onward by itself and killed 14 men in the "flag office" of task force commander (Admiral) Marc Mitscher. As the two suicide planes impacted and set off explosions and massive fires, Rowe was on a catwalk beneath the after flight deck. Stunned by the first impact, he explained before his death in 1988, "I ran out to my battery and yelled, 'What the hell is this?' " Moments later, the after section of the ship a lake of fire, he had a momentous personal decision to make. With his area hemmed in by advancing flames, the only escape was "over the side." But *over the side* meant a risky drop to the ocean far below. Rowe climbed over a gun mount's splinter shield and was hanging on to the outside of it. "It must have been an 80-foot drop to the ocean, so I tried to get back into the gun mount because I didn't want to jump. I couldn't do it, though, and that probably saved me from burning to death." What did he do? "Finally, I let go—it's amazing what you'll do when you have to." Rowe hit the water safely enough, despite the long drop, but he was not yet out of danger. He had no life jacket, and he landed in the huge ship's wake. The tumbling water action pushed him down like a giant hand. He tried to claw back to the surface, "but it was more difficult than I imagined." Finally, though, he did.

He found a floating life jacket, grabbed it, then shared it with an injured shipmate who had none. Soon four survivors in all had formed a small supportive ring in the ocean waters, three helping the injured man.

After two hours, a destroyer picked them all up.

Aboard the *Bunker Hill*, meanwhile, surviving sailors and their officers were doing their best to save the grievously wounded vessel—three of her decks on fire from amidships to stern; flight deck buckled; armor plating peeled away; aircraft elevators hamstrung; the 30 targetted planes in ashes.

Crewmen tossed hot bombs and rockets overboard. The ship's skipper, Captain George Seitz, did his valuable bit by making a difficult, 70-degree turn that shifted the carrier's list in the opposite direction and thus sent quantities of fuel and ammunition spilling harmlessly off the flight deck into the ocean. He also had turned broadside to the wind, a maneuver blowing the smoke and flames away from the ship.

With such effort, the *Bunker Hill* was saved; she limped all the way back to Bremerton Navy Yard outside Seattle under her own power for extensive repair, with William Rowe once again aboard his "apartment" ship—but on this cruise helping to clean up and prepare dead shipmates for burials at sea.

When the *Bunker Hill* arrived Stateside, *Time* Magazine said she "ranked next to the *Franklin* as the most cruelly ravaged U.S. ship ever to reach port under her own power." For both the *Bunker Hill* (see main cover photo) and William Rowe, the Pacific War ended before they could replenish themselves and return to battle. Rowe, like many others, was just as glad.

He heard about the end of the war on board his battle-scarred ship. "I was in the shower getting ready to go on liberty when I heard hooting and hollering. A guy came in and said the war was over. I didn't go on my liberty. Instead, I thought how wonderful it was to be over and that I was alive, and I realized I wouldn't have to go into battle action again. Funny, I could go on liberty like all the rest of the crew, but I wanted to be alone at a time when everyone else wanted to be together."

From interview by John F. Wukovits, *Military History*
Magazine, December 1988

# ■ *Obituary*

The woman before Arthur Goldberg, head of the American OSS' Labor Bureau in London and later destined to serve on the

U.S. Supreme Court, was dressed plainly, even severely. A radical Socialist, she always eschewed make-up and wore her hair pulled back in a tight bun.

She would be one of the first American-recruited agents to infiltrate Germany and Austria in the latter half of 1944, and Goldberg felt "a strange foreboding" as she prepared for her mission.

Code-named "Crocus," she was to establish a network of fellow Socialists in the Vienna area. She would "go in" by way of Switzerland, along with Anne Kappius, another Socialist-labor movement believer. They would then split up, with Kappius joining her already-planted agent-husband in the Ruhr and running courier duty for him back to neutral Switzerland.

Escorting them through reoccupied France to the shores of Lake Geneva, American Lieutenant Anthony Turano of the London OSS' Air Dispatch Section was struck by the severe and studiously drab appearance of both women.

They stayed the night with a French family, and when the host somehow produced a fine dinner consisting of a large roast and white bread, the two ascetic-looking women ate only the bread. Turano felt constrained the next day to shake their hands in farewell, rather than try the comradely kiss that he normally would have bestowed.

While Anne Kappius was soon with husband Jupp and running her courier missions, "Crocus" didn't enter Austria until early 1945. When she arrived, though, she quickly put together her planned network.

Soon the time came for her to return to Switzerland with her information. At the Austrian-Swiss border, however, she was spotted by a patrol of the German SS. A sharpshooter hit her in both legs. Still conscious and reasoning despite the pain, she placed her cyanide-filled "L Pill" between her jaws and bit down. Hilde Meisel, a quiet woman in her early thirties, died before the Germans could reach her.

From *Piercing the Reich: The Penetration of Nazi Germany by American Secret Agents During World War II* by Joseph E. Persico (The Viking Press; Ballantine Books, New York, N.Y. 1979)

# ■ Hellships Three

Relatively few would survive the grim process of elimination at work in the movement of American POWs from the Philippines to Japan aboard the Japanese "Hellships." For one group, the trip meant the horrors of three different *Marus*, since two of the crowded transports were shot out from under the POWs.

The tortuous cruise began late on December 13, 1944, aboard the *Oryoku Maru*, jam-packed not only with 2,000 Japanese women and children returning to Japan, but also with 1,600 American POWs (and 37 British). The Japanese dependents had the topside living quarters for their own; the prisoners, already weak and sickly, were jammed into the cargo holds. For the dependents, the hell would begin the next morning. For the prisoners, it began right away.

Packed tightly together in the dark airless holds, they had to share food buckets and latrine buckets that passed hand to hand, often indistinguishable in the dark until too late. Many had dysentery and uncontrollable diarrhea. The air was foul, fetid. The heat was overpowering. Men could only sit or stand—no room to lie down.

The transport left Manila about 5 p.m., in company of four additional merchantmen, a cruiser escort and several destroyers. Night came. Men starved for water. Men died. Men went insane. Many killed one another. "All through the terrible night, the men in hold #5 fought, clawed and tore at each other for a breath of air. Madness, induced by the lack of oxygen, caused many men to pair off and attack their comrades. They slashed the wrists of the weak and drank the blood. Others urinated into their own canteens and drank the fluid."

The next day was hardly any better. It began with 50 of the POWs already dead. Then came the American planes—the convoy had been caught out. "The prisoners stirred apprehensively, knowing that a successful attack might be their death knell. The entire ship vibrated as each bomb straddled the vessel. After their bombing runs, the planes made wide circles and returned, strafing the ship from one end to the other. In hold #2, ricocheting bullets splattered into the (POW) doctors and corpsmen."

The airborne firepower broke open hatch covers or pierced deck planks, at last giving the POWs a breath of fresh air. At the same time, blood from wounded or dead Japanese on the ship's upper levels dripped down on the nearly naked prisoners through the same holes. Topside, the decks were covered with Japanese casualties. The ship's steering gear was knocked out, and now it headed back into Subic Bay. That evening, it ran aground 300 yards from the beach at Olongapo Naval Air Station. The POWs still were kept in the airless cargo holds, some of them crazed enough to scramble up the ladders and be shot.

The next morning, American aircraft struck again as a lifeboat was leaving the damaged ship with a few of the sickest POWs. They strafed the lifeboat, then went after the big transport itself—most of the POWs still trapped in the holds. The guards fled, and when they realized, the POWs streamed up the ladders, onto the deck above and into the water alongside. But many were killed first in the cargo holds.

Outside, the American pilots now noticed the bodies in the water by the ship were white and "waved in recognition."

By now, 250 POWs apparently had died aboard the *Oryoku Maru*; the rest were herded from the water and marched—barefoot over coral ripping their feet—to a concrete tennis court at the naval station. They stayed there in the heat of the day, the cold of the night, for 5½ days. "Every morning a roll call was made and a burial party was formed for those who had died during the night."

The American pilots still attacking every day knew the prisoners were there and avoided the tennis court with their ordnance. On the sixth and seventh days, the POWs were moved by truck to San Fernando, Pampanga, where they were housed in both a provincial jail and a movie house with its seats removed.

They received their first hot food since leaving Bilibid December 13. It was now December 22. On December 23, 15 of the sickest men were taken out of town by truck and executed by a large open grave—beheaded or bayonetted. On the 24th, Christmas Eve, the rest were packed into railroad box cars for a ride to Lingayen Gulf, where they were "housed" at an empty school. Christmas dinner was "a half cup of rice and one cup of water for every two persons." The men denuded a hibiscus hedge around the school building, consuming berries, leaves, and all.

On December 26, they were marched to the shoreline. They spent another night with no cover—on a "beach" that was sand covering "hundreds of drums of high-test gasoline buried beneath them." The next day, men dropped from sunstroke on the same hot sand. On December 27, too, the men were taken by barge to two more *Marus*—the *Brazil Maru* and the *Enoura Maru*. The

194

two transport ships soon set off in convoy with four others and destroyer escorts.

The men aboard the *Enoura Maru* were in a stifling hold most recently occupied by horses. They had to clean up the manure underfoot with their hands. Horse flies swarmed over them and into their small rice ration. Every hour or so, a man died "from dehydration, diarrhea or untended wounds." Much the same conditions prevailed aboard the *Brazil Maru*. Headed for Formosa, the convoy of six was attacked at sea by American submarines. Two transports ran that gauntlet; the rest were lost. The two were the prison ships carrying the POWs in their cargo holds.

They spent New Year's Day aboard their two *Maru*s in Takao harbor, Formosa. They stayed for several days, except that on January 6, the *Brazil* complement was transferred to the *Enoura Maru*—a total at this point of about 1,200 men still living.

Early on January 9, American aircraft attacked—the *Enoura Maru* was hit by a bomb that exploded against the hull and by at least two more striking elsewhere. Three hundred POWs were killed instantly or mortally injured, with many others wounded as well. "Despite the fact that the *Enoura Maru* was in a heavily populated harbor with doctors and hospitals in the vicinity, the Japanese refused to give any aid to the wounded Americans."

Both the wounded and the dead remained on board. "For three days and nights, the living shadows of men wandered shocked and dazed among the decaying corpses. In the crowded holds it was not uncommon to see men sitting on stacks of dead bodies."

After three days, the exhausted prisoners themselves were ordered to remove the bodies and provide a "burial" party— ashore, the men of the burial party formally saluted farewells as their 300 comrades were turned over to the Japanese for cremation. The remaining 900 prisoners now were transferred to the *Brazil Maru* for continuation of the nightmarish voyage to Japan.

On the *Enoura Maru*, they had died at the rate of about one an hour; on the *Brazil Maru*, as it cruised into colder climes, with an icy blast of air whistling into the cargo hold, they died at the rate of about 40 per day. They called the frigid swirl of air the "Wind of Death." And all knew about the "Zero Ward"—a hatch cover about eight feet below the main deck. "Whenever a man felt he could no longer go on, he would say, 'Well, boys, I have had enough. I'm going to sleep in the 'Zero Ward' tonight." Death was the only escape from the Zero Ward.

Madness still afflicted the suffering men. Back on the *Oryoku Maru*, U.S. Navy Commander Frank Bridget had been a voice of reason among the men trapped aboard the grounded prison ship. "For God's sake, men, don't leave your place," he had warned. "Every move you make generates heat. Keep fanning the air. There are people in the back who are going to die unless you sit still and keep fanning."

Now, on the *Brazil Maru*, sadly, he had suffered too much, too long. "Commander Frank Bridget was wandering about the deck, dazed and incoherent. He was discovered by the Japanese and beaten. He was thrown back down the hold, where he died the same night."

The *Brazil Maru* plodded northward toward Japan over a span of 18 days, from January 13 to January 31, 1945. During that period, and before, Chaplain William Cummings had been "a tower of religious strength" for his fellow POWs. Once a day, in the evening, he spoke simple homilies to them and offered prayer. Three days out from Japan, however, "dysentery finally caught up with the priest." He nonetheless went through with his evening ritual—lifted by others so that he could do so. That night, too, he retired to the Zero Ward, where, in hours, he joined the dead.

By the time the *Brazil Maru* docked at Moji, the nightmare voyage finally completed, only 425 survivors were left of the 900 men who had climbed aboard the *Brazil Maru* two weeks before. Before going ashore, the shivering men were hailed onto deck, told to strip naked and were sprayed on the spot with a delousing disinfectant. Pulling on his clothes a few moments later, one POW officer paused and dropped dead.

Of the surviving 425, in the days ahead, 135 were hospitalized, and 80 died. The others, the "healthiest," were sent to prison camps near Omuta and Fukouka. In six weeks, 235 of *those* men also died.

In the end, that is, at war's end, of the 1,600 who set out from Bilibid in early December, 300 survived. Said one of them: "When you speak of the good and the heroic, don't talk about us. The generous men—the brave men—the unselfish men—are the men we left behind."

In his view, the Japanese had been "bad," yes, "but we—the 300 living—we were devils, too. If we had not been devils, we could not have survived." True or untrue? Who but God would presume to judge?

From A.B. Feuer in *Bilibid Diary: The Secret Notebooks of Commander Thomas Hayes, POW, the Philippines, 1942-45*, A.B. Feuer, editor (Archon Books, Hamden, Conn., 1987)

# ■ *Rescue By Drunk Driver*

Was Corporal Roger Foehringer about to look a slightly flawed gift horse in the mouth? No way, not when it was a fully qualified, bonafide American jeep smack dab in the middle of the town square of Versbach, Germany, just outside of Wurzburg. A U.S. Army jeep complete with driver, that excited-looking fellow sitting on the hood and brandishing a .45 at a ring of Versbach's citizenry.

Foehringer, after all, an artilleryman with the U.S. 99th Infantry Division, had been captured in the Battle of the Bulge. He had been marched through snow and ice as a POW. He had been shipped into the heart of Germany in tightly-packed boxcars. He had lost weight, but survived, on a near-starvation diet. He hadn't seen a sign of a Red Cross parcel.

He and his buddies had worked in a Wurzburg military bakery as forced labor.

They had survived American strafing of a rail yard they frequented. They had survived the British night-bombing of the Bavarian city with incendiaries that turned the place into an inferno—"it was the most tremendous wind you've ever felt in your life, and the whole sky and city of Wurzburg seemed to be in flames."

He and his buddies then spent two or three days helping to clean up the debris and remove the bodies beneath, carrying them first to the street curb, then piling them into horse-drawn carts for mass burial.

197

For the next night or two, Foehringer and his four buddies of the bakery detail "saw the sky lit up and we started to hear rumbles and we knew the front was coming." On Easter Sunday, April 1, 1945, their captors decided to move them back, away from the advancing Americans.

Again, it was on foot, by a side road. At a rest break, the five took a planned nature call in the nearby woods and simply didn't go back. Their POW column moved on without them—no one seemed to care.

Friendly Germans a day later showed them a cave in a hillside near the village of Versbach. They hid there for a few days, with two young boys bringing them food once a day. Then, late one afternoon, the two boys showed up with the news that the Americans had come!

Rushing down to the village square, the five American escapees found the waiting jeep and its sergeant-driver.

The only trouble was, he was what today we call a DUI—drunk! He didn't have the vaguest idea where he was, or how he got there. Moreover, he was far ahead of the front lines—he was totally alone.

A mechanic with a tank destroyer unit, he had been drinking somewhere to the far rear and decided to "go up to the front and find out where his buddies were, the guys that drove the tank destroyers."

Soon lost, he "had just come through the lines with the jeep—nobody had bothered him, he had just gone right down the road toward Wurzburg."

Now, of course, he wanted to find his way back. Foehringer and his fellow POWs were more than glad to oblige—and ride along.

First, they opened up the jeep's foot locker and spread its "goodies" among the onlooking townspeople—cans of food, candy, K-bars and the like. The POWs thanked their benefactors, climbed aboard the jeep and began their return after pointing the driver to the highway back to Wurzburg.

They soon came across the signs of battle—"burning German half-tracks, dead soldiers lying outside the road."

At first there was no sign of their fellow Americans, but then, quite suddenly, "along came a line of infantry on either side of the road and of course it was an American infantry and on their helmets were their insignias." It was the 42nd ("Rainbow") Division—a welcome sight for the escaping POWs. And they a welcome sight themselves for the wary GIs of the 42nd, who were "expecting Germans before they saw a jeep with a bunch of Americans hanging on the sides."

From Roger Foehringer in *The Checkerboard*,
99th Infantry Division Association,
Vol. 42, No. 2, March 1989

# ■ *Aliases For FDR*

It struck Harry Truman as an odd, indeed a foreboding remark. In a luncheon meeting at the White House on August 18, 1944, he and Franklin Delano Roosevelt were discussing their plans for the 1944 presidential campaign. For the fourth time, FDR was at the head of the Democratic ticket, and for the first time, Missouri Senator Truman would be FDR's running mate.

Roosevelt had not attended the Democratic National Convention that nominated them, and so Truman had not seen the President and Commander-in-Chief for a while.

He was appalled at what he saw on this day—a man who "talked with difficulty," who shook so badly that he missed his coffee cup when pouring cream from a small pitcher, who physically was "just going to pieces."

But he was mentally alert. Innocently, Truman said something about using an airplane in the coming campaign. Oh, no, said FDR—"One of us has to stay alive."

The fact is, Roosevelt was suffering from cardiovascular disease and never should have run for a fourth term . . . not in normal times. But this was war, and perhaps that's what he had in mind when he publicly announced he was seeking re-election in 1944 as a "good soldier."

But was he fit to continue as Commander-in-Chief? How would the voters have reacted if they had known just how ill their polio-crippled President was? Only his doctors and the inner circle of the White House were aware that in the three to four months before the Normandy invasion of June 6, 1944, illness kept Roosevelt away from his Oval Office half of the same time period. Only a privileged handful were aware that the same sick man visited the Bethesda Naval Hospital at least 29 times from 1941 to his death in 1945—using 29 aliases, such as "Mr. Delano," "James D. Elliott," "Ralph Frank," "Rolphe Frank," "George Adams," or "John Cash."

That FDR himself felt the shadow looming over him can hardly be doubted, and not only because of his remark to running-mate Truman. They won, of course, and on inaugural day itself in early 1945, FDR huddled with son James to ask help in ordering his papers and other affairs, to explain his will and, on the spot, to pass on a family ring that FDR removed from his own hand.

James was upset, naturally, and later he said that 1944 campaign was his father's "death warrant." From the time of the campaign to inaugural day, January 21, 1945, he only saw his father twice, and, "Each time I realized with awful irrevocable certainty that we were going to lose him."

Eleanor Roosevelt asked the White House staff "not to push the President too hard."

Still ahead for FDR in those closing weeks of the war in Europe was the all-important Yalta Conference with Winston Churchill and Joseph Stalin. Simply to make the trip, much less debate the post-war shape of Europe with such titans of the world stage, FDR had to travel eight days by ship, fly another 1,200 miles (at low altitudes due to his precarious condition) and finally drive 80 miles on a Crimean road so bad that the drive alone took six hours.

The argument over FDR's alleged concessions at Yalta have persisted ever since. Did he, mesmerized or bullied by Stalin, "give away" Eastern Europe? Did he, recognizing the reality of Red Army presence in Eastern Europe already, win Stalin's agreement to FDR's own goals, such as continued support for the establishment of the United Nations? Or was FDR too ill to hold his own in any case?

Participants at the conference were stunned and saddened at FDR's appearance. His Ambassador to Moscow, Averell Harriman, saw "signs of deterioration" that were "unmistakable." And Churchill, old ally and friend Churchill, was unhappily struck, too. "His captivating smile, his gay and charming manner, had not deserted him, but his face had a transparency, an air of purification, and often there was a far-away look in his eyes."

The difficult conference ran from February 4 to February 11. Roosevelt then met with Mid-East leaders in Egypt (and Churchill again), then returned to Washington, where he faced an address to a joint session of Congress. For the first time in a congressional appearance, he spoke while seated, explaining in attempted jest that he was tired out by "so much metal" on his legs (his braces).

With the San Francisco conference launching the UN soon to come, FDR then traveled to his favorite resting place of Warm Springs, Georgia, where he would prepare his keynote address for the UN gathering that meant so much to him.

That was on March 29, and shortly before, somewhat mysteriously, a Secret Service detail appeared on Vice President Harry Truman's circuit for the first time. Margaret Truman, his daughter, later wrote that the assignment was arranged by Truman aide Harry Vaughn, but Vaughn in a post-war interview asserted the Secret Service just appeared one day with no explanation for their presence.

On April 12, still in Warm Springs, FDR awoke with a slight headache. It passed after a light massage, and later, about midday he was going over paperwork and sitting for a portrait when he suddenly started, rubbed his forehead, and slumped forward. His last words were: "I've got a terrific headache."

It was nearly 1:15 p.m., and he remained unconscious but alive until 3:31 p.m., when his breathing stopped. He was pronounced dead at 3:35 p.m. Harry Truman, late that afternoon, was called to the White House. He arrived at 5:25 p.m., and Eleanor Roosevelt, who had not made the trip to Warm Springs, told him what had happened. Truman was sworn in as FDR's successor shortly after 7 p.m. in the White House itself.

Churchill, on hearing the news, felt "a physical blow." Stalin's Soviet Union lowered its flags to half mast and bordered them in black. Hitler's propagandist Joseph Gobbels called his *Führer*, and said: "I congratulate you—Roosevelt is dead." And in Japan, the other great enemy, oddly, Prime Minister Kantaro Suzuki offered the American people "profound sympathy" for the loss of a leader who could take credit for "the Americans' advantageous position today."

From *Hidden Illness in the White House* by Kenneth R. Crispell and Carlos F. Gomez (Duke University Press, Durham, N.C., 1988)

# ◼ *Flowers On Their Graves*

In wartime Germany, "the mood of the people became rather bad." People didn't smile any more. "Many families had lost a son, two sons, a father, or a husband fighting on the Russian front or in the Balkans. Many came home seriously wounded or maimed for life."

Gertrud Breier's two older brothers were drafted. "Helmuth, a flyer, didn't return from a flight over the Atlantic. My older brother, Fritz, deserted the air force and found a safe refuge in Denmark with a farmer."

Gertrud's mother had moved her younger children and their governess Kate to a small cabin in a mountain village, away from the small industrial city of Ludwigshafen, since it was a prime target for air raids.

Gertrud's schooling was interrupted by a year at a labor camp for girls her age—a year spent in Spartan barracks, cold showers, dull, ugly uniforms, and farm work in the surrounding countryside. A friend who was half Jewish fled and with her father successfully escaped to Denmark, where they also found refuge on a farm for the rest of the war.

After the year's labor camp assignment was completed, Gertrud, nearing 20 in age, was not allowed to go home and resume her schooling. "When the year was over, most of the girls were sent to ammunition factories or other important war plants. I was sent to the south of Germany to get some training as a meterological technician."

After that, she was assigned to a *Luftwaffe* base in France, just south of Paris. She found "a nice group of pilots," but, "Those pilots didn't have much to do, as there was no more gasoline for their planes."

Came the invasion, the Normandy invasion of June 1944, and all fled for German territory by road. "Only once did American planes attack us on the highway. Fortunately, we had found a safe shelter and didn't get hit. Over the border we were attacked again, and there were many wounded and several killed. When the caravan reached Vienna, I felt so desperate to feel safe again, but where?"

Gertrud deserted, leaving her mobile headquarters on foot and walking for days back toward the west. She begged food and milk at remote farms and slept in barns, on straw (very similar to the labor camp pallets, actually).

Her "march" through Bavaria and across the Rhine took nearly two weeks, even with an occasional ride on a freight train. Her mother, two sisters and younger brothers were at the mountain cabin—she finally reached them shortly before Christmas of 1944, during the Battle of the Bulge. As a deserter, she "tried not to be seen by the people in the village."

But she wasn't safe after all. "On December 21, 1944, the little mountain village was bombed. It was the most devastating, horrible, indescribable, sad happening in my life."

The American bomber crews had mistaken the small mountain village for another one by the same name five miles away in a nearby valley. The intended target had a railway station, and the small mountain village did not. "No one expected a thing when suddenly small aircraft unloaded their deadly bombs. For days to come the survivors had to search for bodies. . . . Months after the war, there were corpses still being dug out of the destroyed houses."

Gertrud was among those who ran to pick through the smoking rubble for possible survivors. She found a small boy without legs—dead.

During the raid, she and her mother saw one of the attacking airplanes crash into the side of a nearby hill. They went the next morning to look for any survivors.

"When we got there, two dead American air force men were still in the plane. The bodies were already stiff. We had a hard time putting them in the little wagon we had brought along. We both cried."

They took the bodies home, where, as in biblical times, Gertrud's mother wrapped them in hand-woven and embroidered sheets that had been a part of her trousseau years before. They secretly buried the American flyers in "the very back of the cemetery." First, Gertrud's mother carefully saved their dog tags, rings, and watches. "She hid them under her mattress. We knew then that soon the war would be over."

Then, on a beautiful spring day at their village of Esthal, American tanks appeared—they could be seen "moving on the other side of the mountains in the woods."

Gertrud's mother opened an upstairs window and hung out a white flag—ten minutes later, two American GIs arrived at their doorstep. The war was over for Gertrud and her family. Nearly over, that is, since there was one more matter to take care of.

Asking the Americans for an officer, Gertrud's mother solemnly handed over the dog tags and other personal items from the two airmen who had crashed into the hillside. "We told them where we buried them. We took him to the cemetery about eight hundred yards from our house, and what did we see? Someone had put flowers on the grave."

From The Governess by Gertrud Breier (Vantage Press, New York, 1988)

# ■ *Brothers/Sisters Of The Sea*

They were the superships of the war and their skippers an exalted threesome who, toward war's end, would share the same grim fate.

Mounting giant 18-inch guns, *Yamato* and *Musashi* came out of the yards and feverish pre-war secrecy as 72,000-ton behemoths of the sea, the mightiest battleships ever built. Their sister hull, the *Shinano*, emerged by a change in plan as a giant aircraft carrier.

Their combined fate, though, was to contribute surprisingly little to Japan's war effort. *Yamato*, first of the trio to visit the waters of the Pacific, merely stood by in the Battle of Midway, a disaster for the Imperial Japanese Navy (four carriers lost, to America's one, the *Yorktown*). Their first real action was in the three-day, multi-pronged Battle of Leyte Gulf. *Musashi* should have stayed home, and *Yamato* might as well have.

They were with Vice Admiral Takao Kurita's Center Force approaching Leyte in the Philippines by the "back door" route of the Sibuyan Sea on October 24, 1944. At *Musashi*'s helm was Toshihira Inoguchi, sailing his last day as skipper of the powerful warship.

Spotted and attacked in the South China Sea by two U.S. submarines the day before (October 23), Kurita's Center Force came under swarming air attack, with the two giant battleships the main target for the American dive bombers and torpedo planes.

The first wave came in about 10:40 a.m., but the two superships steamed on, their heavy armor-plating allowing them to "shrug off" torpedo and bomb hits. The ordnance tended simply to bounce off.

204

At noon, in came a second wave of U.S. flyers braving the ring of flak around the two capital ships. Again, no serious injury inflicted.

At 1:35 p.m., a third wave of U.S. Navy aircraft appeared. All 29 attackers this time concentrated on *Musashi* alone. And she merely plowed onward . . . it seemed at first.

But no, three torpedoes had struck home in her starboard bow and bent vital plates. Her skipper, Inoguchi, ordered counter-flooding to stabilize his monster ship. Her speed now slowed to just 22 knots. Her doom was near.

At 2:30, another 50 air attackers swept in, and at 3:10, still another 100 swarmed angrily about the Japanese fleet. They focused upon any apparently damaged Japanese ship. In that lot, the giant *Musashi* stuck out like the proverbial sore thumb. She took more and more torpedoes. Inoguchi had been forced to flood three of her four engine rooms to keep his even keel. Her bow was underwater and she staggered along at six knots.

He made for the closest land in order to ground the great ship and prevent at least her sinking. But now her last engine failed. Dead in the water, Inoguchi gave the word to abandon ship.

The first of the three skippers to meet shared fate, he stayed on his bridge—still there when the behemoth suddenly rolled to port and went down, with 1,100 crewmen—and their skipper—still aboard.

Kurita took his Center Force through the San Bernadino Strait the same night, *Yamato* still tagging along, but after encountering a startled U.S. task force of jeep carriers and small escorts the next morning, he unaccountably reversed course before exacting any damage on the U.S. landing force in Leyte Gulf. *Yamato*, turning away to avoid torpedo attacks, contributed little to the morning action of October 25 and retired with the rest of Kurita's Center Force.

*Shinano's* turn came next, about a month later—and quite unexpectedly. Just off her shipyard ways and in her first sea trials, the giant carrier was taken by surprise in Japan's own home waters—the Kumano Sea. The American submarine *Archer-Fish* had found her, an incredible target for Commander Joseph F. Enright's submersible prowler.

Four torpedoes tore into *Shinano's* hull without warning. Her skipper, Toshio Abe, still had faith in his "unsinkable" ship, however, and he steamed for nearby safe haven at 20 knots. Soon, though, the internal fires boiled up and she listed badly. He, too, ordered abandon ship. He, too, remained on the bridge. And he, too, was still there when his ship went down.

That left only *Yamato*, the original of the three mighty sisters of the sea, and *her* skipper, Kosaku Aruga, to face the final days of the Pacific War. And they stayed out of harm's way for weeks, then months.

With the American invasion of Okinawa in April of 1945, however, the admirals of the shattered Imperial Navy decided upon a last desperate sortie to the aid of Okinawa's defenders. *Yamato* would be the flagship for Vice Admiral Seiichi Ito's Second Fleet in the grim run—some say it was a one-way suicide sortie from the very outset, with no fuel available for the return voyage to Japan.

As the last of the Imperial Navy's big ships started for Okinawa, they were shadowed by U.S. reconnaissance planes and submarines. The sortie would be no surprise, and ahead waited the American carriers and their swarms of aircraft.

The action began the morning of April 7, 1945. Wave after wave of airplanes went after *Yamato* in battle lasting three hours in all. Holed by torpedoes and hammered by countless bombs, the mighty *Yamato* soon was staggering, her end obviously near.

On the bridge, his ship dying beneath him, Aruga gave orders to be tied to the compass stand. "I am one with *Yamato*," he told his executive officer, Jiro Nomura.

Oddly, he also said he might work free and swim away later. So near was the end, though, that Nomura was swept off the bridge even while strapping his skipper to the ship's binnacle. Like his two brothers of the sea, Aruga then went down with the third and last of Japan's three most powerful sisters of the sea.

From various sources

# ■ *Greatest Invasion Averted*

As Vice President of the United States, Harry S. Truman didn't know his country was close to perfecting the atomic bomb. He didn't even know that it was being developed under the aegis of the super-secret Manhattan Project.

*President* Truman's first glimmer came at the end of an emergency Cabinet meeting he convened in the White House just minutes after he took his oath of office on the evening of April 12, 1945, to replace the deceased Franklin D. Roosevelt. Secretary of War Henry L. Stimson lingered briefly to alert the new President to "an immense project" developing an explosive "of almost unbelievable destructive power." That's all he told Truman for the moment.

In far-off Japan, the enemy knew even less. The Japanese, clearly on the defensive at this late stage of World War II, were fully occupied with more immediate events. America's island-hopping Pacific campaign was drawing closer to the home islands; from the air, the war already was crashing down upon the homeland.

On March 26, after incredibly fierce fighting, U.S. Marines who first landed February 19 finally secured the island of Iwo Jima, just 750 miles from Tokyo.

Worse, though, U.S. bombers on March 9 had opened a new phase in the air war against Japan proper. Where bombing by long-range U.S. B-29s had achieved only desultory effect before, 325 of the new "Superfortresses" on this night leveled 16 square miles of Tokyo and killed 85,000 to 100,000 persons in a single incendiary raid. Curtis LeMay's bomber force would carry the same firestorms to many other Japanese cities by war's end in August, the port city of Hiroshima one of the few to be "spared."

On April 1, U.S. forces invaded the island of Okinawa, just 340 miles south of Japan, to initiate another fierce battle that would last until late June before final American victory. By now, the invasion of Japan itself looked imminent.

In the West, Roosevelt had died on April 12, to be succeeded by Truman. On April 30, Hitler committed suicide—Germany was just about out of the war. Berlin fell to the Russians May 2; Germany surrendered unconditionally May 7. Japan was now alone.

On July 4, Douglas MacArthur could announce the full liberation of the Philippines from occupying Japanese forces. All U.S. war effort now could be devoted to the invasion and final defeat of Japan.

Okinawa, however, had been a sobering lesson for the American and British strategists laying their invasion plans. For one thing, Okinawa had been the scene of hundreds of *kamikaze* attacks by suicide-bent Japanese defenders. As Winston Churchill noted, though, there had been another kind of suicide, too.

"I had in my mind," he wrote in *Triumph and Tragedy*, "the spectacle of Okinawa Island, where many thousands of Japanese, rather than surrender, had drawn up in line and destroyed themselves by hand-grenades after their leaders had solemnly performed the rite of *hari-kari*." Allied strategists concluded the Japanese would not submit easily to invasion of their homeland—rather than any surrender, casualties would be in the millions.

On July 16, at Alamogordo, New Mexico, however, the secret Manhattan Project, costing some $2 billion, involving thousands of workers, creating two entire cities (Oak Ridge, Tennessee, and Hanford, Washington), inaugurated a new age. In a test detonation, "Fat Boy," the first plutonium bomb, had worked beyond all expectations. News of "Fat Boy's" success was flashed to Truman and Churchill at their Potsdam Conference with Josef Stalin in Germany.

Just a month earlier, Truman, War Secretary Stimson and the U.S. Joint Chiefs of Staff had given conditional approval to Operation Olympic, MacArthur's plan to invade Japan's southern-most home island of Kyushu on November 1—at expectedly horrendous cost. Wrote Churchill later: "Now all this nightmare picture had vanished. In its place was a vision—fair and bright, indeed it seemed—of the end of the whole war in one or two violent shocks."

On July 26, the United States and Great Britain, with China as a co-signer, issued their Potsdam Declaration demanding that Japan surrender unconditionally or face "complete destruction" of its armed forces and "utter devastation" of the homeland.

For 10 days, its Supreme War Council split between diehards and moderates, Japan did not respond clearly or officially. By President Truman's decision to end the war quickly as possible, America's plan to use one or both of its only operational atomic bombs went forward. The first, a uranium bomb called "Little Boy," was dropped on Hiroshima August 6, and the second on Nagasaki August 9.

By some accounts, Russia's last-minute declaration of war against Japan August 8 shook Japan policy-makers more than the blow at Hiroshima two days before. Still, even after Nagasaki, the Supreme Council remained split, until Emperor Hirohito settled the issue August 14 by urging surrender without further quibble.

In the refined language of the Japanese court, he announced

the decision to his people the next day, August 15. "The war situation has developed not necessarily to Japan's advantage," he said—with some understatement. The greatest war in history was over. The greatest invasion in history was averted.

From various sources

# ■ *How To Settle The Peace*

Two months, nearly three, after the Normandy invasion, Major Ed Steiner of the U.S. 20th Fighter Group spent an afternoon as a panelist for a group discussion by about 30 key enlisted personnel, all as part of an Army orientation program.

"I was asked by Station Headquarters to sit on the panel with the Chaplain . . . and two enlisted men to answer questions that were asked by the men," Steiner wrote home from his airbase in England. "I enjoyed the hour of discussion that started off with the question: Should Germany be divided into small states after the war, as it was before Bismarck's time?"

In the discussion that followed, the participants talked about "the causes of the war, the mistakes of the last peace (Versailles) and other related matters."

Steiner wondered aloud how many of those present felt "that it was possible for us to arrange the peace and so conduct international affairs that this would be the last war."

Only five of his listeners thought that this would be the last. Steiner argued otherwise. The discussion "got really good," and he signed off in his letter home the next day saying, "I am convinced that we CAN avoid future wars."

As a thoroughly practical P.S., he also pleaded, "Please send me a package of food."

From *King's Cliffe Remembered*, 20th Fighter Group
Association, Vol. 5, No. 1, January-May 1987

# ■ Obituary

"I write suspense novels," said British author Francis Clifford one time, "because I believe that only when a character is at the end of his tether—be it physically, mentally, morally, spiritually or financially—is his character revealed."

Clifford learned his lessons of character and the *tether* in war, behind the enemy lines, where a man is alone, with suspicion and fear his constant companions, night and day, with no surcease, no letup, no time out even for a wound or injury.

Real name Arthur Bell Thompson, he was born in Bristol, England, in 1917. In his early twenties at the outbreak of war, he was in Burma as a rice merchant. He was commissioned into the Burmese Army, and he soon was conducting sabotage operations against the advancing Japanese—behind their lines. In time, he was welcomed as a member of the British Special Operations Executive (SOE), which, like the American OSS, specialized in disruptive activities in enemy-occupied territory.

Thompson/Clifford's experience in such clandestine and dangerous warfare exposed him to what he later described as "the strongest of human emotions—fear." For him, the war years were "the watershed of my career."

He spent the immediate post-war years as an industrial journalist but began writing novels on the side. The first one published was *Honor the Shrine*, appearing in 1953. After four more books over the next six years, the world still had not taken great notice, but Thompson gambled on leaving his job to become a fulltime writer anyway. He had only $200 in the bank at the time.

After another seven years near the end of the *financial* tether, he finally achieved best-seller status with the *Naked Runner* in 1966, also made into a movie. Then came another success, *All Men Are Lonely*. Two subsequent books, *Another Way of Dying* and *The Grosvenor Square Goodbye*, won the Silver Dagger award from the British Crime Writers' Association.

His last book, another "thinking man's thriller," was *Drummer in the Dark*. Upon his passing shortly after its publication in the early 1970s, the London *Times* said: "His books were as removed from most suspense writing as fine brandy is from common wine."

Also posthumously, it was said that his writings explored, again and again, "the human toll taken and the ethical questions raised when men declared war on each other.'' Lessons learned on that lonely *tether* in wartime . . .

From *Reader's Digest Condensed Books*, Volume 2, 1976

# ■ *The End Is Seen*

Leroy Nicholson was just 16 years old and all of 98 pounds when he joined up in August 1942—''just a little squirt working in a cotton mill.'' That was when the Marines already were going ashore at Guadalcanal. How much war could be left?

Enough so that he saw his action. First aboard the light cruiser *Montpelier*, ship of 26 invasions, of 53 shore bombardments, of 13 battle stars before it all was over.

And so, in the Pacific, as a young man in a quadruple 40mm antiaircraft gun mount, he saw—

• Gun battles at sea, such as the Battle of Empress Augusta Bay the night of Nov. 2, 1943, in which Rear Admiral A. Stanton (''Tip'') Merrill's Task Force 39 of four light cruisers, plus destroyers, took on two heavy and two light Japanese cruisers, plus *their* destroyers, in order to protect the American transports landing the Marines on Bougainville.

Merrill's tactics in that American victory are still considered classic. As the engagement unfolded, however, few on board the *Montpelier* were thinking of textbook naval battles, even if she were the Admiral's flagship.

*When their* (the Japanese) *8-inch shells landed, they threw up enormous mountains of water, and the light from the outer shells colored the water green and red and orange. Our gun tub was close to a passage that led from one side of the ship to the other. When the 8-inch shells started landing on the starboard side, we would run to port. When they started ranging on the port side, we'd run to starboard. There was always a danger of shrapnel from those big, beautiful waterspouts, you see.*

Right on the scene like that, he could really see—

• *You could see the flashes from their guns. And we got a good view of one of their cruisers, the* Sendai, *going down. She was on fire from one end to the other, part of her hull looked like it was glowing. You had to feel sorry for the men on board . . . but not too sorry, because if it hadn't been for Admiral Merrill's getting the drop on them, it might have been our ship instead.*

He had had to obtain parental permission to join up, and now, out in the Pacific, he saw what it was like to be under intensive air attack. He saw that the morning after the nighttime engagement at Empress Augusta Bay—

• *As I remember it, we were too busy to be frightened. They threw about 100 planes at us in the space of seven or eight minutes . . . . Our ship burned up about 6,000 rounds of 40 and 20mm ammo in those eight minutes—it was incredible how much firepower we could throw out.* (Merrill had circled his ships in wagon-train style to fight off the air attackers.) *The prettiest hit I saw that day, however, was not by one of the antiaircraft guns, but by one of the big, 6-inch turrets. It was tracking a plane as it flew off to the north, and when it fired you could see the big tracer just arch out over the water. The 6-inch round landed right beneath the Japanese plane, and this enormous column of water came up and knocked it out of the sky, end over end—just like swatting a fly.*

He was there when *Montpelier* and *Cleveland* traded blows with Japanese shore guns (8-inchers)—

• *I kept thinking how it would be our turn next, and how big a target a 600-foot-long cruiser makes. Sure enough, when we came into line and opened fire, 8-inch rounds started landing nearby. I heard one of them come overhead, right between the mainmast and the smokestack—50 yards shorter and it would have landed on us. Next thing I knew, they bracketed the bow of the* Montpelier. *These were just near-misses, mind you, but the force from them was enough to rip one of the 20mm guns off its mount, and the whole front end of the ship was sprayed with big hunks of red-hot shrapnel.*

He later saw man's most violent weaponry at work, too—

• *We actually saw the Nagasaki bomb go off, a big flash off in the distance. We thought one of our carriers had taken a bad* kamikaze *hit and blown up. It wasn't that at all, of course.*

Strangely, though, it was also at Nagasaki that the late Leroy Nicholson saw an end to the war, and its battles, its hatreds—

• *A month later, when we were allowed on shore, it was a weird experience. What can I say, except that the city looked just like the pictures you see—utter devastation. We didn't know what to expect, but it was logical to assume the Japanese would feel very hostile, so we all went ashore armed with .45s. We were walking down the street when suddenly these little children came out, maybe half a dozen of them, six or seven years old. They were adorable and well-mannered—they bowed politely and held our hands and we walked around with them, gave them some candy, and suddenly it was as if the blackness of the war had lifted from our minds. The hatred most of us had felt for the Japanese during the past few years just went away. We had all been bragging about how, boy, when we get to Japan, we're gonna show 'em who's boss . . . and suddenly, standing there in a devastated city, holding hands with some smiling children, it was impossible to feel that way any longer. I think that was the day the war really ended for most of us.*

From interview by William R. Trotter,
*Military History* Magazine, August 1989.

***About the author:***

C. Brian Kelly is editor of *World War II* and *Military History* magazines, a lecturer in journalism at the University of Virginia and a former newspaper reporter. He contributed chapters to the books *True Stories of Great Escapes* (Reader's Digest Books) and *Who's Poisoning America* (Sierra Club Books ). He was co-author (with Jeffrey O'Connell) of *The Blame Game: How Shin-kicking Litigation Is Hurting All of Us* (Lexington Books). His articles have appeared in *Reader's Digest, Friends, VFW* and other magazines, his fiction in *Yankee, Rod Serling's Twilight Zone, Fantasy & Science Fiction* and *Cats*.

## *What our reviewers say:*

"The very conciseness of some of the stories lends poignancy to the tales . . . an ideal book for the bedside of the World War II vet and the military history buff."
—Byron Farwell in *The Washington Times.*

"Kelly catches the spirit of the moment and brings the epic struggle that was World War II to life once again."
—*Daily Press,* Newport News, Virginia.

"The 101 stories can be read individually, yet together they generate the suspense of a novel."
—*The Book Report,* Columbus, Ohio.

"A fascinating mosaic of this multi-faceted conflict . . ."
—*Army Magazine.*

"Concise, crisply written, and revealing, this book will appeal to all veterans, World War II buffs and history students."
—*Military,* Sacramento, California

"You don't have to read them all at once, even though it is next to impossible to put the book down."
—*The Richmond News Leader,* Richmond, Virginia

"Those fascinated by World War II won't want to miss this book."
—*The Birmingham News,* Birmingham, Alabama

———————

To order more copies for friends, relatives, libraries, schools, etc., send $10.95 for each book (including postage and handling). Signed on request.

Montpelier Publishing
P.O. Box 3384   University Station
Charlottesville, Virginia 22903-0384

Please include your name, address, city, state, and zip code.

(Virginia residents add 4.5% sales tax, for a total of $11.44 for each book.)